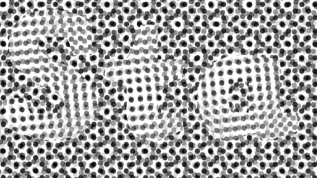
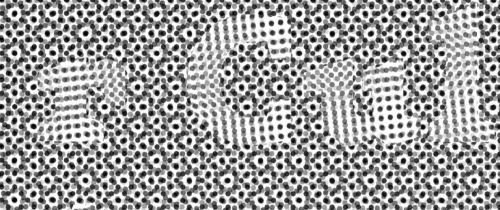
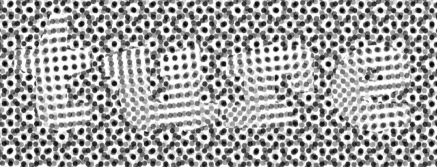

The collected interviews from Dazed & Confused magazine

Phaidon Press Limited, Regent's Wharf, All Saints Street, London N1 9PA. First published 2000.
© 2000 Phaidon Press Ltd. A CIP catalogue record of this book is available from the British Library.
ISBN 0 7148 3955 8. All rights reserved. No part of this publication may be reproduced, stored in a retrieval system or transmitted, in any form or by any means, electronic, mechanical, photocopying, recording or otherwise, without the prior permission of Phaidon Press Limited.
Edited by Mark Sanders & Jefferson Hack. Designed by Gareth Hague @ Alias.
Printed in China.

The show is over. The audience get up to leave their seats. Time to collect their coats and go home. They turn around... no more coats and no more home.'

Rozanov Definition of a Nihilist *quoted by Raoul Vaneigem in* **The Revolution of Everyday Life 1967**

'The history of our time calls to mind those Walt Disney characters who rush madly over the edge of a cliff without seeing it: the power of their imagination keeps them suspended in mid-air, but as soon as they look down and see where they are, they fall.'

Raoul Vaneigem The Revolution of Everyday Life 1967

'The relationship between the famous and the public who sustain them is governed by a striking paradox. Infinitely remote, the great stars of politics, film and entertainment move across an electric terrain of limousines, bodyguards and private helicopters. At the same time, the zoom lens and the interview camera bring them so close to us that we know their faces and their smallest gestures more intimately than those of our friends.'

J G Ballard The Atrocity Exhibition 1970

Today, as in no other time in history, our universe is populated by a myriad of different stars. From the serial killer mutated into a taboo totem, to the rock star's latest televisual confessions, or the avant-garde artist turned pop-philosopher, the sacrament of the celebrity has come full circle: the famous and the infamous have transmuted and transformed into an external vision of ourselves.

Redolent of the internal confusion of post-Cold War consumerism, star culture represents the collective neurosis of our age. Never before have we been so obsessed by the lifestyles of the rich and famous. We gaze through the keyhole but we fail to unlock the mystery. Never before has reputation been a licence of genuine authenticity. Yet within this Byzantine system of focus groups, puff pieces and chat-show trivia, there lies a striking paradox. Determined by the needs of our modern entertainment culture, the personalities and artists propelled by this interstellar overdrive are also imprisoned by it – crucified by the controlling frame of their own celebrity.

The election of modern entertainment culture to a new secular religion now suffocates the world in which we live. The public's unquenchable thirst for more bizarre and cruel forms of amusement shackles the modern celebrity to a Faustian contract where unimaginable wealth and sexual indulgence bear an exorbitant cost. Scrutinized and studied by the media, worshipped and condemned by the public, the modern star is forced to live a life of unending and relentless inspection. Rather than trial by fire, water or combat, we now judge the modern celebrity through the tabloid tradition of trial by revelation. In ancient times, the gladiator's survival depended on the whim of the Emperor. Today, settlement emerges from the arena of public opinion.

Star Culture: The collected interviews from Dazed & Confused magazine confronts this paradox as revealed in the thoughts and ideas of some of our most audacious and spectacular stars. Selected from the first sixty issues of *Dazed & Confused*, alongside a collection of specially commissioned exclusive interviews, it brings together a series of 'situations in print' profiling those celebrities, writers and artists who operate as guides to the structural hallucinations that define the way in which we think. From two-way interviews to fax interviews, self-interviews to invented interviews, this book is but one attempt to excavate the buried discourse of our time.

Dazed & Confused magazine was formed in 1993 as a direct assault on the tired excesses of the British style press. Conceived as a new and independent take on accepted modes of popular journalism, its ethos of collaborative and collective action has led to a series of interventions by leading celebrities and artists within the field of popular culture. The interviews that follow are intended to break the perceived boundaries of style journalism, providing not only a unique insight into the mind-set of the more established artists and performers of the past three decades, but also to create a unique space for an alternative voice to challenge head-on the vagaries of modern star culture.

Dazed & Confused magazine, 9th December 1999

November 1993
Introduction and interview | *Michael Holden*

When Anita Pallenberg was making the film
Performance *(Nic Roeg/Donald Cammell, 1970)*,
Keith Richards, her boyfriend at the time, would
wait in his car all day for filming to end. When
she went to Italy to make a film with Marlon
Brando, Richards caught the first plane to Rome
as soon as he found out. It was time to make a
decision between acting and The Rolling Stones,
between her own career and someone else's.
Pallenberg chose the latter. For a time, it must
have seemed like the right thing to do.

Pallenberg, having previously dated Brian
Jones, now designed clothes for the band and co-
wrote songs; the model-turned-actress was now
a full time Rolling Stone. By the 1970s, it had
started to go wrong. Drugs, bad publicity and
the strains of touring all took their toll. By the
end of the decade, Pallenberg had a heroin problem, busted for being in possession of Tic-Tacs.
Today, having reclaimed her life, she is a degree
student at St Martin's School of Art, studying
textiles and living in London and the USA.

Dazed & Confused | **Don't you wish you'd done
more acting?**
Anita Pallenberg | No, I hated every minute of
it. And I don't consider myself an actress, I just
consider myself a photogenic person. They just
used my face to put it in the pictures. I'd never
done any Shakespeare or what I consider acting.
I didn't like the whole ambience anyway; I don't
really like movie people that much. Having The
Stones in one hand, who were these five guys
who could say 'fuck you' to anyone... there I was
alone and I had these producers and they were
fucking me over. I never got paid a whole
amount for any film I did, and there were
always court cases and being sued and all that
shit; they walked all over me. So I don't have
any regrets about stopping being in that scene.
So now I think it's over, but you never know,
I've still got great legs...
**Would you say you were happy being a
student?**
Oh yeah, I could say that these student years
have been the best of my life, thinking about it. I
never thought they were gonna take me because
I saw all these very talented young people that
were being interviewed and I thought, 'What are
they gonna do with an old fart like me?' Even as
a mature student, I was really terrified of what
they would think of me, thinking that maybe
some freak, some movie buff would recognize
me. Then, in the first week of college they
showed *Barbarella* and they were all waiting
outside afterwards like, 'Anita, weren't you in
Barbarella?', and since then, everyone's been
really sweet – that broke the ice. It's been really
good, I've done things like going to Russia and
going to collections with college, it's been great.
**Was being around The Stones to that extent
a bit like having a job?**
Yeah, because they offered me Ferraris and
things if I did this and that, and then I did 'Get
Yer Ya Ya's Out' – I got that title – and they're
like, 'Oh, we'll get you this and this for getting

Anita Pallenberg, 1993
Gary Wallis

that.' I never got anything out of it, not a penny.

You wrote 'You Can't Always Get What You Want'?

Well, we co-wrote it, sitting in the jungle in Brazil. There was like, this whole aftermath of *Performance*, feelings still left over. So we were just saying that you can't always get what you want, but you can get what you need.

Do you think you got what you needed?

Now, I'm certainly getting what I need, and I'm even starting to get what I want; it's really funny. So it's like *[sings]* 'you can get it if you really want it, but you must try,' so it's, 'try, try, I'm gonna try and try'.

You were once quoted as saying 'With my lifestyle I lost everything, especially the things I like.' Do you still feel that's true?

I felt for a while that I liked all the glamour and the limousines and the comfort, and it was actually quite hard to suddenly wake up and have to make my own decisions and call a cab and get on the bus and all that stuff. But now I've got a bicycle and I'm perfectly happy really, and I ride everywhere on my bike and I couldn't give a toss now if I've got a limousine or not.

Do you think it was necessary to go through those experiences to be able to appreciate what you have now?

Well, I think I always had my feet on the ground. I grew up in Italy after the war and we didn't have much food. I used to pick up grass out of the meadow to make salads. I knew about the simple way of life. So I don't envy any of those people involved with The Stones – it's all right, it's good, for them – for me it's different.

What do you think of The Stones now? Would it be fair to say that you've made more progress than them? After all, they're still going on tour and getting married, at least you've done something different.

Well, I can't really put myself on the level of The Stones. I think they've all achieved an awful lot. From what we were about in the 60s, nobody knew that it was gonna be this big, that thirty years later they'd still be together. It was like tapping in the dark. The thing is that I managed to survive: I was a casualty. I mean, they were just waiting for me to die. I was the so-called weak link in the chain for a long time, you know, the bad girl, the trouble-maker and all that shit. So the fact that I managed to survive and that I've managed to find my own place, that's already a miracle. I feel I've grown. I've just managed to find myself really. I don't see myself as a giant, but I think that they're giants and how they cope with that in their private lives... sometimes I don't agree with it. I couldn't talk about whether I've grown more than they have, it's too pretentious.

What do you think of England now, compared to how it was in the 60s?

Compared to the 60s? I don't know. Because I'm a foreigner, I've always had a problem getting close to English people; they're much more reserved. I still feel like an outsider, like a guest, even though I've lived here... it's still this very odd feeling. In the 6os for me it was mainly drugs and stuff like that; London's always been a good place for drugs. I never saw the big hippie thing because I was working. Everybody was always, 'We're going to do that festival, we're going to do this festival', and I'd always be working. What can I say now about the 6os? It was like five minutes for me, that was how long it lasted. It's like 'What was that? Oh, the 6os!' It seemed to have gone by really quickly. I get confused between 1968 and 1969 completely – drugs or whatever – so I don't know. I like London when it's a nice day like today.

If you imagine you were a young person coming to London now, do you think you'd have as good a time?

I don't know. I went to Glastonbury and I was checking out what the difference was. Everybody was dressed up like in the 6os, all that was the same: to dress down. So I thought, 'What's the difference?' and I realized that today, all that people were doing was walking around, going to see a gig, going to have a hamburger, a beer; they needed entertainment. In the 6os there was not so much media stuff, so we had to create our own thing. Like at a festival in the 6os, you couldn't get a coffee, but you could bring your harmonica or your guitar and sit in a circle and play and sing and make a fire and cook sausages and it's that creativity that I feel is missing. And I feel it here in London. It seems like people are getting too spoilt – they need entertainment. They have to have it all laid out, but they don't actually do anything themselves anymore. The youth is a bit jaded today. Like when you see people in the street, the way they dress, the originality, it's gone. In those days, it was all home-made and here now you can just buy it all. It might look similar, but it hasn't got that kind of personality to it. I probably would have made more money, in those days. Naomi Campbell, she's hanging out with a pop star and it seems like she's doing all the same stuff I was doing. I know she's a supermodel and she's got more money, but it seems like the same road she's taking. To a certain extent, I wish she wouldn't, I wish she'd change something. Hasn't she seen what we went through and how it affected us? Can't she just learn from that? The one thing that I would really like to put across today is that I'm a survivor and I've been through all that stuff and you don't have to do that.

What do you think about drugs now?

Well, that's what I feel. When we started to take drugs we had examples like Charlie Parker and Billie Holiday and you think, 'that happened to them', but you never think it'll happen to you; so we were experimenting really. But now, there's more information and there's AIDS. It's OK to fool around with them, but I'm perfectly happy without drugs. I can have just as good a time. But then I guess I had to go through it. It killed a lot of friends and that really upsets me.

Surely though, you can appreciate how someone might look at a life like your own, inclusive of all the bad things and think, 'Yeah, that might be a fun thing to do.'

Yeah, I totally understand somebody else wanting to do it as well, but good luck to them, because they might not come through it. In those days, drugs were better, let's face it. I found a gram of coke in the toilets at Glastonbury and I didn't touch it. I gave it to some friends and they said, 'This is shit!' Everything gets so big and so all over the place; the quality of it suffers, and I like quality.

If you hadn't fallen in with The Stones, what do you think you'd have ended up doing?

I'd probably have become the kind of Italian Sophia Loren. I had these two lifestyles that I weighed up and I thought, 'They want me to be in the movies, OK.' But then I preferred The Stones' lifestyle: it was all kids screaming and chaos and confusion. Plus, every time I did a movie, Keith would get pissed off, so eventually I had to give it up and have children. I feel as if I'm a late starter anyway. Fashion's always been a part of my life, and now I've finally managed to get round to doing it.

Oasis make you feel good. Their hardline nonchalance is exciting. After the short, sharp, shocked careers of the Mondays and Roses we need Oasis, and in their own, impetuous, cocky, Manc way, they know it. Oasis think they are big – bigger than The Beatles, bigger than Bowie. I met Noel and Liam Gallagher and discovered their alter egos, John Lennon and Ziggy Stardust.

After a lengthy hiatus spent boozing with his mam in Burnage, Manchester, John Lennon has been finally put back in touch with his muse. Since his mam found it in a bucket under the kitchen sink last Easter, the gnarly Northerner has been writing melodious pop chestnuts by the score. Asked how to explain his absence, Lennon spits sardonically, 'Eh mate, I'm the only man in rock who can go on the piss with his mam, so shut it. We get shit-faced on gin and tonic and sit around crying.' Today, thank God, there are no tears. We meet in an existential cave in seedy Soho, where he and his mam are enjoying an all-too-rare day out shopping in the Smoke. Both are wearing new hats and are sucking hard on straws connected to huge barrels of gin and tonic. 'Because the other three Beatles were killed in the Munich air disaster,' glowers Lennon, 'I had to get some new players in. Then the fucking lawyers told me I couldn't use the old name and had to get a new one.' Lennon chose the name Oasis because his uncle owns an arcade of the same name in Morecambe. 'I thought they might give us a bit of sponsorship, like.' The players, according to Lennon, were harder to come by. 'It was obvious I should get our kid in on vocals, though.'

Dazed & Confused | **Where did you steal that song 'Supersonic' from?**
Lennon | I lifted the guitar from 'My Sweet Lord' by George Harrison. Bit cheeky that, eh? It's not exactly the same, but it's similar. That's how I write all the songs these days. I'm not an original songwriter. If I was to sit down and write original songs, they'd sound shit, like the Inspiral Carpets. I listen to records and think 'That's all right, but I can do better.' With the writing of the songs, I take from everywhere, Burt Bacharach even. I've really got into easy listening these days, especially Burt Bacharach, he's a god – 'This Guy's in Love With You' – what a song! I'd love to make records that sound, y'know, like a T Rex record. When I listen to T Rex, I listen in colours. Same as Bowie's 'Ziggy Stardust'... eh up! Here's Ziggy Stardust now. *[Lennon's kid brother, Ziggy Stardust, ambles towards our table swaying to an imaginary rhythm and pouting slightly. He's with Oasis bass player John Paul Jones. They are both eating Chicken McNuggets]*
Give us one.
Ziggy | *[to himself]* It's just got a magical touch; you can't explain it. You can't explain nuffink. It's either good or it's not good.
You what?
Lennon | Look, right, I haven't got a record player 'cause I've nowhere to live and I'm still searching for the perfect pair of trainers, adidas jeans – proper 70s gear – adidas jeans or adidas cords, top gear. Our record company gave us a load of money to smarten ourselves up. I spent four hundred quid on a Paul Smith jacket. I don't even like it. It's like, 'What's the most expensive thing you've got in the shop, mate? Well, give it here.' I don't even wear it. It's right, innit?
Aside from 'Supersonic', how are the rest of your songs shaping up?
Lennon | We've got a couple of tunes. 'Whatever' and 'All Around the World', they're like 'Hey

From top
Liam and Noel
Gallagher, 1994
Alex Szaszy

Jude' but better. It took us four months to record the album and it's gonna take us six months to record just one of them songs, 'cause it's 'Hey Jude' but bigger.

Ziggy | Yer in a band, y'know what I mean, you've got to get the songs done right and live yer dreams.

You're a bit cocky, cock.

Lennon | Why sit there embarrassed? We are narcissists. We get on tables and sing when we hear our songs in clubs, 'I fucking wrote that' and sing the lyrics in people's faces.

Ziggy | That's good; that's the way to be. If that ain't the way to be, if what we're doing is not right, then fuck it all 'cause I don't want to be in no other band.

What about the gin?

Lennon | We've got that much time on our hands so we just do this *[downs another gin]*. Do it again and do it again. Have a fight and run round the street like nutters. Then people say that Oasis are mad. We're not mad, we're just bored. If there was any bands or new music or fashion to get into, I'd be on it, me, but there's not, so we're bored, so we end up fighting with each other. I gave John Paul a black eye yesterday. Oasis are bored shitless.

We don't give a fuck, we're bored and we're tryna humour ourselves.

Get down baby, lay some more philosophy on the table.

Ziggy | Life makes us who we are. We all have experiences that make us who we are. I'm glad of who I am. I wouldn't change anything in my life and a lot of bad things have happened. If we all came from Essex and our dad worked for British Aerospace and he had two Mercedes and he borrowed one to me every now and again, Oasis wouldn't exist.

Steady on.

Lennon | I'm angry that John Smith died. The only time I get angry... we don't write about politics or anything like that. We write about yer local things like how the dreams you have as children fade away. Like about how shit it is leaving school and finding out life is a bag of shit. The only time we get angry is on the day of the general election and we get our polling card and go 'You fucking Tory bastards, let's fucking have it', and you put your cross in. That's it. 'Cause if we all vote together and we all vote Labour... It's like someone from the Redskins once said, 'If we all spit together, we drown the bastards.'

Dazed & Confused | **How do you see your public image?**

Björk | Well, after going through ten years in Iceland with its small-town mentality on your back for twenty-four hours a day – sort of like, 'fuck off, you're ugly, it's bad taste, piss off' – I think I got immune. You just have to do what you've got to do for your own reasons. And coming out here, I think I've been incredibly lucky. I mean OK, eighty per cent or whatever of my public image is bollocks, but at least twenty per cent is not that far from the truth. On the whole, it is quite positive.

What did you think of the Spitting Image sketch?

The fact that your average English person perceives me as someone who sings along to fax machines? It couldn't be better. They actually got me very much to the pin there, like, what I'm about. I prefer a fax machine any day to a guitar solo. I was in a band when I was fifteen, me and another girl, and we'd have a popcorn machine on stage and mic it up and drum to that. Or I would go and record my grandfather snoring and we would use that as a rhythm.

That's quite advanced for a fifteen-year-old.

Yeah, just using normal noises instead of going for the perfect world of pop, where you need ten thousand billion grand and have to work with seventy-five billion session people. That's always been my approach, and you might hate it or you might like it, but if you're going to ask how people look at me, I quite like it.

What do you look for in a man?

Surprises. I think the men I've gone out with have nothing in common, really, when it comes to physical things. It is definitely spontaneous minds and a good sense of humour; to be ready to jump off cliffs with me.

Has anyone held your hand and jumped off a cliff with you?

What, literally?!

No, metaphysically. In your own world?

Ahh, I do that all the time. I'm addicted to that. It keeps me going, definitely. Friend-wise, lover-wise...

Music-wise as well?

Definitely. I mean, I would die if I didn't always have a relationship like that going on, where you don't need words, just to jump off cliffs together.

Do you have a story that symbolizes that feeling?

I don't want to blow my own trumpet, but the lyrics of 'Big Time Sensuality' are just about that: when you meet someone and you just want to do everything in the world and take off and fuck the rest, and 'let's get lost' and all that bollocks.

Are you afraid of letting people near you? Are you afraid that everybody wants a bit of you?

When I was eleven and my record 'Gling Glong' came out in Iceland, I was a bit of a child star so I got that shock then: when you suddenly get a lot of people talking to you because it's kinda cool, and only one in twenty sincerely wants to talk to you. I think it's quite lucky for that to happen to you so early. It rehearses your instinct and you get really good at telling what people are after. You just make sure that certain people don't get closer.

Have you got certain instinctive things you do to make sure people don't get closer to you? Do you tell them to fuck off?

No, I just don't invite them back to my house.

Tell me about the *Story of the Eye* by George Bataille. You refer to it quite a lot.

Everybody's got a book that changed their life. It's the book I read when I was seventeen, and it proved to me I wasn't mad. It's basically about a couple that go on a mission against morality and against perceived ways of behaviour, and basically take it to the extreme and show that if you want to do it, you should. Well that's simplifying it a lot. I mean you've only got one life and if you don't do today what you want to do, you've lost the battle. It's a freedom thing, I guess. Just to really nail it down, you would call it a French Surrealist road book.

Do you see freedom as a childlike state? I mean, is that freedom a child has, similar, say, to abandoning the moral code for the characters in the *Story of the Eye*?

I suppose it's a little book that teaches you how to grow up but to keep that childlike approach.

Is that something you would say you were about?

I try to be as spontaneous as possible and I try not to organize my life too much, and I try to go with the flow and have a laugh. But at the same time, I try to have integrity and the courage to make all the things I want come true – not only the easy surface stuff, but all the way deep. And another thing that is important about this book is it takes away that selfish thing: if you just do exactly what you want to do it is supposed to be completely egoistic and selfish, but it's not.

Isn't that a contradiction?

I mean, the sort of universal side of it... getting really deep now...

You've been writing lyrics all day...

Listen, my lyrics have been really silly, about bouncing teddy bears... That's probably why I'm getting a bit more serious now. It's simple really: if every person takes care of himself and his own needs and dreams, the whole picture will be sorted, but if people keep repressing themselves, it's a sad world. The most generous thing you can do is make your own dreams come true, which is a contradiction in a way, but that's what it's about.

Are there more dreams you've yet to make come true?

Not in the obvious sense, like to sell five million records or something silly like that, but I've got a lot of songs to write. I've always pictured myself writing songs wherever I am, and not in relation to money. But I'll still be writing tunes with knives and forks on kitchen tables and whatever when I'm seventy-five. It's a bit of a mission for me, really.

Talking about bouncing teddy bears, what makes you happy?

It's always strangers who ask you the questions not even your friends would ask you!

Well, all your friends will read the replies.

What makes me happy? I think surprises. Definitely, that's my favourite. Like the bomb today. I'm sorry, people got hurt, so it sounds

Björk, 1994
Rankin

malicious... like the earthquake in LA. Or people being spontaneous and surprising me. Calling me up and saying things I wouldn't expect from them. And going to a club and the DJ putting completely the wrong record on. It just makes me laugh. It makes me very happy. Predictable things: I'm terrified of them. And boredom in general terrifies me. That's what I'm most scared of out of everything – boredom.

Tell me about the last dream you had.

I had the best dream the other day. I dreamt I was Paul Newman, naked with a backsack full of weapons, and I had to go into this white house and Steve McQueen was in this house naked as well, of course, and I was supposed to kill him and I was terrified because I don't want to hurt anyone, especially Steve McQueen, and he noticed how scared I was and he started to make fun of me and throw knives at me.

Which you dodged because you were Paul Newman?

I wasn't quite comfortable about being aggressive and having to hurt people, and then it became quite tense until Steve McQueen accidentally, while picking his knives up, came up to me and I managed to charm him and then he changed into a woman and then

I was relieved and took his hand and put it on my breast to show him or her that I was actually a woman too, and both being women we became very happy about not having to shoot each other and we made mad, sexy love. There you go.

Did you wake up in a cold sweat or was it one that you didn't remember until later?
I woke up like, 'Wow, that was great!', and then I wrote it down.

Do you have a lot of friends?
Yeah, I guess now I've got quite a lot of friends. When I went to Iceland this Christmas I was still convinced that all my true friends were there. And then it surprised me that there were a lot of people I really missed. It takes time, even though you can fiercely love people, or like them, it takes time to get them so into your system that you can't live without them. We went to Blackpool last Friday. I had a special Blackpool gig with my friends from New York DJing and my friend playing oriental film music and Acacia. We got a bus of fifty people, two of my friends from Iceland, the rest English, and we partied really hardcore and it was really special.

Are you looking forward to the festival gig in Scotland?
Scotland's going to be another Glastonbury situation. No sound check, just walk on stage... and it's like Russian roulette really as to what happens. It's very exciting and gets your adrenaline going, that's for sure. Either it works or it doesn't. There's not a lot you can do really if it doesn't. You just have to keep going until the end.

Are you very aware of the crowd, the audience, or do you lose yourself in the music?
I try to work it, because I've done so many hundreds of gigs in my life, and I've been in a lot of really awkward situations, from not hearing anyone in the band, or having smoke covering me, or someone punching his fists up my crotch – a lot of really awkward situations where you still have to do your own thing. And a certain part of it is obviously professionalism, even though you can't hear anything; you still go on till the end.

What female performers do you admire? Who would you like to see live?

I really like Betty Davis. You know that singer?
The actress?
No, she used to be married to Jimi Hendrix – a little bit of rock fact for you.
What was she like?
She's like, completely wild on stage. She used to fuck on stage with someone else while she was singing. In *Star Trek* outfits. The person I most regret never having seen is Sun Ra. I'll never forgive myself for that. I saw Ella Fitzgerald when I was fifteen, and I am very grateful for that. Even though she was sixty-something at the time it was remarkable.
Nina Simone?
No, I've not seen her. She actually played Iceland recently and pissed a lot of people off, because she looked incredibly bored with having to be on stage.
Do you think you'll ever get like that?
Well, that's not a problem: then you just do something else. There's loads of things to do in life – start a school, start a restaurant, become a tour guide or a cook or a nurse or whatever.
Do you feel quite privileged at the moment?
I feel privileged in the sense that I'm working with what I love to do. I mean, the world is full of shoemakers who are doctors, and dentists who are running radio shows. I think radio people doing radio shows and dentists doing dentistry are lucky. I mean, success has got nothing to do with anything; it's just being able to lead the life you want to, you know.
Let's talk about the remix album. The last Sugarcubes album, *It's It*, was also a remix compilation.
I was always the only one in The Sugarcubes that was completely obsessed with remixes, just for the experimental side to it. *It's It* was like a

goodbye to the whole Sugarcubes thing. My new album came about because I was really excited with a lot of things that were going on here, and a way to work with a lot of people, which is quite a modern way, is to get them to remix for you.

How did you choose who you wanted to remix your music?

We did it quite cleverly. I mean, even before *Debut* was finished, Nellee and I would start picking and sending and getting remixes done – like done for excitement – and then we'd put them out for the clubs. And listening back to all the remixes, I got this sudden idea. At first, my record companies abroad were like, 'We want a remix album before last Christmas', to pump out more money, and I told them, 'No way, fuck off, I'd never do anything like that and no, I'm not putting out all the remixes', just six out of twenty, which I thought were timeless.

Remixes that stand up as songs in their own right?

That's exactly right. And I never buy white labels. So I thought, OK, let's put out the songs I don't want to be lost or forgotten. So I picked six remixes to put on an EP, for the same price as a single, with forty minutes of material.

So who are the chosen six?

It's 'Underworld', 'Sabres of Paradise' and 'Black Dog'. Three mixes from 'Sabres', two from 'Black Dog' and one from 'Underworld'.

With all your remixes and even with The Sugarcubes, it's all dance. Why's that? Aren't you interested in other styles of remix, say hip-hop?

Personally, I listen to Public Enemy and I would be dead if they didn't exist. And I listen to a lot of American music, but many people in that scene don't get what I'm on about. I can't blame them. They hear this voice and they just go like 'What the fuck is this?' Some of them have tried to do remixes, but the chemistry hasn't worked.

What's the name of the remix EP?

It's a very long title: *The Best Remixes of the Debut Album for All the People That Don't Buy White Labels.*

That's a very straightforward, no bullshit title.

I just wanted to make sure that it's not a second album. A lot of the record companies abroad

wanted to pretend that it was Björk album number two and sell it full price, and I just couldn't believe that. It's such bollocks, with material you've already paid for, they're just taking the piss. Record companies actually prefer doing greatest hits albums, compilations, remix albums, because it's all paid for.

And that is the most direct action that you as an artist can take, to prevent public misconception of your product?

Yes, to call the album that, and to sell it for that price. I like that. The record will be disabled because of the title, like a person without arms or something, not an independent statement. Because it isn't. The songs have already been written and released, it's not a new thing.

So what is new?

I bought a Sony projector telly. Do you want to see it?

[we go upstairs to Björk's lounge, and play 'Vessel', Björk's new longform video directed by Stephane Sednaoui]

Stephane shot this didn't he?

Yes.

Is Stephane your boyfriend?

Yeah. *[smirking]*

What was the visual style that you were looking to achieve?

I just want it to be really straightforward, because when I do things like videos, I'm quite into being theatrical, experimental, doing little games. When he was doing the documentary I just wanted to be really straightforward and honest. And I thought Stephane was a really great person to make it look flexible and alive.

Do you style yourself?

Yes.

Have you always?

I got some serious support in the beginning from Judy Blame and he told me 'You don't need a stylist, just wear your own clothes.' He gave me a confidence and reassurance at the beginning of my lunacy schedule that is now very, very precious to me.

Who are you working with musically at the moment?

Evelyn Glennie. She's a percussionist from Scotland, same age as me – twenty-eight. She travels around with classical orchestras and she's actually deaf, which is even more exciting. We wrote three songs together. One out of jamming, two songs where I actually wrote the melodies and the chords and she figured out what she would do inside that, but it was very, very exciting.

A lot of the tracks you wrote around the time of *Debut* didn't make it onto the album. Is there a danger that these could also remain unreleased?

I think you never really know. At the end of the day, the reason I'm doing all of this is to make music and work with exciting people, and to continue to do that financially you have to pick out certain songs and put them on a record. And what I sort of aim for is maybe having twenty or thirty songs and then picking out ten and putting them on an album. Sometimes the ten you pick are not necessarily the best ones, but the ones that work together as a unit. And that was the *Debut* album. So I guess I'll continue to do things like that.

Did the success of *Debut* come as a surprise to you?

The surprise was because of how I was trying not to please absolutely anyone, probably the same as you're having with your magazine, like because you're not trying to please anyone, you're just doing what the fuck you want and that's what people want.

And that's honesty.

Exactly. And I am going through all the magazines in the bookshop and I can just tell that the people who are making this magazine just love doing it and they're doing it not because of other people, but because of themselves, and there is a certain enthusiasm involved that is just magic. It's easy to say that afterwards. It's hard for me to judge it that closely. The surprise was, I managed to please the most people I ever pleased in my life, which

is a contradiction, but I think there is a little law in there somewhere.

Are you afraid that people will become Björked out?

Oh yes, terrified.

I'm hearing it everywhere – there are people making love to it, there are people dying to it.

It's out of my hands; there's nothing I can do. I mean I'm not saying it's bad, I'm just saying once you put a record out, it's like you've got a kid: you don't own the kid, you try to educate it, try to keep it warm, try to give it as much nutrition as possible so it can survive on its own in the world. Same when you make a record: you do it the best you can, but I'd much rather be, like everyone, quite little, and still to be discovered, that there is more of a 'coming' sort of thing, rather than being overexposed. But, we'll just see – take it as it comes.

But you are in control of your own life?

That's another story. I am in control of what I do, but not of what people think of it. And I don't want to be. I like all the different angles that come out, and I love the fact that there are people of all different ages, sexes and races that listen to my music. I'm very proud of that, and I'd be very happy if people misunderstand it in as many ways as possible, you know, and from all the different angles.

You once said, 'Warning: this interview won't bring you any closer to the music.'

I still agree with that, because it takes you away. I mean, I don't know how interested you still are, but next time you listen to my record you will listen to it from a different angle, because you talked to me or met me. My favourite thing to do would be to write music in my house and then sneak up behind people and put headphones on them and they wouldn't know what age the person who did it was, what sex he or she was, or where they came from, and you wouldn't even understand the words.

And still like it.

Or just be affected by it, because that's what it's supposed to do. The music is supposed to bring out some things in you that you didn't know you had.

Is there anything else you'd like to say?

No, I always feel like I say too much rather than too little.

'You've reached Harry Crews. You have two minutes. Leave it.' The drawled answer-phone message I've been repeatedly hearing for two months reverberates gently. In Florida, where Crews currently lives, the afternoon is easing past while darkness falls in London. Despite his apparent delight at British press interest, the Southern writer is proving charmingly elusive.

Born in 1935 in Georgia, Harry Crews did not quite have luck and good fortune on his side. Childhood loneliness and the poverty of rural life provided inspiration for much of his work, as did the isolating experience of a freak accident involving scalding water, a post-adolescence spent as part of the Marine Corps, the death of one son in a drowning accident and a decade-long struggle for acclaim.

Harry Crews deliberately writes from the periphery of the literary scene. In the collection Classic Crews (1993) it is his bullshit-free observation and fearless approach to an essentially hostile world that make his work so unique. He is not concerned with left-field concepts of kink or abnormality, but presents his tableaux, however bizarre, within the humble parameters of daily love and common emotion. Love, death, betrayal, greed: part of the reason his name is not as commonly known as it should be is the discomfort people feel with his idiosyncratic, unapologetic matter-of-factness. The gallows humour and determination to describe beatifically the least glamorous of circumstances, while refusing to create artistic fancy where none exists, produces challenging, gritty prose that is part-fable and part snapshot of daily life.

In person, Harry Crews is professionally charming and searingly intelligent. He speaks in perfectly formed, perfectly honest sentences whose sentiments shift between rhetoric, paranoia and cynicism. He talks about the pain of trying to produce his best possible work, yet the only question that seriously throws him is, 'Are you a masochist?' One wonders how comfortably his deep mistrust of the establishment sits with good old American pride, and how well-rehearsed his hatred of commerciality, bigotry and artifice is. Although Crews maintains that 'there is absolutely no romance whatsoever' in his work, his chronicles of disaffection and the perception they're saturated with remain in the mind long after his gruff voice has broken the phone connection.

Dazed & Confused | **Why do you think it is that you've only occupied the margins of mainstream literary culture?**
Harry Crews | It would probably have to do with my notion of the human predicament, the human situation and the subjects of my books. I don't think there are an awful lot of people who, as they would say, worry about that sort of thing. They like to talk about how many freaks I have in my books. I don't call them freaks, I call them people with special considerations. And besides that, I've had all the readers that I've wanted, and I would maintain that art is aristocratic, not democratic, and probably the more people that like you, the worse you are. All you have to do is look at *The New York Times* bestsellers' list: once in a great long while a book of some merit gets mentioned, but what generally gets onto it are what middle-aged housewives want to read about – bosom-busters, romance novels. My stuff is definitely not of that persuasion. **What would you describe as good, or valuable art?**

Art that turns the witness back upon himself. Art is a moral issue. It's a moral occupation practised by not necessarily moral people. It's about good and bad and things that you, the reader, have to make judgements about. Since it's a psychological truism that before you can make judgements about something outside yourself you have to first make judgements about yourself, I would say stuff that is good or valuable is that which makes you re-examine your own values – and heart.

What do you most respect?
Honesty, openness, the willingness to listen even when what is being said happens not to be your own point of view, but you're willing to listen to what the other person has to say before you gas them or hang them or segregate them or pin them up or burn them in a furnace.

What do you see in yourself that frightens you the most?
It's the bloody teeth, the smell of something that's just stormed out of the woods. I think all of us have a very thin veneer of civilization painted over what underneath is a savage and marauding beast, and I know that better than anyone else. I'm up-front enough to admit it, because most people won't. It puts me one step above and over them.

What physical environment do you feel least comfortable in?
The more civilized it is, the more terrified I am. I mean people with suits, with ties and a ring of keys. If you give someone a white shirt and a tie and a ring of keys you'll find out what kind of a son of a bitch he is. Give them to him in the morning and you'll know before noon.

If there is a complaint you have, what is it?
That I'm cut off too much from the land and the woods and animals of all kinds. I grew up with all that and when I got out of the Marines I didn't realize how much I missed being out there and working up an honest sweat with an axe or a plough or a shovel.

What are you afraid of?
My fellow man. My fellow man has given me no reason not to be afraid of him and he's given me every reason to be afraid. I am particularly afraid of groups of my fellow men, groups of almost any sort, organized groups, government. Groups of human beings will skin you alive and leave you hanging, bleeding and dripping from a tree in order to 'save' you. Every son of a bitch and his brother is out to 'save' somebody. People like me, most generally. In order to save somebody, they can kill them, wreck them, bankrupt them, whatever.

How much confidence do you have in other people?
If I don't know them pretty well, damn little. I try to keep my eyes open and my back covered, against a wall or a friend. Because that's what the world has taught me. It's taught me to, as fighter pilots put it, 'cover your six'. (Six o'clock is right behind you.)

If someone put a curse on you when you were born, what was it?
Probably being a writer. I've come to the conclusion in the last few years, it's just about destroyed me physically and emotionally, shredded my nerves. Artists are never allowed to let things alone. They're forever picking at the scabs. Writers, by their nature, spend their time thinking about, wondering about, delving into, trying to understand the very things that the rest of the world doesn't like to think about.

Shakespeare had to have had the most complicated, complex and punishing inner life. It couldn't have been fun for him to write about regicide, incest, betrayal, death. That's not fun. People who think writers are having fun are simply people who've never done it. They don't see you in a room for days, all those years. I think of all the words I've written and all I can think of is, 'My God, how many days and nights have I spent alone when I could have been fishing or dancing or eating a steak or making love?'

Which questions have you yet to find the answer to?
Damn near all of them. Damn near any question

you could ask, I haven't found the answer to: wherein honour lies, wherein manhood lies, wherein courage lies. It's a battle that people who don't have closed minds fight every day of their lives. Unless of course you're just willing to go to the church-house or the university or the school and listen to some bastard tell you the answers to all these. There's no shortage of people who will tell you the answers to all these things, but I've never found any that satisfy me. That's why I write fiction. Fiction is an effort to understand all the questions. The reason why writers keep writing is because they don't have that understanding, they're still seeking it.

What have you discovered that you'd rather not know?

The absolute blind brutality of groups of people or organizations. Somehow in such things nobody has to be responsible. When you get out of a one-to-one situation or relationship and are put in a group of people, the organizations destroy things.

What do you dream about?

Well, I've been having lots of nightmares. Dreams are all metaphors for something else, and I dream a lot. In recent times I've been in danger, going down cliffs, white-water rivers, waterfalls. Real juvenile bullshit things like that. But it doesn't stop them from being scary as hell. A lot of things scare me. Being lost and being convinced in the dream that I'm not just lost now, or for the next fifteen minutes, but for ever.

If you could bring one person who died in your life back, who would it be?

My father. He died before I could know him. I was twenty-one months old. But also my son, whom I loved dearly and deeply. I only had him for four years before he drowned. He was just a baby, four years old. Hell, I don't know. God save me from having to make such decisions.

How important is the concept of family to you?

It's probably the ultimate in importance. The ties of blood, the extended family, knowing one another, supporting one another. Which puts me in a very bad position in the twentieth century, because we're not allowed to know any old people anymore. You're not allowed to grow up with them. We warehouse them, put them in homes.

What do you regret?

Gimme six months maybe I can tell you. I deeply regret that I could not be a husband. I had a wife. One – I thought that was my fair share. She was a good woman but I couldn't live with her. My son and I were tight, close, we respected one another, but I suppose I'd have been a better father if I was a better husband.

Who or what do you feel loyalty towards?

The first thing that comes to mind is my friends, but also my mother. And, as much as I've bad-mouthed the damn country to you. I feel a tremendous loyalty to America. They didn't have to draft me in. I had a brother fighting in Korea and they were killing people over there and I went down and joined the Marine Corps. It's not as though I joined the Foreign Air Force or some other wimp, nerdish service. I joined people that got down and dirty when the fighting began. Because my country falls short of what I'd have it be, doesn't mean I don't love it or am not loyal to it. If I criticize it harshly, it's only because I expect so much of it and it pains me that it falls short of the mark I'd have it reach. But my loyalty lies in the following order: blood relations, country, friends.

You may not have heard of Noam Chomsky, but one way or another you've heard from him. According to The Arts and Humanities Citation Index, only Marx, Lenin, Shakespeare, the Bible, Plato, Aristotle and Freud are quoted more often. So who is he?

Noam Avram Chomsky is a slightly built, American professor at Massachusetts Institute of Technology, with a reputation as the most radical intellectual alive today. In the late 1950s and early 1960s, he revolutionized the study of linguistics with a number of controversial theories about the way we process and under-stand language, including the concept that humans were 'wired for language', in much the same way that we are wired for the interpreta-tion of visual stimuli. While this idea might seem commonplace in an age of home computers, it probably came across like science fiction back in the Cold War era. Nonetheless, having redefined the intellectual territory on which linguistics was debated, Chomsky was soon acknowledged as the leading theorist in his field.

But it is as a cultural and political commentator and champion of human rights that Chomsky has had notoriety thrust upon him. Ever since he was arrested on an early anti-Vietnam protest and put in a cell with Norman Mailer, he has been regarded as the most scathing critic of American foreign and domestic policy. Despite the apparent dryness of his academic background, and for all the precision of his language, Chomsky is not one to mince words. In his 1988 book, Manufacturing Consent, *he stated: 'If the Nuremberg laws were applied, then every post-war American president would have been hanged.'*

Referring to Roosevelt, Eisenhower, Kennedy, Johnson, Nixon, Ford, Carter, Reagan and Bush as war criminals has not endeared him to the Great American Public. Undaunted, he has repeatedly attacked US foreign policy, particular-ly in Central America and the Middle East, which he denounced as self-serving and immoral. This flies in the face of the US State Department's line,

which is that America is only interested in preserving democracy and countering the twin evils of Communism and terrorism.

In his homeland, Chomsky is a prophet without honour, virtually a non-person within the mainstream media. But like many voices of dissent, his is clinical, rational and disturbingly coherent. His towering academic achievements mean he cannot easily be ignored. Because of this, he is in constant demand as a speaker on the lecture circuit. He was recently in London to give the keynote address at the Human Rights Convention organized by civil rights group Liberty. The following unedited interview was conducted in a ten-minute session just before Noam Chomsky delivered his speech.

Dazed & Confused | **There is a train of thought that says that the O J Simpson trial is the end of the American justice system, and has done untold damage to race relations. What is your reaction to those ideas?**
Noam Chomsky | If you really want to know about the American justice system, read serious criminologists, like William Chambliss. For some years now, he has been working on a programme with the police in Washington DC, travelling with them, and monitoring their activities – that means against blacks. And he publishes the transcripts in criminal justice journals. You can't say they're treating black people like criminals. They're treating them like a population under military occupation. Nobody even pretends to observe constitutional rights. If you want to break into somebody's home, grab somebody and throw him in jail, you go right ahead and do it. If someone says: 'Where's your warrant?' the police just laugh at you. There's nothing secret about it.

There are more black males involved in the criminal justice system, either in prison or waiting to go there, or on parole, than there are in college. And the figure is going up. There's just a war against the black population. It's not particularly racist: there's a close race-to-class correlation in the United States, so this makes some sense as part of a class war, and blacks are a very vulnerable part of the working class. They're defenceless, basically.

The same thing happens with the 'drug war'. You want to know about that? Then look at the criminal penalties for possession. There's two kinds of cocaine: crack and powder. Crack happens to be the favoured drug in the ghetto. Powder is what the rich guys sniff out in the suburbs when they come home from the bank. Basically, it's the same drug. But the ratio of the penalty for possession is a hundred to one. Your fine, or period of imprisonment, will on average be a hundred times more severe for possession of crack than powder cocaine. They don't break into the homes of bankers looking for drugs.

And if you want to be serious about it, ask yourself how many bank executives are in jail. The OACD did a survey recently on the profits from the drug trade, and they put the total figure at about half a trillion dollars a year (five hundred thousand million dollars, or $500,000,000,000). Now more than half of that money passes through US banks. You know how much passes through Columbia, where the cocaine comes from? Seven per cent. So, you want to do something about drugs and stop the men who are profiting from this trade? Go down to Wall Street. They're sitting right there. That's where the money is getting laundered. The CIA and the Professional Research Service did studies in the late 80s on American chemical companies, and their exports to Latin America. Turns out their exports are way in excess of that needed for any industrial use, and the stuff that is being exported is exactly what's being used to make drugs. How many American chemical company executives are sitting in jail? What you see sitting in jail is a black kid who was caught with a joint or some crack in his pocket. Because that's what the drug war is for: to criminalize and get rid of the black population.

You have referred to senior figures in the Pentagon, the multinational oil companies and the financial corporations as 'behaving like Mafia dons'. Do you see them that way?
'Mafia' is a colourful term; they don't work exactly the same way. But their goals are very similar: to enrich themselves, increase their power, extend their control over the population, and reduce the infection of democratic participation in our society. And they do it pretty well.

But is it an unconscious, emergent property of their behaviour, or is it calculated?
Well, for the smarter people it's conscious. It goes right back to the beginnings of American history. The country was set up on the principle that the people who owned the country ought to govern it. That was the major maxim of John Jay, who was the President of the Constitutional Convention, and the first Chief Justice of the Supreme Court. The whole Constitution is based on the aim, as James Madison put it, 'to protect the opulent minority' against the normal people; to protect the respectable, the serious property-owners. And that goes right up to the President. So, the smarter people say it like it is; the dumber people sing praises to democracy. But the point is, if you don't go along with it, either consciously or unconsciously, you begin to get weeded out of the system. It starts in kindergarten and continues through school, high school, and into the professions. The threat is always there: if you don't play ball, you'll end up on the streets.

Surely, under these circumstances, it's no wonder that people give up all their hope and turn their backs on the whole thing?
Well, some do. Some join the mad parade. Others struggle and resist.

There's another fashionable notion that the Internet, which has so far managed to remain free from censorship, offers some form of resistance. Do you see that?
It's possible, but it was also possible with the printing press and radio and TV. Technology tends to be pretty neutral. It doesn't care how it gets used. The printing press can be a liberating device, and it can also be used to repress people. It all depends on who's in control of the Net right now. But when people talk about the Internet being free, let's not deceive ourselves: it's free for relatively rich people. You're not on the Internet unless you're relatively wealthy. The reason it's been free is because, ironically, it comes out of the Pentagon, and they don't really care very much. But now the entertainment corporations are getting interested, and Time-Warner wants a piece, and so on. Now, when they get interested, you get a real power struggle. And the question is whether it will be handed over to them, and subjected to their controls.

I wanted to ask you about the bombing of the federal building in Oklahoma. What do you make of the two white men who have been charged with this attack? What do they represent to you?

Well, you can certainly understand them. The guys that have been charged are what you call Angry White Males. These are like, maybe sixty-five per cent of the population, who are basically high-school graduates whose lives have collapsed in the last twenty years. They claim there has been a 'war' against them. Their incomes have dropped about twenty per cent. Their wives have to go to work, to put food on the table. And these are people who have an image of themselves, you know: 'I go to work, I bring home money, my wife takes care of the kids, they respect me, we take a vacation once a year...' And now there's nothing like that. It's all fallen apart. And they've been taught for the last fifty years that you've got to hate the government. Fifty years of intense corporate propaganda, which has managed to hide corporate power completely. These people don't read *Business Week*, they don't read *Fortune*, they don't know that profits went up fifty-four per cent last year for the *Fortune* 500, the world's most profitable five hundred companies, whose annual returns are regarded as an index of market performance. All they see is, 'Well, jobs are scarce, government is doing something to me', so you take out your frustration on it, you blow up one of its buildings.

I talk to a lot of these people. I meet them on the lecture circuit, and their line is: 'Look, we have to defend ourselves from federal government, and therefore we need guns.' Now, after that comes madness, and the country is dissolved into sects of every crazy kind you can imagine. There are a lot of people in the US who think that the federal government is bringing UN troops into the country in black helicopters to commit genocide against the American people. When I laugh about this, people send me letters, and photos of the black helicopters: 'Look, I filmed them...', that sort of thing. And the other thing: a lot of people think they're bringing in extra-terrestrials. In fact, there's a place out in Idaho, a mountain where everybody goes, a short distance from an airforce base. And at that airforce base there are planes flying in all night, nobody knows what's going on. But people go to this mountain in Idaho to see the extra-terrestrials, who are being brought in by the US airforce, to commit genocide against the American people, unless we arm ourselves.

Now, you have to respect the feelings behind this kind of thing. The feelings are quite genuine, but because there is no constructive way to react, and people's minds have been turned into mush by decades of propaganda and crazy entertainment, this is what happens. It's not unlike Islamic fundamentalism. In fact, it's probably more extreme. I've never seen a comparative study, but I'll bet you there are more fundamentalist religious fanatics in the United States than in Iran. Quite a lot more; and they're just as extreme as the most extreme mullahs you can dig up. And they may even hold power over the Republican Party. It's not a small phenomenon. About half the population of the US thinks that the world was created two thousand years ago. That's not a joke. The US is probably the most fundamentalist country in the world.

One of the defendants in the bombing has actually claimed political rights as a prisoner...
Yeah, well, that's because the federal government is your enemy. And the reason they call themselves 'People's Militias' is this streak in American history they're appealing to. There was a time when 'the militias' fought off the British Redcoats. So that streak is somehow hidden in the American consciousness. And if you look at the Second Amendment that these people appeal to for their right to bear arms, it says: 'Nothing shall infringe the right of the people to bear arms as part of militias set up by the State.' See, there was no US federal army at that time, so the States agreed to set up militias in case the British came back. The British were a big military power, America had just fought and won its war of independence, so it was a very genuine threat. Now, the threat is not the British but the federal government, or aliens, or UN troops, or Russians, or Arabs, or anything.

Security is very tight. Have you been threatened yourself?
There are a lot of crazy people around. Even on American campuses, I often have police getting involved. They've asked me before if they can provide a visible police protection, but I always refuse, which means you can see the undercover cops in the crowd. It's not hard to spot a policeman in a philosophy centre. Being followed, being threatened, it's part of the game.

September 1995
Interview | Mark Sanders

*One, two, testing. This tape is being recorded
in the studio of Jake and Dinos Chapman,
surrounded by the aberrations and distortions
of their imaginations: dismembered mannequins,
Siamese fuckfaces, stork eyes, dicks, cunts... Jake
is sitting here in front of me in a shiny white
boilersuit from hell, smiling mischievously. Dinos
has just returned from another part of the
studio. OK, everyone's ready. Let's start, but first...*

Dazed & Confused | **Say something for me to
test the level.**
Jake Chapman | Something.
Dinos Chapman | Something.
Do you have a definable aesthetic?
JC | Yeah, but it is variable.
Can you pinpoint it at all?
JC | Availability; any object that is happy to reci-
procate desire.
So your work is about desire?
JC | Not 'about', but 'like'.
**So your work functions as a funnel for
desire?**
JC | Funnel?
DC | Funhole. *[laughs]*
JC | Or maybe a U-bend for desire. *[laughs]* It
operates desire, it's available for desire.

**So the objects you create are objects that are
designed to pique the unconscious? That is,
the act of ejaculation is the same for everybody, what differs is the object of desire to
which that act is attached?**
JC | We're interested in forms of practice that
dissimulate or conceal their masochistic origin.
**Looking at your work, it seems to delve
into that act of fascination and expose
an aspect of horror and mutilation that
is latent within each of us and in a broader
cultural context. There's a filtered
fascination through TV that deals a daily
dose of death for mass consumption.
Do you consider your work to explore the
unconscious desires that remain deeply
embedded within a mediated sexuality?**
JC | That returns us to the aesthetics of
scopophilia, of obtaining sexual pleasure from
the act of looking. The eyes are an erotogenic
zone. The spectacle of culture provokes the
voyeur to observe that which he or she knows
is prohibited. He or she transgresses that law
and so the oscillation between moral observance
and the bad conscience in perverse looking
becomes the point of pleasure.
**That was what was so powerful about you
displaying your sculpture *The Disasters of
War* in Cork Street last year. That piece
looked out into the street and people just
couldn't help but stop and stare at the
mutilated corpses, they were revolted and
yet excited at the same time, fascinated by
their own disgust.**
JC | A dead work of art. We wanted to produce
a morally ambivalent focus for consumption,
where the mediation itself becomes
physiological, so that, say for the voyeur,
pleasure is heightened by having a smaller

This page from top
Zygotic Acceleration...
de-sublimated model
(detail), 1997
Zygotic Acceleration...
de-sublimated model,
1997
Opposite page
from top
Two-faced Cunt, *1996*
Chromosexual, *1997*

and smaller orifice to peep through. It is the mediation that becomes the pleasure, it is not the object but the mediation.

The act of looking becomes an act of control?

JC | It is also a question of terror. I don't think it means possessing the object of desire. For instance, Sacher Masoch in *Venus in Furs* describes whips and furs as the means by which he terrorizes himself.

The interesting thing about that is the way in which his fantasy and reality become fused. Masoch's desire is completely exposed and turned into an act.

DC | A contract.

And your work manifests itself on that level? Or do you see your work as an anti-aesthetic in any way?

JC | We prefer something more prostitutional, a means of producing desiring objects. We wouldn't want to think they were part of a passive, anti-aesthetic. All right, Nick?

[enter Nick Waplington – photographer]

Nick Waplington | You've both got your Altern 8 suits on today then.

[he points at Jake and Dinos' white paper, forensic-style boilersuits]

NW | They're very revivalist. How's it going?

JC | Nick, you've walked into our interview.

NW | Oh, sorry!

What about this latest exhibition coming up at the Victoria Miro gallery?

JC | Why don't you have a go at explaining it?

DC | OK. We are making the largest and most extreme conglomeration of Siamese fuckfaces...

JC | ...ever known to man.

How large?

DC | There will be about twenty or so figures in it, a frantic, small group of them, irreconcilable, with certain objects inserted.

A ring?

DC | Yeah, a ring.

JC | An anus.

DC | An anus ring. *[he sings]* A ring a ring a roses, we all fall down, with children.

All of them heading outwards?

DC | Not all of them, some are self-reflexively looking back in, a couple are upside down and one is kind of leaning out. They are all recognizable as Siamese twins or fuckfaces, but they look like they're all breaking out into some zygotic, erratic cell division.

JC | Acceleration.

DC | Acceleration, yeah.

JC | It's like *Jurassic Park*. We tapped into this primeval earwax that we found while we were out walking the other day.

DC | It all stems from dinosaur's earwax.

JC | We found some primordial libido, *[laughs]* and we fertilized it with the semen stains we found on a de Sadean manuscript of *120 Days of Sodom* and gave life to this...

Aberration?

JC | Right, a single-cell organism gone wrong – or gone right. It's our scientific projection of how the libido should become – a perfect cathartic device, a pleasure object. A model of how the libido will de-evolve. Superseding adulthood, the world will become infested with fuckface clones.

We will all wear our erogenous zones on our faces.

JC & DC | That's right!

JC | We already talk through our arses. Maybe we are already advanced biogenetically!

Enter fuckface. At least if you wear your penis on your nose, there will be no problem with size. It will be there for all to see.

JC | It's just another means of offering sadistic objects: allowing these objects to permeate into aesthetic matters and encouraging collectors to become Sadean libertines. We encourage the prostitutional role in producing art.

Where is the collector going to put this piece? In a private house, the bedroom or bathroom, or wherever?

DC | It's going to be an umbrella stand. *[laughs]*

That would turn it around once more. As clothes and hats were discarded on top of it over time, it would be as if the system were slowly closing in on the libido with umbrellas and old walking sticks.

DC | I am sure they will do something to it.

What if the collector is someone who secretly wants to destroy it?

DC | There's a point.

And the latest fuckface porn video?

JC | We made a contractual arrangement with a production company where our severed head, with a penis for a nose, was used as a prop. We were interested only in the contract of obtaining a generic porn movie with our sculpture as the star.

DC | It also works as an index for our other work, the piece could stand as an instrumental video for the head. Buy the head, watch the video. Here's the head, now have your jollies.

The head comes with the video? Isn't an Italian collector going to buy six of them? You better put a diagram in there as well, in case he gets confused.

JC | It's OK, he has six orifices.

DC | A mouth, an anus, two nostrils, two ears.

That's the core, isn't it? The moral inhibitions that people have and where they come from, be it socially or culturally. You might see yourself as a very liberated person, but in many ways, we are all shackled.

JC | But we are reluctant to accept that the work is anything to do with a liberating

This page
Doggy, *1996*
Opposite page
Unnameable, *1997*

process, because we understand moral repression or moral inhibition only as formal sexualized practices originating in masochism.

So censorship as a form of sexualized pleasure, then?

JC | Censorship demands that you have knowledge of all the restrictions that you are proscribing against yourself, all of the sick self-suspicions. You can't proscribe prohibitive laws against what you don't know exists, so in a way, the moral person is simultaneously immoral.

The more the level of repression, the more it will out. Religion being a case in point. Abstinence is written into our culture, denial and guilt giving rise to ecstatic sexuality.

JC | It's Newtonian. The more you deny the expenditure of energy, the more that expenditure will be climactically released – like Tourette's syndrome, with its multiple ticks and barks.

DC | Woof!

[Wagner's Ring Cycle *begins to permeate from the next room]*

And the idea of pain as well: St Sebastian with arrows is a potent icon of pleasure.

DC | Like the guy who chopped his leg off because he didn't feel complete with it. Throughout his entire life, he felt like he needed to lose his leg. For years, he would strap poles down the one side of it so he could simulate a prosthetic. He would cut off his circulation and continuously go back to the doctors and ask for it to be removed, but they wouldn't do it.

JC | Oh, so you're awake.

DC | Finally he shot himself in the knee, but when he woke up on a hospital bed, the doctors were telling him that they could save the leg *[laughs]* and all he could say was that he didn't want the fucking thing.

Lose the leg!

JC | It gets stranger because there were two of them. *[laughs]* An American and an English… and an Irish. No, the American shot his leg off while the English one was crying because he didn't have the guts to get rid of his leg himself.

DC | He was going to lay his across a railway track and get a train to cut it off, but couldn't go through with it. There must be a whole sub-section of the species who are desperate to lose their legs!

JC | Crypto-paraplegics. *[laughs]*

The obsessive power of the mind – very Cartesian. What about the American woman who was into necrophilia in a big way?

JC | Oh yeah, that was the woman who wouldn't get out of the coffin.

That's right, she used to steal the corpses and put them in the back of the hearse for dirty weekends.

DC | Was she the woman who drilled through the ceiling of the morgue, or did she actually work there?

She got a job there especially.

JC | She was having sex with one of the corpses and they had her on *Eye-witness News*, on live TV in this hearse. They had all the press and the TV and she refused to get out of the coffin. She was really in love.

And apparently, if you are a corpse in the States, you have no rights, so they could only prosecute her for taking the hearse without permission. I think she got a small fine, three points on her licence, or something. *[laughs]*

JC | That reminds me of an essay by George Bataille. A man is calmly walking down the street and he stares at the sun and suddenly tears one of his fingers off.

Which Bataille book?

JC | It was in *Visions of Excess*; the essay is 'The Sacrificial Mutilation and the Severed Ear of Vincent Van Gogh'... a moment of absolute insanity.

We say 'insanity', but in actual fact it could be read as a moment of utter sanity, of total clarity.

JC | Of complete lucidity, of being affected in the most profound way towards the goal of a particular desire. The police caught him and took him to hospital. It is a medical description, a medical reference, not a hallucination in any way.

That's what makes *The Story of the Eye* such a powerful book, because it is so loaded. The eye as sun, the eye as control and the eye as bodily fluid as it is inserted into Simone's vagina. Religion and desire connected through the eye of a priest.

JC | And Bataille was a librarian.

Well that just about wraps things up.

DC | What is that red light on your machine for?

It's a voice-activated censor. If you touch it...

Terry Southern was born in Alvaro, Texas, in 1924. At the age of sixteen, his phenomenal writing career began with a radical reworking of the tales of Edgar Allan Poe, which he 'translated' into Texan. After the Second World War, he lived in Paris, where he began to exchange jazz records and 'other stuff' between France and the States. In the early 1950s, he and George Plimpton co-founded the Paris Review, regarded as the premier literary magazine of its era. In it, Southern personally burst the Hemingway bubble with a piece entitled 'Face of the Matador', satirizing the macho posturing of much American literature of the time. Southern was also influential in getting writers and poets like William Burroughs, Allen Ginsberg and Gregory Carso published; his friends included Charlie Parker and Simone de Beauvoir.

After Paris, he moved to Geneva to write Flash and Filigree and The Magic Christian. Both were published in the late 1950s to widespread critical acclaim, the latter becoming a best-seller. But rather than follow the well-established route of celebrity novelist, Southern became interested in film, beginning to write original scripts and reworking others. His first attempt was the seminal Cold War satire Dr Strangelove (Stanley Kubrick, 1963), starring Peter Sellers in both the title role and that of an impotent English officer, Colonel Mandrake, who watches helplessly as a lunatic American general single-handedly starts World War Three. A dark, sardonic movie, Dr Strangelove was, like much of Southern's work, well ahead of its time.

Following this, he was drafted in to rewrite Christopher Isherwood's screenplay of Evelyn Waugh's The Loved One (Tony Richardson, 1965). The result was less than the sum of its parts, to say the least. But then Southern went on to pro-duce several classics, including The Cincinnati Kid (Norman Jewison, 1965), Barbarella (Roger Vadim, 1967) and, perhaps most importantly, Easy Rider (Dennis Hopper, 1969), the movie that changed America's perception of youth culture.

His novels include Candy (1958, made into a mediocre movie, not scripted by Southern) and the amazing Blue Movie (1970), which many producers have tried – and failed – to turn into a film. An anthology of his short stories called Red Dirt Marijuana and Other Tastes was published a few years ago (1995), while his most recent work was Texas Summer, published in 1993. This winter sees the publication of The Virgin Story, tracing the rise of the once-independent label, which brought artists as diverse as Bob Marley, Culture Club and U2 to the world's attention.

A resolute anglophile, Terry Southern teaches at Columbia and Yale, drinks Bombay Sapphire or Bass Ale, and speaks with the clipped tones of a British naval commander. His ash-coloured hair is worn long and unkempt; his beard is bushy and overgrown. Now seventy-one, he uses a walking cane, and his owlish grey eyes peer suspiciously over his tinted bifocal glasses. As befits a man of his stature, Southern is regally impervious to the hubbub around him in the bar of the Gramercy Park Hotel, New York.

Dazed & Confused | **Terry, you've been writing for fifty-five, sixty years now. Do you still feel the urge to write when you get up in the morning?**
Terry Southern | No.
Did you ever feel the urge to write?
No.
Then what makes you write? Money?
Well... yeah. And being encouraged by other people wanting to see some of my work.

From top
Terry Southern, 1968
Terry Southern, right,
with director Joseph
McGrath, left, and
Beatle Ringo Starr on
the set of The Magic
Christian, *December*
1969

You don't sound like a Texan, you don't have the drawl...
Naaa, but ah cain ree-vurt to it.
How did you lose it in the first place? Why do you sound so anglophile?
Well, I tried to shake it off. As I would hope that those Australians would try to shake that fuck-ing accent off, I can't stand that goddamn sound. *[does bad impersonation of Aussie accent]*
Some people think the early 1960s and early 1970s was the golden age of rock and that everything these days is just a pastiche – rearranged notions from that era. Do you see it that way?
Yeah, I do. *[defiantly]* Yeah.
A lack of the original threat, perhaps?
Well, it doesn't seem to have evolved in that direction; it seems to have lapsed into a series of abrupt flashes and then fragmentation. Yeah, I don't think much of the present scene.
Were you aware of the punk phenomenon as it happened? Did you have a perspective on that?
Yeah, I was aware of The Sex Pistols, and that was, uh... innovative *[chuckles]*. But apart from that? That was the only legitimate departure I've seen from the path established by The Stones and The Beatles.
Some critics argue that the vanguard of popular music now, the cutting edge, the real threat to the status quo, lies in the black arena, with hip-hop acts. What's your response to that?
Well, it's definitely got an audience, and it's interesting musically, but I don't think it will attract a large non-black audience. Not here in the US.
Surely that's got a lot to do with the way the music industry is so segregated in this

country, with the radio, TV and other media dividing everything into 'black' and 'white' music?

Well, that was the phenomenal thing about Elvis: it was the first time the black sound was acceptable, because it was made by a white person. Otherwise, yes, it is strictly segregated. And it's gone full circle. Now we have race records again, just like we did before Elvis came along.

Did you ever meet any of The Sex Pistols?

I met Sid and Nancy. I used to go and see them at the Chelsea Hotel.

Did you find Sid pleasant company? I heard conflicting reports from close acquaintances at the time, some of whom described him as a grotesque moron, others who thought he was a sweet, battered child.

Well... *[laughs]* you had to catch him at the right moment, at the right part of his mood swing. Part of his head, I think, was devoted to maintaining his reputation, doing his Dylan Thomas pissing-on-the-curtains thing, y'know? He wanted to build on his reputation for craziness, so a lot of the things he did were done in a studied way. Maybe not totally conscious, perhaps, but in an unconscious conscious way, y'know? He went out for the evening thinking, 'Well, I have to do some indoor graffiti writing tonight', or something. And so being in that basic mood, it was easy to get into that kind of, uh, trip.

What about Nancy?

Well, she was pretty feisty. Y'know, she would keep saying to him, 'You are a proper swine! You swine!' And his response was, 'I'm gonna glass you. I'm going to glass your saucy mug', but she wasn't intimidated in the least. And then they would have their moods of righteousness, when they would try and clean themselves up. I think

they were under rather a lot of pressure from the authorities as well, trying to deport them. They certainly had some enemies who had high-placed friends in the immigration office.

Where did you meet them?

The first time I met Sid and Nancy was with Debbie Harry at the Mudd club, one of the early punk hangouts – a basement, dark and packed with people doing all kinds of unspeakable things in the corners.

Aside from the Virgin book, have you been working on anything else?

Well the last book I had published, about a year ago, was *Texan Summer*. But my mistake in terms of not being more productive is that I very often start things but then keep them in abeyance, so I have several things going at any one time.

But in terms of film scripts, I understand you have a body of unpublished work.

Yeah that's true. How many? I probably have twenty unpublished scripts. Yeah, about twenty at the last count.

Terry Southern on Peter Sellers

Well, you see, Peter had been invited to the wedding of this wealthy Arabic couple who sent chartered jets all over the world to pick up the guests and take them to the Middle East for the wedding. And Peter, who prided himself on being able to locate and copy any accent, ended up sitting next to this guy whose accent he couldn't place. Anyway, turned out the guy was Greek, and an arms dealer, see. So Peter was fascinated by that, and the guy was telling him his latest deal was a big arms sale to the Palestinians. So Peter said to him, 'Well I'm surprised you can sleep easily at night, knowing that those weapons will be used against Jews.' And he turned around and said, 'No problem, I sell to the Jews as well.' So when Peter came back he had his minions check out the arms trade – probably the first time any individual had done this – and it turned out that in America, Britain, France and many Scandinavian countries, the number one gross national product income was from selling arms to the emerging Third World nations.

Anyway, he was so upset by this he decided to do a movie, and asked me to do the script. So he gave me some money to get started, and I was in touch with his people, who did the research. And one of the great scenes of the script, if I might say so, takes place on a beautiful, green common in England somewhere, probably Devon, and it's surrounded by razor wire, because they're having this arms bazaar. And at these arms bazaars they demonstrate the effectiveness of their new weapons. And this is not especially high-tech. This is mainly laid on for some of the poorest nations in the world, although one of the great customers in those days was the Shah of Iran. Anyway, that's the script that's currently in progress, called *Grossing Out*. It was written really for Peter, for him to play several roles.

Did you know Peter Sellers before *Dr Strangelove*? His part, the role of Mandrake, I mean, seems to have been written especially for him.

Yes, I did know him, although we were not really friends at that point. What happened was that Peter went wild over *The Magic Christian*. Before I met him, my publishers called me one day and said 'Peter Sellers has just bought a hundred copies of your book.' He actually went to the publishers, instead of the book store. And it turned out he had bought them to give to all his friends for birthdays or Christmas, whatever. And it turned out later that the person who had turned him on to it was Dr Jonathan Miller who was both Peter's and my doctor at the time. He prescribed us both uppers.

What, THE Jonathan Miller? The one who directs operas and does TV programmes about evolution? He was giving you uppers?

Yeah, because of my workload. He was prescribing me Dexedrine, and some other stuff. Methedrine? Yeah, that was it.

So he was a pretty good doctor; he understood the kind of treatment that writers need.

Oh yeah, excellent. Anyway, he had read *Magic Christian* and liked it, so he passed it on to Peter, who liked it to that extent. So we had that background before we met. To answer your question, yes, the parts of both Strangelove and Mandrake were written specifically for him. In fact, the financing of the movie was entirely dependent upon him playing multiple roles, because of the success of *Lolita* I guess [Kubrick,

1961]. In fact, he was also meant to play the pilot who sits on the bomb, but after shooting for two days, he sprained his ankle getting out of a taxi to go into an Indian restaurant. So we had to get someone else, and you can't replace Peter Sellers with another actor, so we had to get a real redneck. We tried John Wayne, but he realized we'd be sending him up and declined. Then Stanley had a flash and remembered that during the filming of *One-Eyed Jacks* [Marlon Brando, 1961] – before Brando got him sacked – he'd met this real cowboy actor called Slim Pickens. And that's how we ended up with Slim as the redneck pilot. And he was perfect. The only travelling he'd ever done was on the rodeo circuit; he'd never been out of America.

Terry Southern on Easy Rider

What were the formative experiences that led you to write *Easy Rider*? There's an anger and bleakness that comes through in that film that made it quite unlike anything else being made at that time.

Well, I'm glad that anger and bleakness came through. Because Dennis Hopper didn't have a clue as to what the film was about. The thrust of the film, from my point of view, the philosophical position, is that it's supposed to be an indictment of the blue-collar thing, the truck-driver people of America, for their intolerance and their support of the Vietnam war. It's supposed to be an indictment of the worst part of mainstream Middle America, as personified by those two assholes in the pick-up truck. Bigotry incarnate. And the final sequence is, I guess, the ultimate statement about that mentality, where these two innocent bikers get blown away because these two assholes don't like their looks. So that's the ending. And when Dennis Hopper read it he said, 'Are you kidding? Are you going to kill off both of them?' Yeah, that's what he said, 'kill off'. *[laughs]* So I said, 'Well, that's the only way it can be, because otherwise we're not saying anything; it's just a little odyssey by a couple of irresponsible hippies. So they've got to serve some purpose, make some point.' Anyway, that shows where he was at.

But you were no kid, you were in your late thirties when you wrote that script. And you were a Texan, not some East Coast liberal. I wonder how you could relate to that viewpoint?

Well, I was no stranger to that kind of experience. I was wearing a peace symbol and had long hair, and did drugs and was subject to that kind of thing, that kind of intolerance and bigotry. But even if I hadn't been subject to it, I still would have seen it and recognized it for what it is. The story was a distillation of many experiences that I had witnessed and heard of and read about. But it wouldn't have occurred to me to write it if it hadn't reflected my personal experience.

How much involvement did Dennis Hopper and Peter Fonda have in the script? Because they're both credited along with you as scriptwriters.

Well, right at the beginning Dennis and Peter had just this one idea, right? Listen, this is their contribution to the whole thing. These two guys, Peter and Dennis, at first they were going to be in cars, so they could do stunts in cars. It was going to be called *Barnstormers* or something. This is what they came to me with. So we changed it to motorbikes, but the idea then was that they would score some drugs and – this is when people are just beginning to realize you can make big money in drugs – so they buy some coke in Mexico, sell it, ride their bikes to Florida, buy a boat and leave the American rat-race; sail off into the sunset. The entertainment aspect of the film, presumably, was to be their pilgrimage from Mexico to Key West. That was it. That was their idea. So I went to work on that, and the deal at the time was that we were such good friends that we had a handshake deal, we'd split everything three

ways. So, uh, I never saw any bread whatsoever out of it.

You wrote *Easy Rider* and you never got any of the money? No percentages, nothing like that?

Well, when it played on TV I would get eighty-five dollars, something like that. But I never had a contract, so their business managers, when the movie was completed, said, 'Well, he doesn't even have a contract. It's just a handshake deal. You don't have to pay him anything.' And the best bit is, I have the letters to prove this, but when the movie was finished, I wrote to the Screenwriters' Guild of America, asking specifically for their names to be credited as writers on the movie. Even though I had written it. And, of course, the Guild wrote back and said, 'These guys aren't writers, they're actors.' And I wrote back to them saying, 'These guys must get credited as writers, otherwise they won't be able to get the finance for their next movie.' And so they got their credit. And I'm still waiting to get paid.

Aren't you bitter about being treated that way?

Well, I'm not happy about it, but that's no secret. Both Hopper and Fonda know that. And I also know that one of the major studios has started developing a script called *Easy Rider – The Next Generation*, and that considerable sums of money have already changed hands. In fact, Peter Fonda phoned me recently to ask me to sign a document relinquishing all rights to the title *Easy Rider*. And he was saying, 'Oh, it's just a pro-forma thing, it's really not very important.' *[laughs]*

And what did you say to that?

What do you think? I told him my lawyers would be in touch.

I met up with Iggy Pop in a photography studio in New York, near his Lower East Side home. I had been a fan of his for ages, so I was a bit nervous about seeing him. Then he came through the door and started walking towards me. He had dyed his hair blond, like it was when I first got into him in the Raw Power *era. I thought I was going to start seizing up and regressing to fourteen, because I didn't know what to say. I just went up to him and gave him a hug and said: 'Whoa Iggy ya cunt, how's it guan?!' He said: 'Hey, Irvine, man, fuckin' cool.' We went round to a Mexican place on Fourteenth Street and spraffed for most of the afternoon, going through hours of tape. This is a highly edited version.*

Iggy Pop | You ever been to Vegas?
Irvine Welsh | **Yeah, I went there. It was horrible.**
It's really, really disgusting. I've gone twice now, workin' both times. The first time it was a nightmare, like, you know, I get there and it's like the Hilton – like the Flamingo Hilton or something. It's just like all these old people, right, like doddering old miserable people going to their…
The fucking gambling machines…
The machines, right, you know, not at all what I expect.
See, in Britain, they go to Blackpool on the Wallace Arnold coach tours, but in America it's flight packages to Vegas.
But what was cool was that I was going to play a gig at this place. This chick who had been a madam saved her money and opened a rock club for kids on the outskirts of town. A regular old bar, right…
Brilliant, man…
It was like three hundred and twenty people

and I mean these people were ready to do fuckin' anything. She warned me right before the gig, she said, 'OK, now look,' she said eh… now how did she put it? She said eh… 'After the show, you boys just point out the ones you like and I'll send these girls back to get their throats cleaned.' Woahhhh! You know! The name of the bar and the name of the place, and her name was something like Hail Mary. And we went out and played and it's like all these… it was the dirtiest group of girls I've ever seen in my life.
Yeah, right.
In the front…
Yeah right there, man.
… they're like, 'I'm fourteen and I've seen everything already. Look at these tits,' you know, 'anybody can suck on these. See, like, I'm here; do I look pretty? Am I making you pretty fuckin' horny, motherfucker?' You know what I mean? With the really nasty attitude.
Just right into their own power.
Yeah, and the guys were all ready just to tear anything apart, and just get fucked up and they really got into the spirit of the music. *[laughter]* It really made me do a really good gig. I really, really thought, 'God, what it must be to be a kid in fuckin' Las Vegas', you know?

And the second time I went was really weird. I went there just last year and opened a Hard Rock Casino. Hard Rock – that horrible chain – they started a casino, a casino hotel. They put me up for three days for it. They put me up in the hotel, and so, you're living over this casino and you just feel the vibration all the time, you know, they're playing loud commercial rock-'n'-roll at all times in the casino in the hallways and you hear it in your fucking room and they turn off for three hours a day, five to eight in the morning. The rest of it's twenty-one hours a day of this shit! I was just shaking by the time I got outta this place, you know?
What do you do banged up in a place like that? Do you read a lot?
Yeah. I go off and on with myself; I'll go for months or so and I'll take printed information from books, newspapers, magazines and everything and evaluate what I'm reading and feel things from whatever I'm reading, and then for a couple of months I won't read anything: I'm just like a squirrel… Living right there and

the fucking second that I'm in, it just goes, 'bing-de-bang-de-boom'.

You probably read a lot more than me, because I'm not that great a reader, though I like browsing dust-jackets in bookshops. It's a weird thing for a writer to say, but I've never been a great reader of fiction. It fucks up all those wankers that review books because they're always trying to place you in terms of what you're supposed to have read...

Oh right, so they say you've read... yeah, yeah, yeah...

... Burroughs and Genet and all this kind of stuff, but I say, 'No, my references are from music', my references are from people like yourself.

Sure.

They say, 'You must've read Burroughs', and I go, 'Well, no. Maybe I got Burroughs off Iggy or whatever...'

Sure. Listen to my shit, you got his shit.

Yeah...

Or some feeling from it anyway.

Yeah, it's the spirit of it, not fucking pieces of text or notes of music or frames of films that matter.

Yeah.

It must be strange for you to be held in such regard by so many people that you've never met all over, well, probably, all over the world. I still get a bit freaked if some cunt comes to me in a club and says, 'Enjoyed the book, man.'

Yeah, it's strange, but you know, OK, since you brought it up, right. I went out with this chick, right? I had this chick out, about three weeks ago. You know, I meet her, I had never met her, it was somebody I had corresponded with for a long time. So the first thing she says to me after we say 'hello' 'n' stuff, she's mighty shaken and she says to me, 'This is like a dream for me 'cause you are a Living God!' and I'm like, at first, there's a part of me goes, 'Woaaah... I don't wanna hear this'... then, you know, I thought about it, and after a while, you know... *[loud laughter]*

Yeah! I'll take it!

Heyyy! Living Goh-hod... I guess that means I can do this and this and this... won't have to have tea first or anything, wooah! It's funny, you know... I actually found myself being on a little bit better behaviour. I spent about a week with her and I found I was catching myself, where maybe I'd normally give something away, I wouldn't, I'd go: 'Wait! would a Living God do this? Hey, hey hold on! Hold on!'

It's amazing, there's this kind of thing, I dunno if it's just a Scottish thing or not but, it's like ma mates in Scotland that are intae you, they've never met ye, don't really know anything about you other than the usual myth shite, but just sort of regard you as one of the boys, like one of the posse.

Well, when I met you I could tell how it was. And it was weird 'cause I was thinkin', you know, 'cause I read I was in your book and shit... I got that far last night, page seventy-five and I thought, 'Did he go to my gig or did he not?' You think, 'Oh fuck! Does this guy really dig me and am I, like, gonna disappoint him 'cause I'm not a fucking Living God?' and all this shit! That shit does go around, but not too much, 'cause basically I'm in a position, I still feel like the cat that got the canary because it's like I was putting out this music for a long time. Some people laughed at me, some people hated me, a lot of people start to listen to this shit, so I feel like a pig in shit. It's kinda neat for me you know. I think 'Cool', you know, it's really like that.

The thing about your music, for myself, and so many other people I've known that have been into it... I mean the first time I heard *Raw Power* was when I was fourteen; my mate Colin bought it and we were sitting in his bedroom playing it and I just thought, 'Aw yeah, this is fucking great, fuckin' brilliant', and that was it, right, gaun roond the Grassmarket looking for long silver

gloves tae wear tae the school and all that...
Right... right... cool!
... that thing about being a kid, but also
going right through the years and knowing
that somebody understands what you're
feeling inside. Somebody's articulating that
and it's out there as a reference point: all
those fucking weird impulses that you've
got and are having to repress 'cause it's like
the values of parents, teachers, work, the
authorities, all that fuckin' shite... and it's
like, 'Yessss... fuckin' right!' Like, you're the
patron saint of expressing what we're
feeling inside. It's like, the thing that
interests me most is the newer stuff, *Brick
By Brick*, *American Caesar*, and the new
album... it's the articulate criticism of
American society, the TV age and all that.
That's the stuff I always play now. I like
listening to the old stuff, but it's the newer
stuff I'm more into. With that in mind, I
was going to ask you – 'cause I read in *The
Telegraph* coming over on the plane – about
The Stooges getting back together again. I
would be disappointed in a way if that happened. If they're your main band, a part of
you wants to see them back together again,
but for me the stuff you're doing now is the
most interesting 'cause it's living in its own
time. To me it's, 'Fuck Dylan and all that
kind of stuff; this is American poetry telling
it as it is.' It makes sense to me about how
the world is; it's fuckin' hitting it you
know? I'd hate you to go retro. There's the
Velvet Underground getting back together,
they're talking about The Sex Pistols next...
Woah, woah, woah...

**Well what do you think of that kind of
thing?**
I don't have a very high opinion of it 'cause it's
the same kind of thing, as, I mean, I heard the
Velvets were going to do it and I didn't think
one thing or the other, then I saw a piece of film
of them actually doing it.

It was pony.
Same thing. It disappointed me 'cause, number
one, the guys looked so... old, for lack of a better
word. It didn't seem like they were actually like,
vibing on this thing; they were just like
grinding through – oh God, you know – and it
seemed so uptight and I dunno if I wanna see

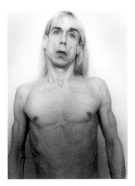

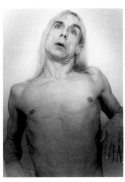

*This page and
following pages
Iggy Pop, 1996*
Martina Hoogland
Ivanow

The Sex Pistols do that either, you know? The thing with The Stooges... the reason that came up, was they'd been asking me, Ron and especially Scott, the drummer, who is my mate and who I have a real warm spot in my heart for as a person, he kept at me for years, you know, 'Let's do something, let's do it.' He even came to New York once; he's not a rich guy, he figured out a way to get to New York was to audition to see if he could be my drummer. I didn't think it was right for me, you know, and it really fuckin' tore me apart to say...

Yeah, I bet...

... 'Sorry, I got somebody else', and every time... I've a terror of doing something with those guys, you know, falling back into this hole.

So it would be you, James Williamson and the Ashton brothers?

No, it would be me and the Ashtons. Williamson doesn't really play anymore. So it would be the original three with a bass player: there's a guy named Gary Rasmussen of that musical circle. He played in Sonic Smith's band before he passed away and he's like us basically, you know? What it is that attracts me is people would ask us to do it for movies, for this, for festivals. I kept turning everybody down, but on a personal level, as a guy, it's like, I don't want to come over as I'm too good now, I've got my life, you know what I mean? And all that kind of shit, right? So what happened was I was fuckin'... oh fuck it, I'll say who it is, I was at dinner with this fuckin' guy Rick Rubin, right? This record producer, right? And he was like asking me so many questions about Detroit and Sinclair and The Stooges, he kept pumpin' me, you know? I was telling him what I thought, knew, about those times. And then, like a couple of weeks later a friend of his says to me, 'Would you play with The Stooges again?' I said, 'No! I wouldn't do that! Da-de-da. Leave me alone! Right?' Obviously, for all the obvious reasons. Then a friend said, 'You know, I was talkin' to Rick the other day. Rick would really like to make a record of The Stooges.' This I had never thought of, oddly enough. That's a different thing from going out and playing your old shit.

Yeah... make an album.

Why not get together and make some fuckin' music, make an album and see what's there? That appeals to me. That appeals.

Would it be a Stooges record though, or would it be an Iggy Pop record with The Stooges as the backing group?

No... no... *[laughter]* because it doesn't work that way with those people. No... it wouldn't, no... uh-uh, uh-uh. I was always the undisputed leader of the miserable band of *[laughter]* savage fuckin' ragged... you know... fuckin' losers. But good question; it popped into my mind. I wondered, could I shed... I mean, would it be different?

Would you want to?

Yes, in the sense that I do things by feel, a lot of things, not everything, but I do a lot things by feel and, like, I have a right feeling toward those people and in some way I think it would be nice if I could make music with them.

The new album carries on in the territory you've marked out in *Brick By Brick* **and** *American Caesar*, **like the criticisms of modern American capitalism and the TV age and lamenting the loss of a more innocent world.**

There's a lot of just 'I' and what's around here, like even in that song 'Pussy Walk'. What got me excited in the song is all the immigrants, that's what that song is really. Like, wow! I don't know these people, how do I talk to her? I gotta find out! I should know about this, you know. There's that, then I'm working on all this real quiet blues shit where I just do it with a guitar and make the music up myself. That's real important to me to do that kinda thing, and I wanna do a... I'm hopin' about a year from now – I gotta tour a long time, you know – I would like to do, they call it bel canto singing, you know what this is? This is like dignified ballads of miserable fucked-up love, broken love and broken hopes. Standards that already exist, with a pianist. I would like to have a shot at that 'cause I really love this kinda singing.

It's like the voice you do... I dunno where this came in, you probably always had it, that crooning voice...

That's it, I wanna do that.

That's a powerful instrument now, you know, it's like a kind of Crosby–Sinatra thing.

I've always felt that I'd like to go over there, but I didn't have a handle on it and then there's this one album by Sinatra I've got obsessed with lately, it's called *Frank Sinatra Sings for Only the Lonely*, and he's in kinda clown make-up on the cover and there's a tear, and it's all these songs about girls that aren't with him anymore and, 'We fucked it up when we thought it could be good, but it doesn't matter 'cause I'm still cool and fuck you anyway.' That's there too. I'm dignified about this! All of a sudden, I guess, 'cause of some shit I been through lately, all of a sudden I really felt that I could sing that shit and so I would like to sing ballads about being wounded, but still walking around. So a Stooge reunion is somewhere down the line, you know, certain elements will pick up on that.

What about the acting, is that still... ye still intae that?

Yeah, I'm doing that. OK, I don't have a fucking agent and I don't have a fuckin'... there's no head shot that exists that's like 'Hey! available for hire.' Guys call me and almost all the ones I take it's... the one I just did was *The Crow* sequel and it was Tim Pope who shot the *Kiss My Blood* video. That's why I got the gig, and Jarmusch used me 'cause he knew me from music; it's all like that, you know. I like doing that shit 'cause at one point hardly any of my albums were in print; I was real marginal in the industry and I was determined I was gonna get all my stuff up there in the light where people can see all this old shit and it's available. The only way to do that was to do shit that impressed straight people, and nothing impresses those people more than if you're in a fuckin' movie. *[laughter]* 'Hey ass-wipe, I'm a cock-suckin' movie star, so you can just lick my dirty brown ass!' That does it, man, when you're in a movie; oh, wow, boy, do they jump! So I got into a movie for all the wrong reasons, I fuckin' just elbowed my way in.

Do you enjoy acting?

No, it's horrible! It's so hard, it's tedious.

Yes.

But what I really do enjoy, the last couple of times I started getting less shitty at it, the last three times. The thing with Jarmusch, and *The Crow* thing, was not so shitty, so I felt like, hey, this wasn't too bad, y'know?

I did a wee bit in the *Trainspotting* film; I had a part in that.

How d'ya like doing it?

Fuckin' boring aroond aw the time man.

Borin' as shit, right? It's miserable; your whole life's going before you, right?

Yeah, it's tedious.

Almost worse, 'cause I was reading your book last night, and I was thinkin', 'What's worse: waiting on a film set, or waiting for junk?'

Junk.

Yeah, really, it's almost as bad as waiting for junk... All that AIDS shit man, I was reading your book, and I get the willies every time that subject comes up, I get the fuckin' willies. 'Cause I'm not ready to die, do everything they say I should do. No, sorry. I'm not really ready to die yet. A lot of people fell like that.

Too fuckin' right! But I mind that I was talking to one magazine about the book and that if I hadnae have listened to you I couldn't have written that book, it would have been a different book...

Wow!

When you see the film, you'll see loads of pictures yourself.

Wow!

Tons of references to yourself.

Cool!

It's an Iggy film, man. An Iggy book and an Iggy film.

Wow!

It's almost strange without you actually being in it. You're in it, without being in it!

That's really good!

What do you reckon to the whole acid house thing, the house club culture, the ecstasy culture?

I know fuck all about that, because my problem with that is, for one thing, I can't handle drugs any more. So, you know, you really don't wanna see me stoned. I don't have a rule – I do take shit sometimes but I get really silly and I have not

thought, 'Woah, I'm in love; this girl's gonna put me up in her flat for ever and ever. She loves to fuck me, everything's cool. Everything's fine, you know. I can't cross the street without being led by the hand, but it's OK you know.' But, you know, there's something to be said for that.

Certainly, in Britain, there's a vibrant culture attached to that. You have the odd ecstasy-related death, on no scale compared to alcohol-related deaths, and those are attributable to false information. People were told to drink loads of water, now they're overdosing on that and dying – washes out all the sodium level and other chemicals we need to regulate the body. It's just like drinking too much alcohol. The advice should be, 'Take water, but don't go over the top. Dance for about twenty minutes at a time, then sit the fuck on your arse and chill out for a bit.'

That's wild... washing precious metals out of your brain.

Designer drugs have become so popular with the young, the brewers have started their own to compete. They've got this alcoholic lemonade now, to get kids hooked on their drugs in an attempt to recapture some of the market. Ten per cent proof some of that shite is. It's knocking every cunt for six. The thing is, people aren't stopping taking the other drugs though. They do the fuckin' lot.

In Europe, I have heard some interesting shit.

I think in 80s Britain, you had the rampant egoism and the politics, and after punk, the star system reinstated itself. But the music was shite. House was great because it empowered a lot of punters who the government and authorities were constantly harassing and telling them they were shite and fuck all. The punters though, they took their Es, went along to the do, and they were the stars and they knew better than the sad fucks who were trying to make their lives miserable. The DJ was an anonymous figure behind the decks, giving the crowd what they wanted, feeding off their energy. Creating spontaneous music through the mixing.

That's what I always hoped for when we started playing music and I never got it for about ten

taken ecstasy, so I guess... maybe I'll go...

Very, very different.

I wouldn't go to a rave unless I was gonna get down with the chicks there, right?

Cool.

I was really not even thinking about things like that for years. I got to be almost a work machine. And now, just in the last few months, I'm opening up a bit more, so maybe I can learn about it.

You'd enjoy it.

Really?

You'd enjoy it the most, man.

Wow! Cool! OK. The ecstasy isn't too terribly strong? Some of my friends say that it's real nice...

People feel very positive on it.

Wow!

It's... eh... a very, very different type of experience from any other drug.

I had MDA – used to shoot that, years ago. I was thirty, penniless, barefoot, but it was great. I

years. In the late 60s they used to just stand and stare, and I always hated that. The first time it ever really happened was in Britain, all of a sudden it's po-going, spitting... fuckin' wonderful! Then it happened sporadically. When you get a lot of people doing something together, man... Once there was this festival in Belgium where sixty thousand people started throwing bottles in the air at once. That's a lot of bottles and it looked incredible. But I know that a good electric dancebeat can be really unifying to people. I was curious about jungle because I like the name and a lot of my friends...

Fuckin' brilliant!

... A lot of people of Caribbean descent go to these clubs?

It's the only genuinely multi-racial form of dance or acid house in Britain.

I got one record sent to me, but it didn't do much for me; I guess it wasn't a good record...

Yeah, but I don't think that you can... it's never really done it for me on record. I mean, a lot of acid house I don't think does it purely to sit down and listen to. You have to go to the club, get the vibe, be with your posse, neck your pill, get right into the whole fuckin'... total participation.

OK, OK... I'm just gonna have to try it. I dunno about the pill, that scares me.

Naw... it's...

You gotta take the pill?

You gotta take the pill, man.

This guy... *[laughter]*

You got tae take the fuckin' pill, man! [laughter]

You gotta take the pill... you gotta take the fuckin' pill... *[laughter]*

Ye must, man. [laughter]

You goddamn got to take the fuckin' pill, man. *[laughter]*

It's amazing how people become converts to that whole thing. It's got to be done at some point, man, 'cause it is another thing, another thing, but part of the same, if you know what I mean. It's funny in Britain with house, it fucked the guitar bands for a while, but they're back again. Now you've got like, Oasis. It's like it's come round full circle. The whole Manchester scene with Stone Roses and the Happy Mondays... Have you heard Black Grape? Ye gottae check that

yin oot, man. How did you get on reading *Trainspotting* with the language?

I had almost no problem 'cause I've got a friend who's a Scot who I've known for fifteen years. I knew from him and I've been to Scotland maybe eight or nine times, and more than doing just gigs. I've been there to wander around and hang out and shit, so if I stopped and figure out what it means, oh, that 'fae' means 'from'. Most of it I can figure in my head. The 'fae' word was a bit of a problem. It means 'from' right?

Yeah.

Like, 'I ain't gonna take that fae you.' See, most of the people I spend time talking to in my life through choice, most of them don't speak English too well. So I've developed a good ear; I have an ear for that shit. I don't like to hear people talkin' right, 'cause it don't really sound so interesting. I even figured out Hibernian was another name for Hibs, man. I figured that right away.

When you're touring, do you get a chance to hang out, see the place, away from the airport, coach, hotel syndrome?

Yes. The touring is pretty gruelling, but now I try to build in a couple of extra days to get a feel. Sometimes you meet great people working in the hotels. When you do better, you can be a bit more creative with hotels and avoid the airport. When I stay in Glasgow, for instance, I don't stay at the Holiday Inn, I stay in a regular residential block off the Great Western Road, a sort of five-roomed place. In France, I'll stay in a chateau in the countryside, a little village, so you don't have to be in the fuckin' Hyatt or something.

I was delighted and relieved that Iggy was a brilliant guy. He's a man of great humour, warmth and charm who has time for everyone. In his company, Manhattan shrinks to the size of a village, and I enjoyed hanging out with him later on. Unfortunately, the space provided doesn't allow us to get through other issues such as cinema, Anglo-American imperialism in culture, British music, novels etc., but that's the way it goes. I've personally now realized an ambition. In Pat Stanton, Jock Scott and Iggy Pop, I've now met three of my heroes and none of them has disappointed me. You can't ask for more than that.

March 1996
Introduction and interview | Mark Sanders

South African-born performance artist Bruce Louden defies the imagination. For over a decade, he has been cutting off parts of his body and displaying them in galleries all over the world.

He has severed over twelve pieces of his body, including toes, fingers and an ear. The remnants of these performances are documented and then sold to collectors. Occasionally, he keeps a body-part and records its slow decay. But this January, Louden raised the stakes, completing his most hazardous performance yet. In Kwazulu-Natal, in a secret location on the outskirts of Durban, he severed his own tongue and documented the act on film. The tongue is now due to be exhibited in a London gallery this March.

Body-art is nothing new. Ever since the 1960s and the rise of the Orgy Mystery Theatre and the Viennese Actionists, artists such as Hermann Nitsch and Gunter Brüs have entered into the dark realms of self-mutilation and self-sacrifice through the use of slaughtered animals and scarification. In the early 1970s, Chris Burden had himself shot through the arm and 'crucified' on the roof of a Volkswagen. Today in LA, Ron Athey's performance pieces are centred on the ritualized scarring of his body, and this month saw the death of one of the most famous sado-masochists of our times – Bob Flanagan, whose activities included the nailing of his genitals to a plank of wood. Yet, over the last ten years, the disturbing activities of Bruce Louden have called into question exactly where the line is drawn between art and annihilation. His personal acts of dismemberment are rooted in an auto-erotic desire to dissect his own flesh and blood.

Chillingly matter-of-fact in his observations, Louden gave the following interview on the Internet while he was still recovering from his latest performance in Durban.

Dazed & Confused | **Why did you first decide to cut off parts of your body?**
Bruce Louden | Curiosity. I was fascinated that my body produced so much shit. It seemed that so much time was spent converting useful material into bodily waste, so I wanted to extend the proposition by converting useful parts of my body into waste.
Do you see yourself as separate from your body?
No. The self is only an organ. It just seems to have precedence over all the others. The soul inhabited the heart three hundred years ago; after psychoneurology the self inhabits the brain. It is a part of the body and can never be separated.
How many body parts have you cut off?
Twelve pieces.
Can you list them off the top of your head?
No, and I can't count them on my fingers either.
Is there any part of your body that you would never consider cutting off?
All parts of my body are expendable. There is nothing that I would not consider worthy of the surgeon's knife. It just depends on how quickly or slowly I intend to terminate the project.
When you say 'the project', do you mean 'life'?
Yes.
Are your acts of self-mutilation politically motivated?
No. Bodily processes don't serve any political or moral goals. I prefer to think of my activities as being auto-erotic reductions rather than mutilations. The term 'mutilation' implies abuse. I perform a pleasurable disappearing act where I disassemble a given anatomical structure.
You mean yourself?
Yes.

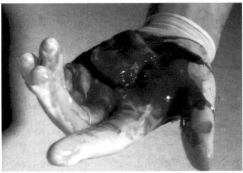

Do you enjoy pain? Are you a sado-masochist?
Quantify 'enjoy'. I can only judge the experience of pain or pleasure against myself, but I do enjoy the writing of both de Sade and Sacher-Masoch.

We are conducting this interview on the Internet because you have cut your tongue out. There seems to be an obvious difference between the severing of a finger and the loss of a tongue.
Different parts of the anatomy perform different functions in relation to the world. A finger negotiates the world by means of touch. By detaching the tongue, I have sabotaged the means by which I can explain the reason for my actions. In that sense, I have cut myself off.

Why did you choose the inability to speak?
I am interested in mediation. Denying speech means that interaction has to occur at a different level. It's like people who lose their sight and are forced to adopt a sensory, rather than visual language. Their language becomes more refined, more erotic.

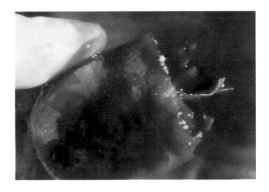

So the lack of a tongue represents an erotic escalation?
Yes.

An escalation based on a fundamental loss?
All eroticism contains an element of loss. Inherent in any erotic act is a sense of failure.

Do you see yourself as an artist?
Yes. It's a system of enquiry that interests me, simply because it consistently raises questions about limits without imposing limits.

Are you yourself limited in how far you will go?
Anatomically speaking, the permutations are limitless. To say I am limited would be like say-

ing a painter's colours are limited when they're obviously infinite.

But you don't have an infinite number of body-parts.
I don't mean to split hairs, but if I wanted to, I could get micro-molecular about dividing body parts, which, in the eventuality, might include splitting hairs.

Do you include toe-nail cutting as an artistic act?
Yes, but only as maquettes.

Are you aesthetically prepared for your death?
Death is impossible to imagine or conceive of as an idea or event, but the biological imminence

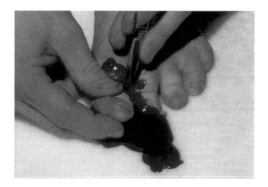

of entropy means that death is aesthetically ready for me. I'm sure I will be uglier than I am now.

Are you religious?
I experience bliss.

Do you draw parallels with your activities and the work of the Viennese Actionists?
I am suspicious of their vulgarity.

Vulgarity?
Of their Teutonic theatricality and angst.

And yet you yourself are involved in some kind of theatre by documenting your performances.
Yes, but the theatre is mediated purely through the image and is never experienced first-hand, except by those who assist me. That mediation disinvests it of any appropriate emotion and causes the spectator to become alienated – severed from the reality of the act. In that sense, we negotiate the event from isolation, unsure of how to achieve a correct response.

Is there a correct response to your activities?
No, but it is a function of theatre and art to incite the viewer to make that mistake.

So your theatre is punitive?
Only if punishment leads to pleasure. The viewer can always make the decision to shut their eyes.

Even your assistants?
Even they have a choice.

How many assistants do you have at any one performance?
It varies according to the level of significance that I attach to that performance. The severing of a finger is obviously less dangerous than the severing of a tongue. My latest performance required two assistants: one surgeon to apply the anaesthetic and conduct the operation and another to cauterize the wound and to stem the bleeding.

What do you do with the body-parts after you have finished with them?
Once they have been detached, they are documented and become available for display. I relinquish all control over them.

Where do they go?
They travel well. My anatomy crops up in galleries all over the world, to such an extent that the demand is beginning to exceed the supply. I considered the possibility of biogenetically cloning parts of my body but it conflicts with my desire for entropy. I considered progeny, but that implied immortality.

Do you sell your body-parts?
Sometimes. But it would be far more lucrative to sell working organs on the black market.

How much do you sell them for? Do you have an anatomically scaled price list?
It depends on the collector.

What kind of collectors are they?
Art collectors, people who collect art.

Have you ever considered becoming a registered organ donor?
[no response]

Bruce Louden's tongue was exhibited at the IAS (Independent Art Space) in March 1996.

April 1996
Introduction and interview | Susan Irvinz

Camper than a drag queen, cooler than Carla
Bruni, a one time champion leg-wrestler and a
mighty fine woman, Jerry Hall, the original
supermodel and rock star wife talks about Mick
and her renaissance as a catwalk queen with
Vivienne Westwood.

Jerry Hall is ensconced at a table drinking
tea. Bleached-blonde locks fall over one shoulder
of her almost matronly silk shirt. Supermodel
style point: a matador's felt cape lined in scarlet
is flung over the back of the sofa. Round Jerry's
neck, a rope of raw, uncut rubies: 'Mick gave
them to me this morning – isn't that GRRREAT?',
with which she toys repeatedly during our nat-
ter. She has just got back from an African safari
in the Masai Mara with Mick and her three kids:
Elizabeth Scarlett (twelve), James Leroy (ten) and
Georgia May (four).

Dazed & Confused | **What was your upbring-
ing like?**
Jerry Hall | Well, it was a household of
women 'cause my father was away a lot, driving
explosive chemicals across the country. He's
part Indian an' he had a li'l problem with
drinking and gambling. Back home, it was my
mother and my grandmother and us five girls.

We were lucky 'cause we inherited our mother's
genes... tall, attractive.
**I remember reading in your autobiography
Tall Tales that you had your 'cherry bust' by
a cowboy.**
*[Jerry laughs nervously and lights up a
Marlboro]*
Weeell. My first boyfrien' was a bullrider.
Bullriders were our heroes. They were the
coolest; just sooooo good looking. An'... umm...
that was what was goin' on in our town.
How old were you?
Fourteen. He was called Tommy Lee Bryant.
What was he like?
*[Jerry pauses and takes another drag on her
cigarette]*
Maaaay-jor beefcake. *[laughs for a long time]*
He was Indian. Black, black hair. Sooo gorgeous.
And two of my sisters married firemen.
They're real heroes. We always liked the heroes.
My mother said the reason she married my
father was 'cause he looked like Rhett Butler
in *Gone With the Wind*. We used to watch that
movie over and over and over. We were very
into fashion and beauty treatments. My mother
used to make our clothes: the most beautiful
things. When I went off to Paris, she made a
whole wardrobe, and I think that's part of
why I was such a success out there because
everyone just went 'wow!' They couldn't believe
the clothes.
How did you break into modelling in Paris?
I went to the South of France, and the first day
I lay on the beach in this very expensive pink
crocheted bikini. Everyone else was topless.
I went to the bathroom and this man followed
me and he said, 'Here, would you like to be a
model?' And he gave me his phone number.
I put it in my bikini bottom and later I called
him up. And he really was an agent. He was my
agent for two years. So there I was in Paris,
staying in an apartment with these other two
models and one night we went out dancing to
Club Sept and I wore one of the outfits my
mother made me and I met this fashion illustra-
tor, Antonio Lopez. An' I started working for
him, posing. An' he said, 'I'm gonna introduce
you to this great photographer.'
Helmut Newton?
YEAH! We worked together the next day. It
was for *Photo* magazine. All the clothes were

ripped, and there were chains everywhere and everything. I was really worried. OOOOH! And I said to him, 'Ah don't really like to do this kind of pornography. I want to do FASHION.' An' he said, 'Oh you're so STOOPID! This is not pornography. This is ART. But if it's fashion you wanna do, we'll do fashion.' So two weeks later, he phoned me up and booked me for *Vogue*. We did the cover of *French Vogue*. I was biting a man's cheek on the cover. It was GRREAT!

So your career just soared immediately?
Uh-huh. Everyone was like, 'Oh, wow! Helmut's got this new girl.' I did the cover of every single magazine the next month, and I was all over the news-stands. Then *Newsweek* came along and did this story on like, 'Here's the newest model taking Paris by storm.'

Were you having a wild time?
I was just having the most AMAZING time. I started living with Antonio and two other guys and they were all artists and things, and we were like going out every night and all of our friends were drag queens and TRANSVESTITES! They taught me how to do my make-up. I was hanging out with Grace Jones and Pat Claveland.

Were you going out with anyone?
Well, I was going out with Antonio for a while and then I found out he was GAY.

How did you find out?
The hard way. But we remained best, best friends until he died. He taught me how to pose.

You've just come back from doing the Vivienne Westwood show in Paris. How was that?
That was GRREAT! She's fabulous, really brilliant, one of the greatest geniuses of fashion, very talented. And she understands that catwalk is about acting.

Which models do you think are good now?
Models who pose well are Linda Evangelista and Kristen McNenamy. And I love Kristy Hume, she's great. Fabulous; she's GRREAT. She's also a great poser.

How did you meet Bryan Ferry?
He hired me to come and do the cover of the *Siren* album for Roxy Music. We did it in the rocks in Wales and I was like this mermaid. It came out so great. Bryan was there the whole day, and I thought he was SO cute. He's still handsome. *[laughs]* My mother thought he was the most beautiful man she had ever seen in her life because he looks like Clark Gable.

What did she think of Mick?
She thought he was the DEVIL. She likes him now, though. But with Bryan, we went back to London and started dating and then got engaged. We were engaged for two years.

So what happened with Bryan?
We were kinda apart too long. He was away for two months... er... it was completely my fault. I started having an affair and I got caught.

Mick?
Yeah. They were friends. Y'know, Mick was very rude. I was very young. Love? It was like I had a major crush on him. He was very persuasive.

Because you had been persuaded?
Well, yeah. I mean he had asked me out a lot before, and I kept saying NO. And he turned up at this dinner and we were sitting next to each other and that was it. *[laughs nervously]* – I behaved very badly.

Don't give yourself a hard time over it, that kind of thing happens.
[shrugs] No excuse.

Did you know he was going to be the love of your life?

No, I didn't. I thought it would last maybe a couple of years. Amazing it lasted.

One of the most amazing marriages in rock. How long?

Twenty years.

And how old are you now?

[sips tea for a bit] Thirty-nine.

What's the secret?

I think part of what Mick liked about me was this thing that I was – you know – independent. It's kept him on his toes. He doesn't like the idea of someone being kinda clingy and possessive. Mick is quite a tricky man – do you know what I mean?

Yes. And then you had those dreadful Carla Bruni incidents to cope with.

[lights a Marlboro, drinks some tea and adjusts her rubies]

My theory is, the more you let 'em go, the more they come back. You can't take anything for granted in a relationship. The thing with rock stars is that women just keep CHASING after them; they're not like normal guys. With normal guys it's bad enough, but things calm down. My girlfriends are always saying, 'I could never do it. I don't know how you can stand it.' Because after all these years, all these girls are still chasing after him. I do admire Mick though, for staying on top so long and keeping himself so attractive. Mick works out like a fiend all the time; he's much better than me. I kind of do it five days before I have a job. He's not into relaxing; he's hyper.

Are you still acting?

I've got a movie coming out with Richard Harris called *Savage Hearts* and then another one that's out in America called *Vampire in Brooklyn* with Eddie Murphy. That was fun. I enjoy acting, but I've not really been very ambitious about it because… I just haven't. Mostly, I just do some acting when I meet some director at dinner. Mick has started a film company. He's doing *Enigma* with Tom Stoppard and something with Mike Figgis. It's really great. I just keep hanging around and saying, 'Hey, anyone got a part for me?' And Bailey and I are working on a talk show together. Beautifully shot, me all dressed up, and really INTIMATE. We'll just interview all our friends.

How else do you spend your time?

I see friends, usually work a coupla days, and I LOVE spending hours arranging knick-knacks and things. I love the theatre, I love the ballet. And I LOVE shopping! Shopping is, like, my hobby. I LOVE goin' to Phillip Treacy's hat shop, it's DIVINE. Sooo glamorous. And I love going to Manolo Blahnik. I'm a shoe maniac.

What's the secret of your fantastic skin?

Kiehl's Diaper Rash Cream. It's GRREAT!

Finally, Jerry, whatever possessed you to dress up as a chicken for that Bovril ad?

But that was a GREAT dress! It was Las Vegas! It was like… chicken couture. It's OK to be made fun of, y'know? It's wrong to take yourself too seriously. It's all fun in the end.

April 1996
Introduction | Jefferson Hack

Radiohead's Thom Yorke likes to think a lot. He says he worries too much – worries about losing the plot. Yet his explicitly personalized, emotive lyrics have made him the anti-hero in a new generation of British rock-'n'-roll stars. Whether as a genius outsider, madman or tortured artist, Yorke has always been the subject of black and white, one-dimensional media profiles. In this self interview he faces his multi-dimensional other selves and, for the first time, we get a close-up, full-colour snapshot of the real Thom Yorke.

It's been a year since Radiohead released The Bends and now one of the best rock albums of 95 is back by popular demand, firmly entrenched in our national charts at number four. Amazingly, the Brits failed to award them one of four nominations. Their penultimate single, 'Just', a charity record for the Help EP, was even refused a play list by Radio One on the grounds that it was not 'radio-friendly'. Yet despite the lack of media support, Radiohead have gone supernova through nakedly brilliant song-writing, stadium-tilting sound, non-stop touring schedules and just being themselves.

Twenty-seven-year-old Yorke is a difficult man to define. Like the difference between his one slightly sleepy eye and his other wide eye, there's a distinct contrast in his personality. One side of him is inward looking, the other looking for answers from the outside world. The band are an internal support group, each member with their own neatly cohesive responsibilities. But as the focal and vocal point, Yorke is pressured to play out the roles defined by the music. It burns him up inside, saps the poetry from his soul and conflicts with his passionate belief in artistic responsibility.

In The Bends, we see Yorke's collective voices compressed and decompressed, like reflections in a hall of mirrors, into comically exaggerated lows and anthemic, epic highs. On stage, his self-deprecation evokes an empathy and hysteria rarely witnessed in pop audiences. Seeing Radiohead live is less a group experience and more a personal revolution. During climactic moments, like the chorus for 'Just', when he sings, 'You do it to yourself, just you, you and no one else', it's as if he's speaking to each and everyone there.

So, does he ever have a laugh? 'Whenever anyone puts a microphone in front of me, I'm serious, because I want to get these noises out of my head. At home, I've got a puerile, juvenile sense of humour. The people that make me laugh more then anyone else are Jonny and Ed. We've known each other since we were fifteen, so how can you not mercilessly rip the shit out of each other? It's just like when you're a kid; it's not different.'

The Bends was an ecliptic moment in Radiohead's trajectory; a point where the pressure of producing a follow-up to their two-million-selling debut, Pablo Honey, saw their fears and desires overshadowed by an honest attempt to find themselves. And just as The Bends was an evolutionary progression, so their new recordings, according to them, see Radiohead continuing to experiment, redefining their sound surroundings with some purely computer-originated songs, others being stripped down, unplugged and semi-acoustic. Radiohead have already gone through several pop cycles. The New Wave failed to pick up on the not-so-new Radiohead, and, in its arrogant and self-perpetuating publicity-driven schemes, the Britpop establishment ignored them. They carved their own niche in the collective consciousness of the record-buying public. The Radiohead of *today are anarchists in a highly politicized pop game; art students who didn't believe in college; rock-'n'-roll stars who don't write about cocaine. They're doing it their way.*

Thom Yorke | **This is a quote from Raoul Vaneigem's *The Revolution of Everyday Life* (1967), and I think this is you: 'The history of our times calls to mind those Walt Disney characters who rush madly over the edge of a cliff without seeing it. The power of their imagination keeps them suspended in mid-air, but as soon as they look down and see where they are, they fall.'**

Thom Yorke | Well, am I looking down? I don't think I'm looking down. I sort of understand the Walt Disney bit, though. The cartoon character bit. I understand running off the edge of a cliff, the expression on the face as they look down. I suppose it means something about the suspension of disbelief, and I suppose what you are trying to ask me is, 'What are you doing?' I can understand that, but it's better than working in advertising, which is what my dad wanted me to do. I'm looking down and I'm not falling.

No, but other people in your position do. Why should you be any different?

I don't say I'm any different at all. I just worry about losing it, you know? I spend most of every fucking day worrying about losing it. I've got to stop swearing as well, because some woman just wrote me a letter saying she really likes my music, but she's fifty years old – our music *[laughs]*, and she doesn't like the swearing! *[laughs]*

Really? That's really interesting that you'd actually get worried about that.

It's pathetic, isn't it? You're really, 'be nice to everybody', nice big grin, shake hands,

one day im gonna
do something, *1999*
Stanley Domwood
and the Chocolate
Factory

worry about wasteful packaging, worry whether people are going to break into your home while you're asleep. You worry about not having written back to fan mail. You worry about what to say on stage in front of people. You're just a worrier. You're about as intuitive as a brick. You spend half your life worrying, more than half your life. You should fucking get a life, you should be enjoying what you're doing. Get on with it, enjoy it. Suck it up. All those lovely people being nice to you. It's what you always wanted.

I didn't know what I wanted. I don't think anybody knows what they want. We did a show in Los Angeles. It's a Christmas radio show they have there every year, and everybody does it who wants to be liked by the radio station that year, and we did it. And we thought we were going to hate it, but we turned up and everybody there... Lenny Kravitz and people like Oasis were talking to us and saying: 'Hi, you know, I really liked that song', or something, and you're going, 'Er, thanks very much.' And that was great. It was like being at your own birthday party, but you don't know anybody, but they know it's your birthday and... I don't know. No, that's bullshit. Anyway, it got a bit out of hand because all the people there – except for a few like Oasis and Lenny Kravitz who we have respect for – were just fucking clinging on, you know? And they got this crazy look in their eye, and apparently a lot of them were on coke. I didn't know that; they said it's the coke paranoia thing.

There was one particular ex-celebrity, who I can't name, who was really ready to punch me and was giving me a lecture about not behaving in the correct manner towards him because he came up to me and he says: 'Hey man, you know, I really love you, man, you know, your album's great, you know, we want to make music like you.' I'm talking to somebody else and I'm thinking, 'Well, I'm not impressed, and it's not like I'm having a fucking go or anything, I'm just not into talking to him simply because he's another famous person, ex-famous person, in this business. I'm sorry, but I didn't get into this to sort of go to the parties and fucking talk to other famous people. I got into this because I really love what we do and I really love the

other blokes in the band and that's why I got into this, and get out of my face', you know? But I didn't say any of these things, I just sort of said nothing.

And there was this famous model there and I snubbed her because I was a bit out of my head at the time and I was a bit stoned. Anyway, I couldn't do it, you know? I wasn't really able to communicate with anyone except for people I really knew. I suppose the novelty of these people has worn off and I just sound like this sulky kid who has had a big birthday party, but didn't get the present he wanted and, you know, someone should just slap him around the face. And this guy was quite prepared to do that.

OK, this is an obvious question. Why did you want to be famous then?
Because I wanted to meet REM and Elvis Costello. *[laughs]* And now I have. But really, we just started making tapes when we were younger. First me on my own, and then me and Jonny, and then with the others. And we'd play them to people, and they'd really like them and they'd take them home and they'd actually play them at home and I was really into this. Or I'd be at a party or something and someone would give me a guitar and I'd play a song. I mean this is all when we were sort of fifteen, sixteen, and it was the first time that I found something that I really loved and I supposed that I just loved the attention, so I wanted to be famous; I wanted the attention. What's wrong with that? But there's also something really seriously fucking unhealthy about it.

You haven't really answered the question. You've said, 'Oh, I want to be loved.' And that's not the real fucking reason, is it? I think you're a bit of a fucking prat.
Yeah, I agree. Um... other reasons to be famous.

hahahaha, *1999*
Stanley Donwood
and the Chocolate
Factory

I think this discussion is so fucking lame.
There's no point in continuing it, really. My
favourite answer is: 'Because that way more
people get to hear what we do', but that would
be a lie. I'm sure if you asked other members of
the band they would agree, but it isn't the only
reason. I just get really wound up, because I
think that when we got involved in what we do,
we were so naive. I still think we are naive and
I used to sort of want to hide it and now I'm
proud of it, because I think the most offensive
thing about the music business, the most
offensive thing about the media in general, is
the level of cynicism and the fact that people
really believe that they can pawn off endlessly
recycled bullshit with no heart, and people will
buy it. And people do buy it, so I'm wrong and
they're right.

　　Just to end this one: whenever I get lost
about this, then the others always pull me up.
And this is not just about me; I mean, I'm doing
this interview on my own because I think it's a
good idea; because I'm not very good at dealing
with day-to-day press interviews. I'm not that
precious about the way people think about me,
but I'm precious about offensive stuff that
people write and I'm precious about headlines
like the one that was put in the *NME*, 'Thom's
Temper Tantrum'. This was a while ago, before
Christmas. As they put it, I threw a tantrum in
Germany and left the stage and nobody could
understand what had happened and everyone
was really pissed off and the whole audience
were really angry and wanted their money back
or whatever. The article was run like that, and it
was sort of second- or third-hand. What actually happened on that night was that I'd been
really, really ill for quite some time and I didn't
know whether I would be able to do it or not
and it's very difficult to tell, but after a while, if
you're doing a tour, there is a point where you
have to just carry on. It doesn't matter how ill
you are, you still have to get on stage, and that
really fucking does something to your head
after a while. When I tried the soundcheck, I got
really worried because I couldn't sing anything.
And when the show came round, people had
driven hundreds of miles to come and it was
snowing, and it was like three or four foot deep,
and I thought: 'There is no way I'm not doing
the show because these people have come this

far.' So I got up on stage and I thought it would be all right, but after three songs, I lost my voice completely and I was croaking and I just got really fucking freaked out. I got tunnel vision and I don't really know what happened. I threw stuff around and threw my amp around and drum kit and ended up with blood all over my face and things. I cried for about two hours afterwards. I want people to know what happened that night. I'm sure no one gives a fuck and I'm sure the *NME* don't give a fuck, but what they wrote in that piece hurt me more than anything else anyone has ever written about me.

I think you've said enough about your fucking precious bullshit. It seems that you're a graduate of the Sinead O'Connor school of media handling and don't you feel it's about time you grew up a little? Stamping your little feet comes across as rather laughable under the circumstances, don't you think?
I think that has a lot to do with the expression that's on my face. People are born with certain faces, like my father was born with a face that people want to hit. *[laughs]* I do stamp my feet out of frustration really, but I don't do it as much now, because I feel that we're in more control of what's happening.

Do you think that people who read this find this level of agonizing pretty offensive?
I think the only reason that I'm able to think like this is because we've been off the wheel long enough, and I've been at home long enough, to start to see a lot of things for what they are. What worries me more than anything else is the whole notion that I'm who people focus on, like it's of significance, you know? People look at me and think that it's a complete existence. What really fucks me up in the head

is that basically, I'm supposed to be endorsing this sort of pop star, 'wow, lucky bastard, he's got it all' existence. What frightens me is the idea that what Radiohead do is basically packaged back to people in the form of entertainment, to play in their car stereos on their way to work. And that's not why I started this, but then I should shut the fuck up because it's pop music and it's not anything more than that.

But I got into music because I naively thought that pop music was basically the only viable art form left, because the art world is run by a few, very extreme, um, privileged people and is ultimately corrupt and barren of any context. And I thought that the pop music industry was different and I was fucking wrong, because I went to the Brits and I saw it everywhere and it's the same thing. It's a lot of women who couldn't fit in their cocktail dresses and lots of men in black ties who, essentially, didn't want to be there, but were. And I was there and we were all committing the same offence. All my favourite artists are people who never seem to be involved in the industry and I found myself getting involved in it, and I felt really ashamed to be there.

It sounds to me like you're going around in ever-decreasing circles.
Yeah, I agree. I don't know if anybody else has this feeling. When you're walking down the street and you catch your reflection in something, like a car window or a shop window, and you see your face and you think, 'Who's that?' You know: 'That's not me, that doesn't represent who I am.' And I think I've recently discovered what the problem is and it's a feeling that essentially you're just reflections, but basically it's all meaningless because you're just trapped and you put yourself there.

I've realized recently that it's actually worrying about it that's the fucking problem. It's actually saying, 'No, this is me, that's not me', and being precious about who you are, because I believe, now, that everyone changes all the time. I think the most unhealthy thing for a human being is to feel that they have to behave in a certain way because other people expect them to behave like that, or to feel they have to think in a certain way, because what happens then is, basically, your mind goes round in circles.

I was getting really freaked out the other day because I was talking to Jonny when we were in the studio, and I woke up one morning and discovered that during the night, as a dream or something, my mind was going round in a trap. Like it was going round and round and round and round. It was like four or five words just going round in my head and it went on for about an hour and I couldn't stop it. And Jonny said he had the same thing. He went to Israel with his wife after a tour and he'd just got out of the bath, and picked up a towel to dry himself. Then before he put the towel down on the floor, he stood there completely freaked out for half an hour because there were so many different places to put the towel. He'd become paralysed and got really, really scared, because his mind had gone into a lock and wouldn't stop. So I get scared about my mind going round in circles, but I think that's only because I'm constantly aware of my own reflection and I feel that's an extremely unhealthy thing. And I feel sorry for anyone who actually starts to believe their own reflection, because I've done it. What a wanker!

I think you're being very dishonest. I think that you're a little shit like every other narcissistic little boy in a pop band. Your particular angle in life is being the tortured artist, which frankly is already appearing fairly tired. It's about time you lightened up.
You're right. I'll lighten up. At the moment, I'm really excited about what we could do, but just as much, like fifty per cent of the time, I'm thinking how close it is to just being completely banal. I guess that's what's supposed to happen. The best thing for us is to just keep turning stuff out and not worrying about what people think. The thing that paralysed us for the first two or three months of recording *The Bends* was the fact that we were paralysed about what people would think. We were paralysed about who we were supposed to be.

It's pretty difficult not to love the attention. And I kind of went through a phase of going to London a lot and going to parties and things. Part of me really wanted to do that – wanted to go out and sort of soak up this beaming fucking sunshine coming out of my bottom or whatever it was, but you know... Maybe I should have done it, but it's not my thing, that's all. I'm not good at taking compliments, but I do it. I think it's more that people have put this level of significance into it, to the point where it's really taking the piss. The reason I'm proud of the fact that people have jumped to the *The Bends* now is because I know how difficult it was to make. The record is a document of a period of time and that was a difficult period of time and the fact that people really like it makes me very proud. I don't really care who wins Brit awards because nobody else does.

It sounds to me like you're desperately trying to find something to fight against.
I didn't come here to be attacked by you. Just fucking lay off, all right? [*laughs*]

No wonder you don't talk too much: you don't seem to have much to say, Thom.
I don't think I do have.

Do you enjoy getting drunk on your own, then, Thom?
Stuff comes out, and I like it because there's a sort of comfort in it: being pissed out of your head and on your own. But it's a bit softer. I think that I should ask you some questions now. You're the one that's been trying to pick a fight with me. Why do you follow me around everywhere?

What do you mean 'follow you around'? I'm just another voice in the tape recorder, part of the interview. What do you mean, 'follow you around'?
You know what I mean. Why do you make me do that stuff? Why do you make me hurt people?

You sound like some dodgy John Hurt serial killer character.
I don't mean 'hurt people'. People say I get in a state, and I think it's because you're around.

I think you're just creating this as part of a convenient excuse for your bad behaviour.
You've always got a fucking answer, haven't you? You've always got a fucking answer.

I think it sounds a bit too much like a very bad 80s thriller, or something. You're trying to create some sort of persona thing. Anyway I don't think this is really for the public domain. Do you?
No, but this is the first time I've ever talked to you.

No it's not. That's bullshit.
Everyone has different sides, and at least I don't go and harm anybody. Except maybe the fish in the pond. I think maybe this house is haunted. I'll tell you about the fish. It was during a Christmas and I bought these oriental fish that lived in a pond at the bottom of the garden and my other half went away for a few days and one of the things that was left on a note was 'look after the fish', because at that time there was ice and snow covering the ground. It was like two foot deep or something ridiculous. Now I let these fish die because I couldn't even be fucking bothered to get my shit together to go down to the bottom of the garden and knock a little hole in the ice to keep these fish alive. So when I eventually remembered that they were there, I saw them belly up in the ice and one of them was... his little mouth was right next to the last hole that had been made there in the pond. A last gasp for a breath of air and I couldn't even fucking manage that.

Poor little Thom.
You're the wanker that wants me to sleep with all these women. But I haven't done it, and I won't.

But you know they're still there.
I don't think it's any of your business.

Of course it's my business.
OK then, but I don't think it's anybody else's business.

Everything is their business. That's the whole point, Thom. This tape's running out. Have you got anything else you want to say in this somewhat random interview that we've been doing?
I want to say that I did this for a reason. It was a good idea because I wanted to just take a different photograph. You know, a different reflection in a different shop window. But maybe I just kind of forgot what it was I wanted to do. I wanted it to be some sort of deep, psychological experience. I wanted to be locked in a room for a day, but my life being what it is, I couldn't do that.

So let's find you a cheery question to end this, shall we? After all, this is the media. Do you think you'll ever get to Heaven, Thom? Or maybe just the top of the charts?
Only if I get rid of you.

Absolutely no chance whatsoever.

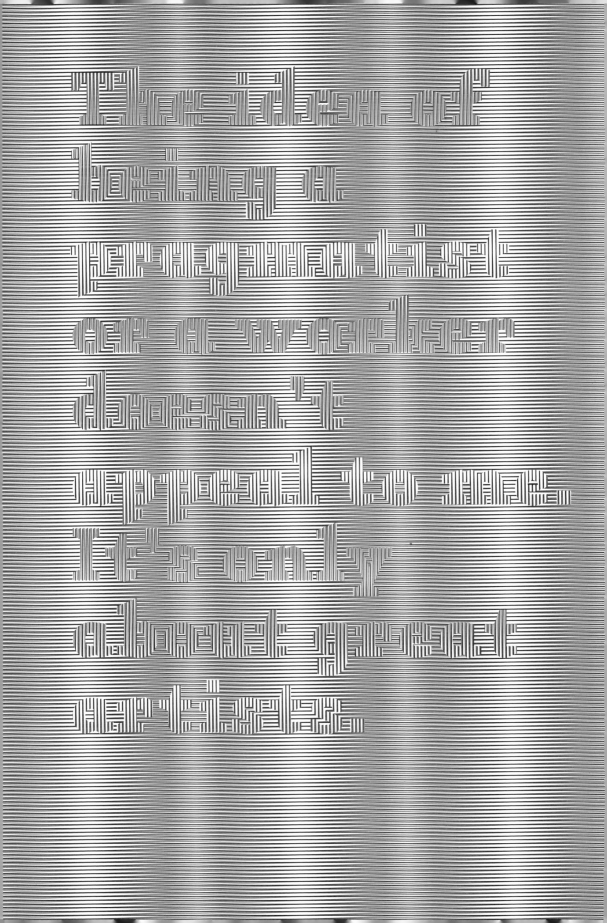

Kate Moss, 1998 Rankin

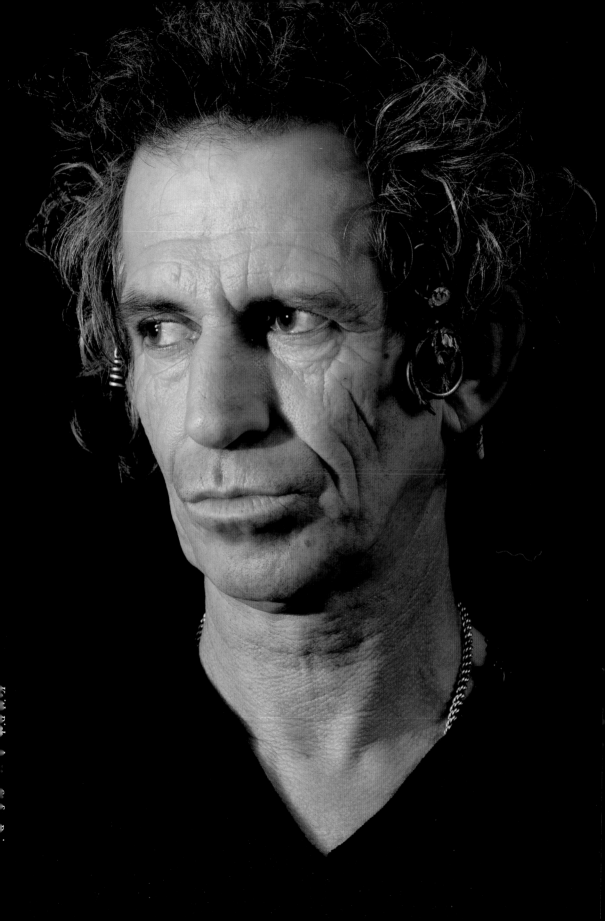

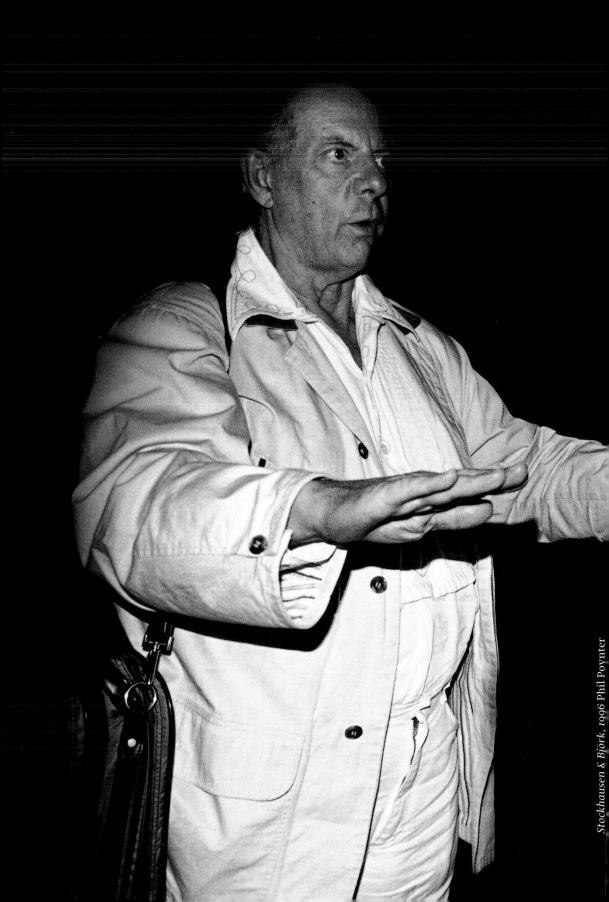

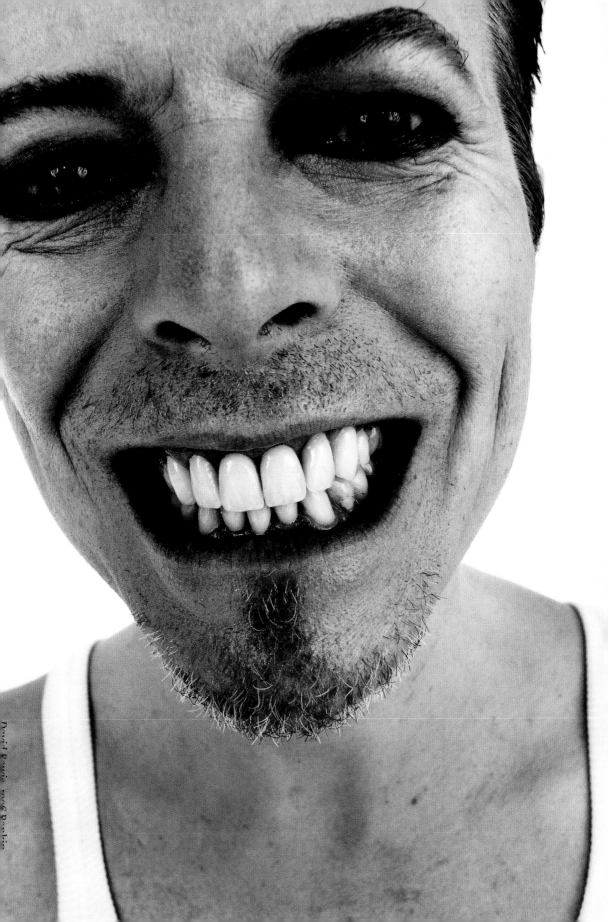

I can't
cure the
world
of illness
with
clothes

Film is the place where words and music come to life: a magical, moving moment when the imagination is overwhelmed in a two-dimensional suspension of disbelief. Film is what brings Paul Auster and Lou Reed together. Both are highly accomplished storytellers. Both are resident New Yorkers, and both have a deep respect for each other's work. For the first time in print, cigar-toting Auster and nicotine-free Reed discuss their collaboration in the films Smoke and Blue in the Face (both 1995), and how they got to be where they are now.

Reed's largely improvised monologue in Blue in the Face, *in which he plugs his invention for flip-lens reading glasses, brings to light his rarely seen good-humoured side. It seems that Reed has neatly folded away the ubiquitous shades, let his hair grow, come out of a depressive state of bereavement that snowballed into his last two albums,* Songs for Drella *(1990) and* Magic and Loss *(1992), to rediscover his quick-witted, charmingly effusive other self. It's a welcome return and nowhere is it more apparent than in his new album,* Set the Twilight Reeling *(1996), which reverberates with provocative, exciting guitars, distortion, a sense of urgency and intimacy. There's an elliptical, momentarily time-warped crescendo at the end of the title track that leaves you realizing that the legendary Lou Reed has weathered far more favourably than his pruney exterior might suggest. 'Egg Cream', taken from this album, is also part of the soundtrack for* Smoke, *and contains the lines, 'When I was a young man, no bigger than this, a chocolate egg cream was not to be missed.'*

Set in a cigar shop in contemporary Brooklyn, Smoke *is based on 'Auggie Wren's Christmas Story' by Paul Auster, which Auster originally wrote for* The New York Times *in 1990. Auggie Wren, played by Harvey Keitel, is the central character and his cigar shop is the central location, in and out of which weaves an unpredictable web of crossed paths: most importantly the relationship between novelist and cigar-shop regular Paul Benjamin (William Hurt), whose life is saved by on-the-run Rashid (first-time actor Harold Perrineau). Keitel's absorbingly natural, second-nature acting is as fine as a Cuban hand-rolled.*

*Both films were directed by Wayne Wang (*The Joy Luck Club*) in collaboration with Auster, who wrote* Smoke *and detailed character studies for* Blue in the Face. *Shot in only three days,* Blue in the Face *is set in the same cigar shop as* Smoke. *It's a high-spirited celebration of everyday Brooklyn life. The improvised performances, based on Auster's notes, also feature an array of New York personalities and actors as diverse as Madonna, Roseanne, Jim Jarmusch, Michael J Fox, Mira Sorvino, Jared Harris and Lily Tomlin. It's a funny, intriguing, spontaneous and quite mad hour and a half.*

Paul Auster is first and foremost a storyteller. His first book, New York Trilogy, *a collection of three short detective stories, used simple but highly crafted narrative devices to establish the unique writing point that has run through nearly all his books: truth is stranger than fiction. He constructs inventive and highly effective twists and turns in his stories in order to blur the lines between reality and fiction, between character identities and the identity of the reader, between what it means to be alive and why we are here. He is an acrobatically graceful and strikingly skilful writer, and one of America's most important contemporary novelists. 'I remember thinking that Lou was flat, not at all in good form,' he relates, 'and that none of it would make the final cut of the film. Lou was of exactly the same opinion. We walked back to my house together for a drink after the day's work was done, and we both felt disappointed, shaking our heads and trying to shrug it off. "Well, that's showbusiness," we said, and then went on to talk about other things. As everyone who has seen the film now knows, show business proved us both wrong. At every* Blue in the Face *screening I have attended, Lou's performance provokes the most laughter and the most comments. He steals the movie.'*

Paul Auster | **When did it occur to you that music might actually be something you would spend your life doing? Were you in high school?**

Lou Reed | I must say, no! I mean, I had wanted to do what you do. I wanted to be a writer. A formal writer. I was writing through college. However, in high school I made a record, and I was playing all these very funny bars on Long Island. Then I went off to college: one of the arguments for that was to stay out of the draft of the Vietnam War. And in college, we just had bar bands every year I was in school, which augmented my income a lot. But we were terrible. We were unspeakable; we actually had to change our name quite often. Were you writing when you were young?

I think I started writing when I was about nine or ten. So right around the time you found the guitar, I found the pen.

That's kind of interesting!

I loved it. When I got to be about fifteen, I read *Crime and Punishment*, the great novel by Dostoyevsky, and it absolutely turned me inside out. And I think it gave me a feeling about what novels can be. And I think it was that experience that made me determined to do it myself. I said, 'This is absolutely how I am going to spend my life.' And all through high school I wrote. In fact, from that point on, I wrote seriously. I mean as seriously as I write now. Much of it, for many years, was real garbage.

You should hear my first record! No, I mean the 45! – 'Lever For Me'/'So Blue' by The Jades, made at age fourteen.

I can imagine. Everyone starts out...

You know what is funny about that? There is a Velvet Underground compilation that is out,

From top
Paul Auster and
Lou Reed, 1996
Bruce Louden

that should be pretty good, and on it, apparently, because I haven't listened to it, is a very, very early tape of us at the very beginning. And I've seen in print, people say, 'It's unbelievable. Their writing and sound is so derivative of other people.' And my response to that is, 'Everybody has to start somewhere.'

It's absolutely true, and I can even go further than that. Having taught writing, for my sins...

Where?

At Princeton, back in the 80s. I did that for about five years. Now, I always felt that the most talented kids were the ones who were turning in the worst work. If I saw a twenty-year-old student able to turn out something that looked like a John Cheever story with a certain degree of power and accomplishment, I realized that there was no hope for that person, because he had already limited his horizons. He wasn't pushing the boundaries, he wasn't testing himself, he wasn't trying to do something new, he was just regurgitating what he felt his elders wanted from him. And the kids that were all over the place and taking risks and blundering about, those were the ones I had hope for. You know, too much accomplishment is not a good thing. I don't think you develop.

I certainly didn't suffer from it! It's not anything I had a fear of. I made my first record at fourteen. It was played on the air once and nose-dived and that was the end of it. And then I was just in bar bands, and then I was writing for this awful schlockhouse that did nothing but cover records. So as far as what I was gonna to do in real life for a living... I remember – it's very funny to think back, I haven't thought about this for a long time – I used to look at *The New York Times* ad. section...

As we all did...

... and I would look at that, saying to myself, 'If you had to get a real job, what in the world are you qualified to do?' Which, as a liberal arts person, meant I was qualified for nothing, as far as training... For what? It didn't exist. I would look at these ads, 'Starting salary: da-da, da-da', but I couldn't picture myself in a suit, going with a resumé... It makes me laugh to even think about it. Applying for a job as a what? Copywriter,

probably, something to do with writing...

Junior salesman of ladies' shoes and accessories.

Did you think, 'I've got to make a living, I've got to do something'?

This was a great torment for me.

Did you ever have a real job?

I've had hundreds of jobs.

I mean a real one.

No. I never had a real job, nothing that could be qualified as a 'career'. I just had odd jobs.

I was a copyreader for two weeks. I filed – actually I had a job in high school, filing burrs off nuts that had been recently manufactured. And I remember the guy next to me, who was thirty years older than me, saying, 'You know, there is a future in this.' And I couldn't imagine what it could be!

I had a lot of blue-collar jobs as a kid. One of the most interesting jobs I ever had was working as a census-taker in Harlem for the 1970s census.

[laughs]

It was an extraordinary experience. I was part of a team...

Now, how do you get a job like that?

I had just graduated from college and I needed to get some work. I needed to make some money.

That's what your degree got you!

That's right. We were part of the crack crew to go out and knock on the doors of the people who hadn't sent back their forms.

[laughs loudly] Who didn't send back their forms! *[laughing]*

But, you see, what it all...

Did they talk to you?

Absolutely. In fact, there was one old woman who must have been ninety,

maybe even close to a hundred, and I realize now that she is the origin of Granny Ethel in *Smoke*. This thought didn't occur to me until a few days ago.

Oh really?

I knock on the door and this nearly blind old woman lets me in. I tell her I'm from the census. She is very polite and the lights are out in the room because she can't see much anyway. At one point, she peers out at me; we were sitting on two beds on opposite sides of a narrow room. She peers out at me and says, 'You know, if you want to turn on the light, go right ahead. I mean, I don't really need it but maybe you do.' And I said, 'Thank you.' And I pulled a string hanging from the ceiling. 'Pop', the light goes on and she squints back at me and looks very carefully and says, 'Why. You're not a black boy at all!' And it turned out that I was the first white person who had ever set foot in her house. We spent a long time together. Her parents had been slaves.

And she couldn't tell by your voice?

She said, 'Well, I thought from your voice that you weren't black.' But it was just inconceivable to her that a white person should have come into her apartment.

All the way up there.

It was amazing. Anyway, what about it? When did you think music might be something you could do professionally?

It's a really interesting question that you are posing. And I think in some ways I could say, 'A year and a half ago.'

[laughing] Right.

You know, I was so shaky in so many ways, that I still say, 'Well, now we are really gonna get to do what we're really gonna do. This has only

been phase one.' At a certain point you realize it's a long race – if you think of it in those terms – and we are only so far down the path with this. And there are a lot of people clamouring for you to stop. Saying, you know...

'Enough is enough.'

... quit right now while we still think something of you rather than...

Right, right.

When did you think you could make a go of it? That, for better or worse, you were...

I sort of stumbled along for about ten years, writing little books of poems that nobody read, published by small presses. Writing articles...

Supporting yourself by other means?

Well, translation mostly. I was translating books – a job that I grew to hate. It's very grinding, poorly paid work. But I always wanted my so-called freedom. But then I became a slave to my own poverty. It was a very bad situation.

Yeah, I know exactly what you mean.

I was trapped, and finally went into a tailspin and had a very bad crisis in the late 70s. And during that time, I didn't write much at all. I thought I was finished. It went on for a year or two, and then slowly I got out of it. Some things happened; I became engaged in it again. I became hungry to do it again and that's when I started writing prose. Up until then, I had only been publishing poems and essays.

Really? See, it's very funny the time span you're talking about, because in the mid to late 70s, I had a terrible crisis. And that is when I found out that I had some hits! I could pass for what is called a 'rock star'. Except, I had no idea what I was doing! I kind of marvel at people who, at that early age, do know what they're doing. I was like a real loose canon. And I found out, in Australia, on a tour, that every single royalty I had ever gotten had been stolen! And that I hadn't had taxes reported for the past five years; that I was in contempt of court – there was a warrant out. I had no money in the bank, no apartment and I had been taken for a ride by these people! And I had about fifteen dollars in my pocket!

What a comforting thought!

Talk about a crisis! That got me involved in a

law suit that lasted ten or so years! So I always had this threat over me that I could lose this law suit and they would put a line on me for everything.

But that was an external crisis. I mean, you didn't doubt yourself as someone who wanted to keep on doing what you were doing, if you could.

Which is what I chose to do. But it certainly made me doubt my intelligence. How could you get yourself into something like this?

So you made some bad mistakes.

Beyond belief! But so many people that I know have variations on the same awful story. Did you run into any problems like that?

You see, you have to understand, as a writer there is no money involved. It's really so little. All I was interested in was literally paying the rent and putting food on the table. That's all I have ever aspired to. It has only been in the last few years that I've had any cushion at all. So I've spent most of my life really being on the edge! It's not a good way to live and yet, if you believe in what you are doing, and you feel you have to do it, what choice do you have? You don't have a choice.

You're right! Because when you think about some of the advice you're given, like: 'Fall back on a real job with security.' What security? These people are being fired left and right, and seniority are the first people to go!

I also see what people look like at my age who have been working in corporate America for the last twenty-five years. They look ten to fifteen years older than I do! Easily! I think rock keeps you young.

I think writing keeps you young. Any art keeps you fresh, because you never retire. You just do it until you croak! You're also not having your blood and juice crushed by a job that doesn't let you express any of it! If that's the thing that gives you air!

So the price you pay for your freedom is struggle. But it's funny; when I was broke, say fifteen years ago when Siri and I first started living together, we really were getting by on pennies. But we were desperately happy and everything was fine; we were both doing good work, and she would lie in bed at night and start worrying about how we were going to pay the rent. And I was always very optimistic, just like Mr Micawber: I'd say, 'Don't worry. Something will turn up. Everything is going to be all right.' I was oozing optimism all the time. Now that we have a cushion, that money is coming in...

[laughs loudly]

... she feels much relieved and happy, and spends money with a certain gusto, and I'm more than pleased for her to get whatever she wants. I'm the one now who is anxious. I keep thinking, 'Things are going well, but just wait, you know. Some stone is going to fall out of the sky and hit me on the head.'

That's what I may have been suffering from after the induction to the Rock-'n'-Roll Hall of Fame: things are going so well that if you dare enjoy this stuff, something very terrible will happen to you. But I was talking to a friend of mine, Patti Smith, because one of the guys in the group had died, sad to say, and she said – and I thought this is a great way of looking at things – 'Because the other person can't be there, you owe it to them to enjoy yourself twice as much.'

Good advice!

And then she added a little addendum to it. 'And that's really hard!' But I thought of that and I tried to take it to heart. You can't waste that moment. It's so easy to cover yourself up.

Let me put it this way. We are at a certain age now; we have as much behind us, probably more, than we have ahead of us...

At least halfway down the line.

... So many people that we've loved and cared about are not here any more, but you carry them around inside you. The older you get, the more your life becomes a quiet conversation with the dead. I find that very sad and at the same time, very comforting. You know, the older you get, the more of a spiritual being you become. You are living with ghosts and they have a lot to tell you. And if you listen carefully, you can learn a lot.

Well, I find myself re-examining things that were said... It's a favourite theme in writing: 'Say something now. If you wait too long, something happens and you might not get a chance to say it at all.' And it turns out to really be true. I had an incident: a friend of mine thought that he had heard one of the Velvet Underground had died and he thought, for some reason, it was me, and I found this incredible message on my machine and I called him up, and he said: 'You're OK!' I said: 'Yeah!'

Resurrected!

Yeah! It was very, very, touching for me.

Well, a moment of true feeling. You understood how he felt and...

I certainly did! But you were saying that you were getting by on nothing and now things are better, and in some ways it makes you even more nervous. But did you ever think, for instance, 'Maybe I should do something, a one-shot commercial thing that would really bring in some money and then I could take a breath'?

Well, I tell you, during that bad crisis period I actually did two or three crazy things. I had money schemes. I was desperate to try to make a quick killing to get the coffers full again. I spent a lot of time inventing a game, you know, a card game...

Jesus! I did the same thing! I swear to you...

... and I spent months of my time on it. It was actually a very good game. I went to all kind of companies, the Toy Fair here in New York in February..,

You went further than I did. Mine was a board game. It was called Rock-'n'-Roll. And it was like a Monopoly board. The object was to get into the Top Ten.

[laughs]

But things would happen. You roll the dice, you move it ahead and it would say: 'You just got a recording contract. Advance.' Then you advance; then you throw something, maybe pick up 'Chance', and it says: 'Your bass player OD'd' or 'Go to rehab or your record company drops you.'

Mine was a baseball game, with cards...

Don't you think it's remarkable that one of the things that occurred to both of us was 'make a game'!

A solution for people who don't want

to work! You want to make a quick and incisive killing!

But it's the kind of thing that people who live on their imagination do: their idea of doing something that might make some money. We'll take what's serious and make it a game!

That's right!

Look at this, I'm talking about a game called 'Rock-'n'-Roll', where all these terrible things keep subverting what you're trying to do! Ah, it's so funny! Was the game rejected?

Yeah, it was rejected. It almost worked, but it didn't quite. And then I wrote a detective story under another name. I mean it's perfectly decent, I'm not ashamed of it, but it was done strictly for money. But the problem was, willing as I was to prostitute myself, nobody would really have me!

[laughs loudly]

And I ultimately made about nine hundred dollars publishing that book! I wanted to sell myself! I was ready. And it didn't work.

Someone once said to me about one of my albums, 'This is real prostitution. Don't you feel you're selling yourself?' And I hadn't even thought about it! And I said, 'As a matter of fact, I would have if I could have! But no one would have me.' There are fans of mine, other musicians who say to me, 'How could you let someone re-record your song?' Now, I can't stop them, but above and beyond that, I'd say, 'What do you mean?' And they would say, 'It's a degrading thing!'

It's actually a compliment!

[laughs loudly] Yeah!

It really is. If someone else wants to do something with what you've done, it's an honour. Really!

I'm just wondering whether you get anything like this? Where they don't want anything you do, for instance, to be made into a movie, or have a synopsis made of it, or have it changed or altered for another format.

No, it's different. It's altogether different. Most people make compromises at one time or another, but not everyone. Think of Harvey Keitel. I mention his name because we both know him. Harvey told me not long ago that he turned down a movie offer for three million dollars. He said, 'I just couldn't see myself doing it. I hated the part. I hated the movie and I couldn't do it.' And he obviously could have used the money to great advantage. And that's the thing I like about him so much.

He could have made *Blue in the Face* with that!

Are you kidding? He could have made two *Blue in the Faces*. He's one of the few well-known actors who hasn't sold out. It's not as though every movie he is in is good. But he thinks it might be good, and he goes into it with a truly good spirit. And I respect him a lot for those kinds of decisions.

Would you like to mention, by the way, the miracle of *Blue in the Face* and *Smoke* and how they came about?

Smoke started from that little Christmas story that was commissioned by *The New York Times*.

I remember reading it in the *Times* and loving it!

That's great. Well, Wayne saw it in San Francisco and thought it might be a good premise for a film.

Can I ask you a question? Now, I get asked the same question all the time, and it's great for me to ask you. Did you really meet someone like Auggie who was taking a picture every day from that corner?

No, everything is made up. In fact, I wrote it in the *Times* in such a way as to confuse everybody. I tried to blur the boundaries of what is real and what is not real and the proof that it worked was that Mike Levitas, the editor, hired a photographer and half the letters that came to the *Times* were letters of protest saying, 'Why didn't you publish Auggie Wren's photographs, how could you rip that poor man off?' When he doesn't exist! Anyway, so Wayne read the story and thought a film could be made on the strength of it. And for over a year, I didn't participate. I didn't want anything to do with writing the screenplay. Little by little he lured me in.

But you gave him permission?

I gave them permission because he's a good filmmaker.

So you said, 'If you want to pursue it, go ahead, I'm not gonna stop you', right?

Exactly. But Wayne led me into it and I enjoyed working with him a lot. He brought me in as a real partner. He's the only filmmaker in the history of American films, I think, who has actively courted the collaboration of a writer and has worked with him hand in glove to such a degree that finally both our names are on the film. It's an extraordinary thing.

'Thirtieth Smash Week!' I remember passing that and saying, 'That must be a very pleasurable thing to see.'

It was very nice: we didn't expect anything like that to happen. *Blue in the Face* was born during rehearsals for *Smoke*. Harvey was there with Giancario Esposito and they said, 'Can we improvise just to warm up?' And of course they could and what they did was so funny and interesting that Wayne, in one of his bursts of enthusiasm, turned to me and said, 'Why don't we make another movie when we're done with *Smoke*?' So we started working on that too. That's when you and I spoke. And why did I call you? Simply because we had become friends and I like you very much and I admired your work and I thought there's something about your voice that's going to work in this film, because it's a New York voice. We didn't have any plan – as you know we were winging it – and it worked. I'm glad we did it. It was a very nutty project. Six days to shoot and ten months to edit.

But back to you, Lou, there's something else I wanted to ask you. As you keep making music, do you feel that it gets easier or harder? That you have learned anything? Or are you constantly having to teach yourself all over again?

I have to teach myself all over again, but it's much quicker, because I've done it before and I remember, and I remember fairly fast.

You get to your mark faster?

Absolutely. I have learned some things not to do, and I'm careful not to do them.

I find that it gets harder, that I get stupider as I get older and have to keep relearning or teaching myself all over again. The only thing experience has helped me with is not to get too depressed when it's not going well. That's a very big improvement. When I was younger and got stuck – which writers do all the time, you run into dead ends and go down the wrong path – I got desperate. I couldn't work my way out of the problem. Now, I run into that wall and I say, 'All right, time to stop. Just leave it alone. Just walk away and come back in two or three days. Maybe a night's sleep is all you need.'
That's the thing. If experience only taught you that, you'd be miles ahead of the younger you.
I am in that respect.
I think of it as a trick. If you're sitting there and saying, 'Oh my God, it's gone, it's this, it's that, I'm finished, oh, da-da, da-da, da-da'... But in fact, you say, 'Now I'm gonna get a pizza...'
Exactly; read the sports page...
... Maybe watch the Nicks. 'We'll come back to this and not be worried.' It's the lack of worry. Everything will be OK. It's a natural ebb and flow taking place. I think it's the single most important thing I've learnt. And there's one other thing that I've learned, when the flow is going, stay out of the way. Don't get hung up on a word or a single detail, or you'll stop it.
Yeah, just keep pushing ahead.
Keep going in a straight line. You can always come back, but if you intrude, you can do something that can derail everything and then you'll go into that panic state of 'uh-oh...'
OK, last question, because this is something that I don't do and I can't share with you. After all these years, does performing still thrill you?

When I haven't done it in a while, I can't even imagine how you do it. That's also true though, for me, regarding writing: if I haven't written anything for a while, I can look at the lyrics and I can't even imagine who wrote it. It's very, very strange and I wish that didn't happen. I really wish that I could look and say, 'I know exactly how I did that. I know how to get it back', but it's not true. With performing, I know that I really like playing with the guys and I know the show can be an enormous amount of fun. It's just at this particular stage of the game, I can't for the life of me figure out, 'Who does that?'
It's like contemplating swimming. It's a chilly day and plunging into the water seems like the most unappetizing thing. Then you're in the water and it feels good.
I know that, I do it. I know I get off on it. It's like one of those things you were saying about trying to teach yourself to remember. It must be something like that. But I'm gonna be remembering real soon. But every time I do it I really love it – there's nothing like the exhilaration of a live show.
I've given many readings, but it's not quite the same thing. You're just reading your book; you're not really 'performing' it.
Well, reading is performing, isn't it?
In a more subtle way, perhaps. It's much more subdued. Although I must say, my friend Art Spiegelman and I read at Summer Stage in Central Park last July...
I did that.
... on this big rock-'n'-roll stage with five thousand people in the audience – that was a new kind of reading for me. Mosquitoes in your face, helicopters whirring overhead...
Don't you think there's acting involved? Don't you think it's a performance?
Definitely. But it's not as though... It's just something I do every now and again.
Don't you think of putting some music on the back of it?
[laughing] No. We can try that sometime.
Like jazz. Like those old 50s guys used to do.
Bongo drums. [laughing]
This is a good place to stop.
I think so.
The melding of word and music.
We're all on the stage here.

May 1996
Introduction and interview | *Alix Sharkey*

How do you start to write about Larry Clark? Perhaps by explaining his unconventional path from drug-addled obscurity to international recognition as an unflinching observer of youthful hedonism and its twilight states: and how, through photo-books like Tulsa *(1971)*, Teenage Lust *(1983)* and Perfect Childhood *(1993)*, he has come to be revered as one of America's most startling and original photographers, to be copied by countless lesser talents.

Or you could pre-empt this by pointing out that Larry Clark is afraid of death, terrified of the very notion of dying. You can see the fear in his eyes when the subject is raised; his daily routine of good food, exercise and energy conservation is a giveaway. Having spent too many nights and days trembling in a speed haze; having all but razed his central nervous system by cranking up speed throughout his early adulthood, he must now lavish care and attention on the body he once abused if he is to live long enough to realize new-found ambitions.

You could ask why the only really devised character in Kids *(1995)* is Jennie – a character who finds out she's going to die; someone who is made to confront the reality of impending death. Clark admits that he cannot yet confront the idea of old age. Perhaps he's still lost in those 'outlaw years', when he drifted through the American Midwest with his prostitute girlfriend, robbing chemists' shops for speed and whatever other drugs he could find; perhaps still wondering why he ended up doing two years in Oklahoma State Penitentiary, 'for shooting some guy in the arm'. And maybe he's trying to decide what he discovered, and what was lost for ever, as he injected amphetamines with his beautiful speed-freak friends in Tulsa, and took the photos that would eventually secure his reputation.

You might notice the way he almost starts to stutter again when he talks about his traumatic adolescence, and it's not hard to imagine him looking at the teenagers whom he befriended and cast in Kids and wondering: 'Are they smarter, or more clued up than I was at their age?' The answer, of course, is both 'yes' and 'no'. That is what he has found and described in a film that is a masterpiece of its genre.

You might start by pointing out that Clark, a man who began his working life as a baby photographer, is obsessed with youth, as is the protagonist of his film, Telly, who wants to 'fuck those little baby virgins, man'. And then you could acknowledge that in this respect, he is no different from anyone else. We all share this obsession. Our entire advertising industry, the mirror of our dreams and aspirations, revolves around images of youth and its sexual potency, images so commonplace that they're practically invisible. Kids shakes the picture up a bit, and lets us see our desires with a new clarity.

The most disturbing thing about Kids is not the sex, or the profanity, or the drugs, or the violence, or the supposed immorality. It is the fact that it presents us with a microcosmic picture of our bizarre environment. Kids depicts the implosion of a society fuelled by infantile desire, obsessed with sex and eternal youthful vigour, thrashing around wildly in its attempts to find freedom without responsibility. That's what really makes many people feel queasy when they see Kids. They feel at once so far removed, and yet totally connected to the characters on the screen. This is the real shock – the impossible distance between what we want to believe and what we know to be true.

But then again, you might just begin with a simple statement, like:

Dazed & Confused | **I understand it was through taking your son skateboarding that you met the people who helped you make *Kids*.**

Larry Clark | I was interested in skateboarders and their culture, because the kids have this incredible freedom, and they're looked on as outlaws, I mean, everybody hates skateboarders, man. And it was like, it took a twelve-year-old kid to figure out the whole city's a concrete playground. So I was interested in it visually, and in the culture, and then these kids seem like actors to me, they're out on the street, they're in confrontations all the time, so they have to act, they gotta have an act. So I started hanging out with them, and I bought myself and my son a skateboard, and we started skating.

Tell me about how the story came together.
I met Harmony Korine in the Washington Square park; he was a skater for six years. When I met him, he was in high school, and he said he was going to stop skating and write screenplays and direct movies. And he told me about a thirty-page screenplay he'd written in high school, it was about a thirteen-year-old kid who lives with his mother, and she's separated from his father, who's an alcoholic. It's the kid's thirteenth birthday and it's his father's weekend to look after him. So his father comes and gets him, takes him out, they go to bars and throughout the day his father gets drunker and drunker, and in the evening he gets this thirteen-year-old kid a prostitute, a streetwalker, for his birthday. So I said, 'Harmony, does he fuck her?' And he says, 'Oh yeah, he fucks her. It's hardcore.' So I said, 'Man, this is odd for a high school kid to be writing a story like this, right?'

A year later, when I got the idea for *Kids*, I knew it had to be written from the inside, and I thought: 'Well, I'm not a writer', and you couldn't get a writer to come in and like, y'know, get in with the kids; they wouldn't accept him. So I said: 'Well, wouldn't it be great if it was a kid who could write, but y'know, there are no kids that can write, I'm just having a fantasy.' But then I remembered Harmony. I thought: 'Wait a minute, this kid said he could write, I wonder if he could or if he was just bullshitting me.' So I called him up, and he brought over this little

screenplay he'd written and it was good; he could write. So I asked him to write *Kids*. I just gave him the bare outline of the story, about this skater who likes to fuck virgins, because he likes to be first 'cause it's safe sex, and the rest of the story. And from that he wrote the whole screenplay. The story came from stuff I saw, just hanging out with these kids.

Why choose an AIDS theme?
I called the summer of 92 'the Summer of condoms'. They were going to instigate a condom giveaway programme in New York high schools, and the whole city was polarized – the Catholic Church was freaking out; they were preaching against it, y'know, so it didn't happen. But people from, like, Planned Parenthood who were pro-education were in the parks and on street corners, giving condoms away. So in the park, the kids had condoms; they wore them round their necks like decorations; they would give them to me. And they were talking about safe sex, man, all the information. And I thought: 'This is great; these kids have so much information, so much education, that they're fucking, but they're having safe sex, right?' Then, after about six months, y'know, I was their friend then, they didn't censor their comments: I was just one of the guys, amazingly, even though I was much older. And I like, find out that nobody's using condoms, it was all bullshit. None of them would use condoms on a bet! They had me completely snowed, y'know, that they know what they're supposed to be doing. They're kids, and kids don't wanna use condoms; nobody likes to use condoms, you don't wanna use them, I don't wanna use them, nobody's using them, it's all bullshit. And I knew these two kids whose idea of safe sex was fucking virgins. And

I watched this one kid seduce girls through the summer; he would come to the park and pick out these thirteen-year-old girls, and just focus on them, y'know, total attention. And then de-virginize them. So that was how I got this idea for the story, and realized that would be the dramatic hook for the movie, and then you could show everything about what these kids do during the day. Because I wanted to do a movie about the kids' world when adults aren't around. Because it's a totally different world; adults don't have access. But I was allowed in, I had access.

The only adults in the film are the two females in the clinic.

And the taxi driver, right? Whose advice is 'If you stutter, don't talk.' *[laughs]* So I wanted to make a movie about this world that nobody ever sees. All these teenage movies; everything is so silly, it's all comedy, it's all fluff, it's bullshit. And I had access to this world, a totally different universe. And I wanted to show that energy, that kids have fun, that they're out there just living for the moment, and the main thing they're thinking about is they don't wanna miss anything. They wanna be with their friends, right?

People forget how difficult it is to be an adolescent; how utterly traumatic it can be on an hourly basis. There are a number of levels on which *Kids* operates, but for me, the most powerful thing was the distance between these characters' lives and my own, and the realization that I was once just like them. It was like watching myself twenty years ago. I said and did almost exactly the same things. But I'd conveniently forgotten all the fights and lies and petty crime and general shittiness, and the incredible energy and humour that comes with living life so intensely. When you get into your thirties, when you've had money and jobs and friends and some kind of life, you feel that you've got access to everything, and you rewrite your character so that it seems you always did have those things. But at that point in your life, when you're a street kid, all you've got is people your own age. Hopefully. If you haven't got them, you've got nothing.

That's what I wanted to capture, that secret world, so the audience is kinda eavesdropping. I wanted to blur the line between documentary and drama. And Eric Edwards, the director of photography, he got it. He did an incredible job.

Who shot the video sequence with the kid who lies down on the skateboard as he's going across the intersection?

That was taken from a famous skate video; a guy who's probably the best skateboarder of all time, Mark Gonzalez. He's incredible.

How have you managed to stay in touch with that energy that comes through in the film? Is that because of your experiences with your earlier work?

With my early work, most of it was autobiographical and it seemed that I had a bottomless well of experience to draw on. And having kids of my own now, I was interested in what was going on. I've done a lot of shit in my life, and uuh... I hate to say it... but, uh... I was actually shocked by some of the shit that was going on. Only because I'm older now. You do forget. And, like you, I hate to admit that.

That's kind of encouraging for me.

But the film is not autobiographical at all. I've always been a story-teller, so it made sense for me to do film. And it was very comfortable directing them. It was like, 'Man, I'm home. This is easy, so good.' It was hard work, but I knew what I was doing. The film looks exactly like what I wanted in my fantasy and my dreams, it looks exactly like it. But this story is about contemporary teenagers; it's not about me, even though my earlier work made it easier for me.

I saw an interview with you, conducted by Gus Van Sant, where he says, 'Our whole society is youth-oriented, nobody cares about old people.'
Yeah. It's probably true.

Why is that?
I don't know. Because everybody wants to be young, I guess. Who wants to get old, y'know?

Because everybody's scared to die?
Nobody wants to age gracefully; everybody wants to be out there.

We have no concept of ageing gracefully in the West; no idea how to do it, right? We don't understand how to do it, right?
Well, it's true. I think about myself. I'm fifty-three now. So if I live to eighty, that's nearly thirty years... *[pause]* I think about all the work I want to do. I'm really in a hurry now. I really wanna do a lot. I have a few films I wanna make, y'know?

Do you feel, then, that you've wasted your life?
[pause] I really don't think in those terms. *[laughs]* I'm sure I've wasted a lot of time. But there's nothing we can do about that.

If you can use the experience you've got from that time, and hopefully you can, if you remained conscious, then you haven't really wasted it, even if you were slumped in a motel room for two years.
Well, I've always made work, and I guess that's what saved me. Doing the books, doing a lot of shows in New York and elsewhere, y'know, installations and so on.

What kind of kid were you, Larry?
I was a really fucked up kid, y'know?

Where'd you grow up?
In Oklahoma.

Oklahoma City?
Tulsa.

Tulsa?
Tulsa. Tulsa. Tulsa.

Tulsa. Right.

Um, and... um... I was a really fucked up kid. I guess I musta had ADD to the max, y'know? Attention Deficit Disorder, I guess that's what they call it now. I had something. I was really hyper, hyper, hyper, hyper, hyper. I was the kid always in the principal's office, always in trouble, always talking in class. I was a skinny little kid, and um... uh... I had a late puberty; I was skinny and little and I stuttered like mad; I could hardly talk – terrible stutter. Uh... uh... and uh... then I started um, um shooting amphetamine when I was like almost sixteen.

What was your home life like?
My mother was a door-to-door baby photographer. It was called kid-napping. And when I was fifteen, I was forced into the family business. I would go out with my mother to small towns in Oklahoma and Kansas, knock on doors, talk my way into the house, and photograph the baby in the house, right there and then. I'd have a pulldown background, like a small movie screen; I'd throw a blanket over the coffee table, set up the Roliflex and the strobe and take a picture of the baby. Six five-by-sevens for ten dollars ninety-five. And then a week later, I'd bring the pictures back and sell them. And I did all that. I had to knock on doors and call shots for my mother, y'know, call shots. I stuttered; it was horrible, man – I hated myself. I was this fucked up kid.

When you say 'call shots', you mean you had to doorstep these people?
I had to go out and make the fucking appointments. And when I was sixteen – you get a driving licence in Oklahoma – I had to go around photographing babies. I was a baby photographer. And I had to, like, put stuffed animals on my head and act silly. Can you imagine being sixteen and hating yourself and

stuttering and being skinny and being totally fucked up and having to make a clown of yourself, and do this shit? Horrible, horrible, horrible. And then I went back and sold the pictures. I mean, I worked in the family business so... but... it served me well, only because I had a camera. And I never thought of photographing anything but babies. But when I was eighteen, I was sent to commercial photography school. I guess my parents thought I could come back and take over the family business. But it was in the basement of an art school, so I started hanging out with the painters and sculptors. They were, like, beatniks and so right away I wanted to use photography to express myself. So right away, I was trying to be an artist with a camera, and I started photographing my friends, and that became the *Tulsa* book. I photographed them for like ten years. And while I was doing this baby photography, I started using amphetamine. So I was shooting amphetamine, so I was skinnier and stuttered even more. I was like a speed-freak for three years, before the term 'speed-freak' came around.

Going into people's houses, photographing their babies, putting fluffy toy animals on your head, flying high on speed?

Oh, fucked up. I was speeding my ass off, right? It was a nutty, nutty time man, a horrible time. But that's where I come from. My father never spoke to me, never. He was totally isolated; he used to go up to his room and stay in his room and uh... *[pause]* everybody liked him. My mother was always saying what a great guy my dad was, how everybody likes the guy, y'know, real personable guy, but he didn't like me, he hated me.

Were you the only child?

No, I had two sisters. I was the middle child. I mean, maybe he didn't hate me, but that was the impression I got. 'Cause he never did nothing with me, he never took me anywhere, never talked to me, never spoke to me, and um... so... he didn't pay any attention to me. So that was, uh, my uh...

What did he do for a living?

He ran the business. He named the business Lou Clark Photography. My mother and I would go out and take the pictures, this was 50s shit, right? And he stayed up in his room and ran the business. He used to go out and sell pictures for a while, but then he just ran the business. So at least it put a camera in my hand, and so then when I'd work and then go to my buddy's house and we'd shoot some shit – amphetamine – I always had my equipment, the Roliflex and a strobe. At first I didn't photograph, but I always had my camera. So later, when I started photographing, it wasn't like oh, 'Larry has a camera!', 'cause I'd always had a camera. It was a very natural thing, so I could photograph my friends because Larry had always had a camera throughout his whole life. It wasn't forced. It wasn't like someone from the outside coming in, and I wasn't taking photographs for any purpose, I was just practising my photography. I wasn't thinking about doing a book or a film or anything. It was just practice and it turned into... well, here I am today. So it's odd how we all start, where we come from and why things are the way they are.

A photographer called Adam Howe showed me a copy of *Tulsa* nearly ten years ago, and I was shocked at the beauty and frankness of the pictures. Speechless, like, 'What the fuck...?' But since then, I've seen many photographs that owed a lot, to say the least, to that book and the others that followed it. There are celebrity photographers who've made careers out of homoerotic photographs that are practically copied from your books. Do you ever get angry with all those fuckers ripping you off?

Yeah, well... obviously my work has influenced a lot of photographers, but they can't really copy me. Like a lot of fashion photographers now; they're doing stuff, taking off some of the stuff I did, but it's stupid y'know? It's selling

Clockwise from
top right
Tulsa, 1972
Still from Kids, *1997*
Untitled (Kids), *1995*
Untitled (Kids), *1995*

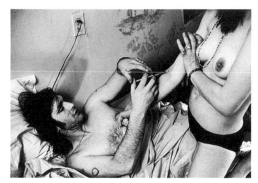

clothes, it has nothing to do with me, it's just
fashion shit. If you look at that work of mine,
there was a reason behind it. If someone has
their clothes off, there's a reason behind it.
When I was photographing those kids on Forty-
second Street for the *Teenage Lust* book, these
hustler kids, there was a reason. And with *Tulsa*
there was a reason. It wasn't like, 'OK we're
doing fashion; take off your shirt' y'know? It
was photographing the ways that different kids
were growing up in America. And, like, you
take the homoerotic photographs you see,
and they're different. They're like photographing someone as an object, or because they're
sexually attractive, and it's, like, that's it.

There's nothing else, no kind of depth there. But in my photographs, there's meaning on all kinds of levels.

Do you ever get asked by art directors and ad. agencies to pastiche your own work? After all, other photographers are getting paid to rip you off, so why don't they just give the money directly to you and get you to rip yourself off?

Well, I get offers, but I'm not going to do commercial work. I mean, if I had done that I wouldn't be sitting here, I'd be a millionaire, millions of dollars, right? But, uh... but a lot of those guys don't just copy me, they copy a lot of photographers. I mean – I don't even know the names – something like Herb Ritts, right? Someone oughta throw that guy out of a window, man. I mean, this guy rips off everybody y'know? Doesn't he have a book-cover with a photograph of a diver spinning in the air? That's a total rip-off of an Aaron Susskind photograph; it's a copy of an Aaron Susskind, a great Chicago photographer, and these guys don't even care, they just rip 'em off, steal any idea. It goes back, though. Like Penn, the famous Irving Penn, did a whole book of people in corners, portraits of people, like butchers in their work clothes. And it was a straight rip-off of August Sander. Look at Sander and then look at Penn. And I never heard anyone say, 'This guy is doing August Sander', or 'This guy is doing Aaron Susskind.' But uh... uh... it's just the genre. These people are shameless.

With *Kids*, it seems inevitable that someone will accuse you of promoting underage sex and all the rest...

Well, if they say that, man, they haven't seen the work. Look at the work; it's not about that. But somebody sent me a British newspaper where this woman in Parliament got up and denounced the film. Emma Nicholson MP, I think. And this was before the film had even arrived in this country; she had never even seen it. So how can this broad describe it as 'paedophile porn' or whatever, when she'd never even seen the film? How can you guys vote for people like that? Who is she to talk about stuff she's never seen?

A lot of the language used by the kids in the film is very brutal, calling each other 'nigger', 'bitch', 'whore' and so on. It's got harder over recent years, street language. Perhaps this is disturbing for people who have lost the defence mechanisms that you have to develop when you're fifteen, sixteen, seventeen years old; people who've forgotten how tough you have to be just to survive. Because even your friends will fuck you over emotionally and it's all about jockeying for position. You're trying to work out your position in the world and, of course, nobody wants to be on the bottom, so if you can put your hand on someone's face and lever yourself up, you're back in that world without any warning or preparation.

Oh, kids today play rough; they play rough, man. But, well, I think kids have rendered a lot of this language meaningless. They, like, use the works y'know... in the park I saw junior high school kids walk up to each other and say, 'Hey, bitch, suck my dick' and the girl will say something back likewise. And I'd say to myself, 'Boy, they're really mean to each other.' But it means nothing, because they've taken the language and, like, turned it inside out. And it's like, whatever will piss off adults or disturb grown-ups, kids will always do that, and we're always gonna do whatever, y'know, we're gonna take stuff and turn it inside out, so no one can understand what we're talking about, and at the same time it makes the grown-ups crazy. But, you know, the film is fun, there's a lot of laughs in the film. I tried to capture the energy of the kids and show them having fun. It's just the end of the film: everyone comes out of the theatre in shock with their mouths open, and they forget the film was fun and there were a lot of laughs. But maybe it will make people remember what it was like to be a kid. It's not just this awful depressing thing.

June 1996
Introduction | Paul Moody
Interview | Jon Savage

Timing has never been the Manic Street Preachers' strong suit. Whilst the world draped itself in the utilitarian workwear of baggy, they chose to be mascara-eyed glamour-pusses. When FM America finally tuned into grunge, they constructed a stadium-lite rock LP and, just as the world had gone Britpop-happy, with ironic high-jinks being the order of the day, they made one of the bleakest and most densely constructed albums ever. And now, they're back with the masterful Everything Must Go, *surrounded by the dressed-up, self-satisfied glitterati of 96, looking and sounding as reflective as they've ever been.*

And all we can really do is trust them. Because with the release of their quite splendid new album, the Manics have reached some kind of virgin territory for a pop group. What the record represents, before you even get to the music, is a safe arrival following one of the most harrowing journeys any pop group has ever encountered. One that has sent them through a maze of contradictions and dark confusion, all stemming from the day, almost fifteen months ago, when Richey Edwards walked out of Room 516 of the Embassy Hotel in Bayswater, and out of their lives for ever. In those agonizing months since, the group have suffered everything the media has been cold-hearted enough to throw at them. Grim, pessimistic tracts about the likelihood of Richey being dead; sombre reports about how his body would never be found if, as the evidence suggested, he'd jumped from the Severn Bridge on the morning of St Valentine's Day, 1995; even unforgivably, rumours that Richey's disappearance had been staged. All had to be dealt with as diplomatically as possible.

Meanwhile, the group, bewildered by the entire episode, have been forced to reconsider their future in private and deal with the whole sorry affair as best they can. Nicky and Sean retired to a surreal serenity as home-loving DIY enthusiasts, whilst James embarked on a demon-exorcizing career as semi-permanent London gadabout. The band, up until now, stayed firmly on ice.

Yet to dwell too heavily on the events of the last twelve months is somehow to miss the point of the Manic Street Preachers. For, ever since their electric-yell of a debut single, they've managed to exude a wildly maverick survival instinct. 'Motown Junk' spat in the face of cloying fan-worship, 'You Love Us' swore vengeance on the doubters, and 'Stay Beautiful', with its glammed-up insouciant howl of a chorus, 'Why don't you just fuck off!', practically redefined outsider chic. And that's way before you get to the epic spitefulness that characterized parts of the last album, The Holy Bible, *which, for all its obsessions with the Holocaust, serial killers and self-abuse, still managed to include the splenetic dazzle of: 'I am stronger than Mensa, Miller and Mailer, I spat out Plath and Pinter' amongst its lyrics. A sign that, as long as Richey's words were supercharged by James' last-chance howl, the band would never veer off into the realms of introspective depression.*

For the Manics have always been desperately keen to show their resistance to any sort of limitations, from their refusal to record in Wales, to their early disdain for most of their contemporaries, through to the remarkable recent shows supporting The Stone Roses and Oasis. There may be an incredibly fraught history surrounding them already (the stuff of legend, unquestionably), but the Manics, as they stand, represent more then just a group freed from twelve months of self-induced torpor. They've peered over the abyss and come back, indeed, with 'A Design for Life'. Perhaps this is best expressed by a lyric from 'Australia', a key song on the new album: 'I want to fly and run until it hurts.' Three-quarters of the Manic Street Preachers, at least, have already proved themselves to be golden souls, untainted by the slings and arrows of pop stardom. As for the fourth, it's to be hoped he's still out there some-where, listening to it all and smiling in the wings.

Jon Savage | **What inspired you when you were growing up to want to do this?**
Nicky Wire | Certain things inspire you along the way, but I do think you're born to it. I still believe that everybody in the world is born with a talent. It's just a lot of people never get the chance to use it. I started writing poetry a lot around the time of the Miners' Strike, because my village was heavily involved with all that, the pits and scabs and all the rest of it, and that was mixed with a sort of leaning towards androgyny and a bit of Morrissey and then The Sex Pistols and then The Clash: I think they were kind of the motivating factors really. The Miners' Strike was really important in terms of writing.

So was it in the valley, or just in your village?
There were twelve pits in our valley and, of course, there are none now and it politicized you at a very young age. I wrote a song; it was a really terrible song, and I gave it to James when me and James were fifteen, and that's the first song me and James ever wrote together.

What was it called?
Ohh, *[laughing]* it's something absolutely dreadful; I can't even remember. I probably don't want to remember; something to do with mines.

Everyone's sort of forgotten about the Miners' Strike, haven't they? I just remember that was the moment when you really realized what the Conservatives were doing, wasn't it?
It was the start of the demystification that working-class people had any power, it's 'No. Now you haven't.' The start of the Conservative destruction, really. It had a big effect on me and James. It didn't sort of hang around long, but as

a catalyst it certainly got me and then I became sort of much more artistic, and Philip Larkin was one of the first things that inspired me poetry-wise. My brother was really into the Beat generation; he'd just come back from America, so that followed on Kerouac and Burroughs. All I played at the time was classic Clash and *Never Mind the Bollocks*; it was a pilgrimage to try and understand those records.

I've started listening to The Clash again, recently. I underrated them for ages, but I'm just remembering that I saw them do two of the best rock shows I've ever seen in my life. It was the *White Riot* tour and the tour they did in the autumn that year, in The Rainbow and the Manchester Apollo, full of kids going mental, completely out of control, tearing the place apart. It was so exciting.
Yeah. *[laughing]* The thing for us, it was all second-hand, I mean, when it was the tenth anniversary of punk, which was 86, Tony Wilson did this re-run of all the Granada shows, and The Clash doing 'Garageland' on there from, I dunno, one of those dodgy gigs. That was completely... we wanted to be like, on stage, because we'd never seen a band that moved, that moved around on stage y'know? The Pistols were more arrogant anyway, more stare you in the face and psyche you out, but seeing The Clash in that video had a massive effect on us.

There's one great scene in that Granada footage where The Clash finish one song and, just at the end, Strummer trips over a monitor and goes flat on his face.
[laughs] That's the one, exactly! And he just bangs his head right on it. He tried to smash a bottle as well, and when he goes, 'Here we are on TV, what does it mean to me? Fuck all!!'

I just love it. When we saw that, it was just fantastic.

So the four of you were all watching this kind of stuff. What were the first groups you ever went to see?

Well, James, Richey and Sean were real Echo and the Bunnymen fans. I think that was their first gig for all of those three, and I really had a phase on The Smiths, but it did wear off very quickly for some reason. Loved *Hatful of Hollow*. Played it to death, but I went off it really quickly. I never went to gigs anyway, Jon, to be honest. The first band I saw was The Primitives and Tallulah Gosh.

Well, The Primitives were good. I liked that record, *Crash*.

Yeah! Well there used to be this club in Port Talbot, which is about fucking eighty miles away, which put on indie bands like, you know, The Shop Assistants... all those 1986 bands. We used to go there because it was about the nearest place really. If you were slightly weird, you liked The Smiths, you liked Echo and the Bunnymen, they were the starting point.

Do you think the problem now is that a lot of particularly indie rock used to be about the outsider, is so much to do with being 'lads' and being top forty groups?

That's why I think we exist outside those perimeters totally. At the end of the day, 'A Design for Life' is still a very serious, intelligent lyric. Well, it tries to be, anyway. It's not exactly a joyous song, it's kind of heroic. But it is worrying, just celebrating the actual being in a band, but people do, they're just happy to have their record deal and get a record out and get on *Top of the Pops*.

One of the things I liked about the video for the single was that you still had slogans and ideas, and it seems to me that not everybody's interested in ideas. Can you talk about a couple of the slogans?

A lot of the slogans like 'A House is a Machine for Living In' and 'Tomorrow is Too Late', they were all designers' and architects' quotes. 'Useful is Beautiful', that kind of stuff. It's the sort of council state mentality, if you know what I mean. 'Destroy Your Own Houses', you know, when working-class people should – if they are going to destroy anything – at least go to somewhere rich and do it. *[laughs]*

Don't you think then, this whole kind of *Loaded* mentality business plays into that very trap? Surely one of the most exciting things about pop, again which came through very much in the punk movement, was the fact that people who weren't privileged, whether they were working class or middle class or wherever they're from, could actually have access and make wonderful things and be beautiful and be intelligent and be extraordinary?

Yeah, well exactly. The one thing I despise more than anything else about working-class people is when they destroy themselves. And they do it every single day. I don't think the access is there so much any more, you know; you've got to be extraordinarily talented to be given the chance in this day and age. People just play up to that *Loaded* image more and more. They just can't see beyond the sort of partying and destructive element. The thing I liked about reading back in history, the fact that every Welsh town had an institute with a library and a swimming pool, which every miner had paid fifty pence a week specifically for. Those kind of things, they do help, but every single one of those institutes has been closed down except Blackwood, and sold off for blocks of flats. One of them was taken down, and every brick was taken to a museum and rebuilt sixty miles away! *[laughs]*

So, it's like, all the stuff is heritage?

Yeah. Of course, there's no place for it now. It's not worth it. But I think the working class helped themselves then, and I don't think we take enough responsibility any more.

Do you feel completely alone? When you were starting out, there were no other Welsh rock bands, were there?

We were worse than alone because the only

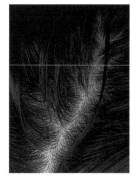

other one had been The Alarm, so we were like minus ten at the start. We got Gorkys on tour and I quite like them, and I think Super Furry Animals are very good actually, I'm getting quite surprised by them. I heard their new single and it was like twelve-bar mixed up with sort of Brian Eno; it sounded really good.

Do you think the English hate the Welsh?

I don't think there's much difference between Northern English people and Welsh people, but I think Southern English people are pretty antagonistic towards the Welsh.

You see, I think Southern English people hate everybody!

[both laughing]

Well, they do! They hate Northern English people, don't they? But still, Welsh people have taken over the Irish for the butt end of a lot of jokes. Irish people have got over that – the 'Paddy' mentality. But I must admit, it's the first time I've ever been... 'patriotic' is not the right word, but it's the first time in my life in the last couple of years when I've felt at ease about being Welsh, within myself. I have felt like a second-class citizen for so long, I've actually kind of come to peace with myself about it.

I hate petty nationalism. The only hope for Great Britain is for London to lose its power and for the power to go to what is rather patronizingly called the 'margins'. And so Northern Ireland, Wales – north and south Wales – the North West of England, the North East of England and Scotland have equal power to London. The kind of nationalism that is being celebrated at the moment is so South Eastern, it's all fucking Paul Weller!

[laughing] Now, Jon...

He is the 'house of god' of the whole thing!

I know what you mean. There is an insidious kind of plot, isn't there?

It seems that way, but I'm sure I'm just being paranoid, and it's like, if you put most of these bands up against Nirvana, it's like, 'No!'

I know. Put virtually every other band against Nirvana and they still, to me – and I know I'm not meant to say it 'cause I'm supposed to say British music's brilliant – but you know, Nirvana is still the greatest band of my generation by a long way.

I put on *In Utero* the other day for the first time in about a year, because you know, it just got very painful to listen to, and it's fucking amazing. Nobody in this country would have the balls to write a song like 'Rape Me'. It's an incredible song.

I don't even know if they'd have the intelligence to. If it was Damon from Blur, he's just inventing a character – Mr Wobbly from fucking Piccadilly instead – who was doing it and playing golf. The third-person disease in this country is just... Everyone's afraid to write about themselves anymore. Everyone's obsessed with this fucking characterization of South East English culture.

Yes, because in South East English culture, particularly as you see it in Fleet Street, as soon as you reveal yourself, people use it as a weapon to be turned against you. And also, what happens is people start censoring themselves.

Yeah, well even us as a band, we've come across that; even me as myself, I just think, 'I can't slag things off any more.' I'm just gonna go back to my old ways and try to keep so much in and it doesn't matter so much at the end of the fucking day; if people like your records, they like your records.

I've got to ask you this: is it still difficult going on stage without Richey?

Yeah. Well I mean we did a warm up before these gigs; we did the Hacienda on Friday and, well, without being a drama queen, it was just the most terrible feeling I've ever had when I came off stage and, you know, just uncontrollably crying... it's, well, only the second time after Richey's been missing that I've cried.

Why now?

Just 'cause it was so intimate. I was worried about it anyway, because the anonymity of our support gigs has been really helpful because you can't see anyone but, you know, James found it really terrible as well. I was just like a blubbering idiot for no reason when I came off stage – well it was obviously for a reason, but it was just terrible. It was a relief getting on in front of thirty thousand Oasis fans who didn't know who we were!

Yes, and of course, grief does take you in all sorts of unexpected ways, that's the problem with it. And you think, 'Oh my God I'm not acting like I usually am, what's going on? I'm losing my mind.'

It was terrible. The next day I woke up and I was fine. I thought, 'Well, it was going to happen some time.' And funnily enough, his mother had called me that night as well and she'd been really upset. Must have been a bit of karma in the air. Sean was speaking to Peter Hook on Friday night. Peter came up to Sean and was quite nice and said, 'Sorry to hear about Richey' and stuff, and Peter goes, 'At least we had a body!' Which, to me, that's brilliant, that's what I want someone to say. To a lot of people that would just seem cold, taking the piss, but I thought it was such a lovely thing to say.

Well, New Order always made jokes about it. Also it's not exactly the Manchester style, just to wear your heart on your sleeve, but I mean if anybody ever doubts that they were absolutely put through hell... I just think a lot of people who write about music and think about music, or a lot of people generally, don't realize that the people who do it are human beings.

Well, you know, that's the old Kurt Cobain thing, with the coma, everyone was kind of laughing and thinking he couldn't do it, and then a few weeks later he's dead. I think perhaps that jolted people a bit because they seemed to be feasting on it, when he failed. There is that thing, like failed suicide can fuck you up more than anything. Every failed suicide tries to do it again, virtually.

So what are your plans now? You've got the LP coming out, haven't you?

It's May twentieth, I think. Just take it from there, really; we got a British tour. We haven't got a plan, to be honest. It's completely day by day now. There's no world plan for Manic Street Preachers domination. If we can just survive day by day and keep the hits rolling in!

Were you surprised the single did so well?

Well, I was surprised. I mean, I had complete faith in the song, I think it's one of the best things we've ever done, but I was really surprised when it went in at number two, just the fact that it sold ninety-three thousand copies in a week, which for us is like, hard to comprehend, you know, it's a lot for us.

It's by far the biggest hit you've had.

Yeah, it's obviously connected a bit, and it is gratifying. I can't pretend that success doesn't mean anything, because it makes you feel a bit better.

Well, the other thing, Nick, is that it's actually a properly constructed song.

Yeah, it is very 'classicist', as James would call it. Like I said when he called me up and it was like, 'Oh I got this Ennio Morricone and a bit of REM and I got some Motown, it's the best song I've ever written', you know. I think we knew when the song was written it had to do it or we were fucked commercially. We are pleased; I can't deny that it didn't give me a thrill.

Well, you need it. You really, really need it.

So how's the book coming along then, which you showed me proofs of last time?

I'm just terrified of saying stuff that's going to piss everybody off. It's so easy, you know, and often it just looks awful, and I've to try not to.

Got to control your temper.

It's so hard. I did a lecture this week at The Photographer's Gallery and it was about this Dutch photographer called Ed Van de Elsken, and he took photos of beatniks and Lettristes in the 50s in Paris. The Lettristes were people who eventually became the Situationists. The lecture was full of these kinds of wasted youth. This guy in the end puts his fucking shades on and says, 'I think it's disgusting how I sat the whole way through the lecture without hearing anything about the fact that the Situationists were a revolutionary movement.' You know, whenever I give a lecture I always think there's one asshole and you hope you're gonna get through without encountering one. So I said, 'Oh, I don't know!' [laughs], and I completely lost my temper, and I said, 'The reason I haven't talked about the Situationists is because I'm fucking sick of them, 'cause I had to read their texts for years, all that nihilistic bullshit, and it used to drive me crazy!' Did you ever read that stuff?**

Yeah, well I've read all that; I like a lot of it. It's great when you're young, isn't it? But I don't think it's a philosophy for living, I have to say.

No, it's too dead end. It's a fantastic critique, but it doesn't actually enable you to build a life. [laughs]

I like Camus, because he came out a bit after the... I think something like *The Plague* was one of my favourite books ever, the symbol of the Nazi occupation, and I think he kind of rose from it, but a lot of it, like you said, was too bleak.

Well, you've got to find something to get through it and that, in fact, is the problematic thing. In a way, that's the thing that has to happen, particularly for men, who I think grow up slower than women. I think that has to happen in your late twenties really.

Yeah. What was that thing you said to me about twenty-seven-year-olds? 'That's the prime time', is that what you said?

I have the sensation that a lot of males don't actually grow up, begin to leave their adolescence, until they're about twenty-

seven. And what happens is this astrological thing called the Saturn Return. Saturn is all about responsibility and basically what that means is you've got to face up to your responsibilities, take control of your life. In fact, I was twenty-seven in the year 1980, when I stopped taking cocaine, which I used to take in the late 70s. I remember I just blacked out one day and I thought, 'Uuuh, my body's trying to tell me something.' And it's also the age when a lot of rock stars died: Hendrix, Joplin, Brian Jones, Kurt Cobain, Richey disappeared, Ian Curtis was a little bit younger, but I think that was partly forced by having a baby early – it's a similar deal, and it's one of the reasons why people go crazy, in fact, like Valentino and Dean, it's the same deal. A lot of the tragic people who die young, die at that age. It's a symbol of people who failed to make that transition from adolescence to adulthood, and that, to me, is so much what pop music is about. Everybody always focuses on the adolescence bit, as they should, but then, you know, what are you supposed to do when you actually pass through that stage? Are you supposed to die? And this, in many ways, is one of the fascinating things in the music industry. It's the sort of youth medium, yet people do survive and continue to make good music, but they're often completely denigrated because of that.

Well, I've done quite a few interviews now, and a lot of them, especially the newspaper ones, have been fishing around trying to make out, you know, 'Richey had a tormented childhood'; 'Was he abused?'; 'Did he have this terrible life?' And it's exactly the opposite. He had such a blissful childhood; that's the thing that fucked him up, because when he came to adolescence, the responsibility and everything else, he could never kind of shake that off. He had a great childhood. It's the opposite to all the insinuations.

Well, I think that goes back to what we were saying about a complete lack of understanding. It must be very hard for you because you've got to deal with stuff that's really personal in a fantastically public way.
It was horrible, everybody snooping around. I used to play football with Richey; he lived up the street, I lived down the street. Every Sunday we'd have a competition. I was the kind of 'posher' street, he was the kind of 'scummier' street. I used to call him 'Teddy Edwards' – he was like a teddy bear. Just 'cause he did what he did doesn't mean he had a distraught and horrible childhood.

When was it that we first met? Was it at the Heavenly party?
Yeah.

Was that Christmas 90 or Christmas 91?
I think it was Christmas 90.

I just remember you and Richey were really funny.
Yeah, Richey did have a fantastic sense of humour, you know.

I remember you had your girls' blouses on, your sisters' blouses and I said, 'Don't you get attacked for looking like that?' and you said, 'Yeah!' and I said, 'Well?' I think you and Richey said, 'Well, we don't care because we're pretty.' And I thought, 'YES! That's what I want to hear.'
I think the last six months of his life were obviously different. I think he probably lost that sense of humour. Fair enough, you know, if you're that fucked up, but he did enjoy a lot of things. He really enjoyed drinking. He loved having a drink; he really looked forward to it. He'd say, 'Oh I'm lying in bed, I've got my whisky and the ice cubes are clanking around', and I'd just think, 'Oh this is brilliant, you know? It's beautiful.' I know it's romantic, but he drank earlier on, 'cause he enjoyed it; he loved the sensation of passing out! But there you go anyway.

It's kind of fascinating, passing out. I'm terrified of it. I hate losing control.
And me. Yeah.

up 'profanity' in the dictionary and it says 'blasphemous'. If I look up 'blasphemous', it says 'irreverence'. I challenge anybody to tell me how the word 'shit' is going to send me to hell. 'Shit' has nothing to do with it. The only word that can be considered irreverent would be 'Goddamn', used in the sense 'God be damned'. Words aren't blasphemous, they're just slang that your daddy would use as exclamation points. I'm the dude who could tell you 'fuck' is the most beautiful word in the English language. You can use it in every way: as a noun, a pronoun, an adjective, compound it... It's like: 'Fuck!'; 'I'll be fucked!'; 'fuck off!'; 'how the fuck?!'; 'Oh my fucking God!' And when you finish with it, a conjunction, predicate... you look at it and it's three or four of those motherfuckers. It's the only word in the English language that can be used like that.

Great word!

It's a beautiful motherfucking word!

True.

Next. What we doing? We'll fuck on stage.

Let's fuck on stage?

I've seen it. The only nasty thing I saw... It wasn't nasty, but I was offended by it. Two motherfuckers getting to get down, gay guys. I mean, that's their thing right? But I didn't want to look at it on stage. I didn't want to be confronted with it doing my four hours. They was testing us, seeing if we were going to stop. I was like, 'You win the prize!' I ain't got nothing against nothing.

I can't watch it.

I can't watch it.

You got anything on the backstage?

Oh yeah, 'No head, no backstage pass.' That was the first T-shirt, right?

George Clinton | Remember when we did the New Music Seminar and everybody was talking about 'no censorship'? And everybody agreed. I said, 'I'll see about that shit' and I did 'Niggerish'. I did it to see if they really meant that shit. When I did that poem, a black chick from one of the papers came up to me and said, 'Why did you do that? We was in agreement 'til you done that. You know we gotta censor that shit.' If there is an exception, then they're full of shit.

Ice-T | **That's right! I've been through it. I know I ain't the first, but I've come to the conclusion now there ain't no free speech.** Free speech costs too much. *[laughs]* We said that a long time ago; we can't afford free speech.

Yeah. So, as an artist, just be prepared and know that they're going to censor it.

You know, 'Nigga' is a pop word now. White groups are learning how to say it. *[laughs]* 'Nigga', not 'nigger'. And the only way you going to get rid of it is to say it to death. If you hide it, it gets more steam and becomes more of a bad word.

When I go to college lectures I say, 'I'm going to use extensively all the vernacular available to me.' So what you call 'profanity', I really don't understand. I look

I'll never forget it. I was on tour with Jane's Addiction. I was in the audience and they were playing, and some girl was, like, singing a song. I was trying to get it with her and I was like, 'You want to go backstage?' Shit like that. I was being nice. I said, 'You like Jane's Addiction?' she says, 'Yeah.' I was like, 'You want to meet Perry Farrell?' Perry's standing backstage with his wife. I opened the door; this girl moved on Perry across his wife. Perry looks at me like, 'What the fuck are you doing?' She's gonna go down on him right in front of his wife. He looks at me, like, 'Why did you let her at me?' I said, 'I thought she was going to shake your hand, dude. I thought I was getting points from letting her meet you', but no. That backstage shit is a trip. I know that shit... Or the hotel...

I got so used to it, my room wouldn't be full, it would be the *fullest*. I would leave. You ain't gonna be throwing motherfuckers out. You wouldn't want to wreck the vibe. It was like, 'I love you too.' I like what Ice Cube says: 'Dude, get off my dick, and send your bitch over here.' That's some funny shit.

What's the wildest thing anybody ever said?

Motherfucker, six foot four, just got out of prison says, 'I ain't no motherfucking fag, but I'll have your motherfucking baby.'

Oh no.

That one, I told him, 'You win the motherfucking prize.'

What would scare me is when I would run into the girls with the Ice-T tattoos. Tattoos are real.

I got one for that one! Las Vegas. A chick said, 'Funkadelic taught me ignorance.' She pulls up her dress and I say, 'Oh goddamn.' All the girls were saying, 'Oh George, you got her.' So even the girls were rooting for me. She pulls her pants down, she'd shaved her hair off down there, she's got 'George Clinton'. I'm thinking 'It's coming off.' She says, 'No, it's not coming off, it's tattooed.'

You got to double-check. When it comes that good, it makes you think.

I'm saying, 'George; what the fuck?' My ego trying to creep up, I'm holding that motherfucker back. She says, 'You want to feel this?' She pulled the rest of that thing down, she had a posturepaedic mattress under that thing. A Kotex this thick! Nasty motherfucker! Again, you have to give that motherfucker five! *[laughter]* Nasty!

The wildest thing that ever happened to me, this girl came and she was dope! And she says, 'Ice-T is God.' And I was like, 'OK, this sounds like *Fatal Attraction* to me.' What we did was handle this with care: 'You ain't fucking nothing like this, because this is on another level.' So I'm, 'OK. Give her a T-shirt, treat her real cool.' Because somebody love you that much will kill you. Don't do the wrong thing!

Anyone who likes me on stage, I'm scared of that person already. Motherfucker choose me and like me? I know what I be portraying up there. 'Yo, baby, I know what you're saying, but I ain't no guru. I'm looking for a joint and some pussy. As a matter of fact, loan me a dollar.' That's how you get the real. You're down to street level then, because they really don't want to have you up there anyway. I ain't going up on no pedestal.

Due to the fact that you guys were kings of the whole [sings] Funk can't stop it, anybody ever come at you because you were playing lots of guitar work? Did you ever run into confused individuals?

We were too black for white people and too white for black people. But the mothers that like us, both black and white, are still around today. It's slow, over a long period of time.

How could you be too white for black people?

Maggot Brain. His guitar was too fucking loud.

Can't black people understand guitars?

When guitars started first getting popular like that it was Duane Eddy. He was a twangy motherfucker. His twangy wasn't BB King, it wasn't blues.

Hendrix?

Jimi Hendrix was like... he was gone. We knew him as Jimi James and the Flames, as King Curtis with the Isley Brothers. So I knows how good he could play. But when he came home, he had these big motherfucking things he called 'amps'. See I had these Fender twin reverb pick-ups...

Came back where?

From London to audition for The Animals. They came back; there was three of them. They made more noise than a hundred motherfuckers. They was precise like a jazz group. That was an experience. That was before Buddy Miles, with Mitch Mitchell. They'd start off together and then they like... didn't sound like they was with each other. They were gone! And I read that Pete Townsend, Eric Clapton, they weren't even that close themselves. They calling each other, and saying, 'Who the fuck is this motherfucker on television?' Here's a motherfucker who was playing where they were going, except this motherfucker was there.

Your clothes was so dope that... when Dr Funkenstein come out that shit with that white mink...

From out of space.

[gets up and gesticulates in excitement] Nigga was just... God! That white shit was just clothes. And niggas were 'Oh, shit. Pimping down!'

The first coat that I had was ermine tails for real. Seventy-five dollars a piece. Ermine tails, like minks. Real ones. That coat was like ninety thousand dollars...

And you could feel it. It was real.

I used to take the motherfucker's tails off and give it to a pretty motherfucker. They said, 'You can't do that. They's too much money.' So they started making me ones that looked just like them and put them back on.

Last question. This is for me and everybody. You know, like me, I'm on my sixth album and everybody thinks I'm doing something incredible... anything in giving anybody a longevity tip? What's the key to staying?

There ain't nothing anyone could do to hurt my feelings. By the time you've wasted time on what a motherfucker has done to you, you've lost so much energy. If I don't get another hit record, fuck 'One Nation...', I will make the next record. If I don't get a new one, fuck me. Then all the other shit you do will be right.

July 1996
Introduction and interview | Mark Sanders

Dubbed 'The dysfunctional father-figure of LA art', performance artist Paul McCarthy may look just like the cuddly uncle of your dreams, but lying beneath that furry beard and matted hair is a man whose art has created more shock waves than many.

As far back as the late 1960s and early 1970s, he was causing consternation through using his body as a vehicle for his expressive gesticulations. Jumping out of windows, spinning into walls and crawling across gallery floors drenched in white paint was not usual. Covering himself in food, wearing women's lingerie and fucking bits of meat, even less so. Once pushed to the sidelines of the art world as a bizarre oddity, his performance art has now entered the mainstream. Less confrontational, yet equally compelling, his collaborations with the likes of Mike Kelly and more comical solo work have led to an official stamp of approval, culminating in the recent video performance, The Painter, staged at MOMA last year.

In recent years, however, McCarthy has also concentrated on the construction of fantastical installation work developed from the various props and artefacts used in his performances. Revealing more than just a passing fixation with Disney and the abject, not to mention the Alpine, he has fashioned entire settings from disused Hollywood sets and then populated them with what he calls his 'robotic' sculptures. Often taking the form of hybrid mechanical mannequins and sporting an array of mutant heads and working genitalia, these bizarre manifestations portray a perverse, kitsch scatology, a carnal visuality.

Having recently visited London to work on a major publication of his work, due to be printed in October, McCarthy is presently working on his latest installation for the Luhring Augustine Gallery, New York, to be shown this September.

Dazed & Confused | **How did your performance art evolve during the 1970s?**
Paul McCarthy | I started doing performances in the late 1960s. I was influenced by Yves Klein and the Happenings of that period. I began doing actions that involved repetition in 1970, using my body as material. Pieces about endurance, or pieces affecting my perception such as spinning. I spun for up to sixty minutes. By touching the wall each time I went round, I could keep my balance and make a smudge on the wall, leaving a trace of the action. I also made rooms inside rooms. There was something about architecture, the family house, hallways, or school rooms that was important to me. But the action changed in 1972 when I started using food and personae or characters. The performances stopped being about repetition and began to be a kind of convoluted narrative. I went through a series of characters/personae such as 'The Sea Captain' or 'Pigs'.
Did you ever get into trouble with the police over any of your early public performances?
More likely the audience would leave first. The performances were not in public spaces that often, and when they were, the police would come. I was also interested in that kind

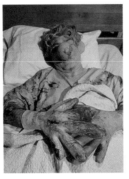

This page from top
Death Ship, *1985–1999*
Painter, *1994*
Opposite page
Colonial Teacup, *1997*

of confrontation. In a performance festival in the 1970s, staged at a large hotel, everybody had been given a room to perform in, but I had decided that I wanted to perform at the top of the hotel staircase. So I told the people in the festival and they agreed; when I got there, I realized that the television cable for the whole hotel was also at the top of the stairs. It was a large hotel, you know, two or three hundred rooms or something. So anyway, I just disconnected the cable and linked up my video equipment, so the performance was transmitted to all the rooms in the hotel. *[laughs]* So that was what they saw – me. That was when the action really began, because no one had informed the security guards that the performance was going to happen, or even what it was. They thought it was a nut on the top floor. Maybe it just appeared really disturbing to some people.

What were you doing?

I had these little dolls that I had lowered over the edge of the balcony and I had stuck some up my arse. I also drank a lot of ketchup. I had a broom between my legs, that kind of thing. I was dressed in a business suit, with a mask of Arafat on. The performance was titled Political Disturbance. There was a lot of fear of terrorism then. There still is. Police and hotel security came after about thirty minutes, but in the end, I managed to escape over the roof.

Your current performances continue to explore the dysfunctional elements of the self and our contemporary culture, but they seem to have become more overtly comic in style. I'm thinking of your recent performance, The Painter, staged at MOMA last year. You spent large periods of time howling 'de Koooooooooning!'

[laughs] That tape ended up being more overtly comical than most. It came out of these cartoon drawings I had done years ago about this painter. It was a kind of joke. I never intended it to be about de Kooning; it just evolved that way. Originally, I bought a wig and when I put it on, I thought, 'Warhol' but then I went, 'no, de Kooning. I like de Kooning!' *[laughs]* I had this idea for a sequel, where this guy who loves de Kooning comes to the studio to have an affair with the painter – and they both looked like de Kooning. *[hysterical laughter]* None of it was planned, it just kind of appeared. Even the other people in the performance had no idea what they would do. As they entered, I would just put a nose on them and say, 'Why don't you be the dealer!? Why don't you be the collector?'

So it was all improvised on the spot?

Yeah.

Even when you end up severing your fake finger with a hatchet?

I originally thought of cutting off the ear, like Van Gogh, but decided against it. The finger is more phallic. It becomes about castration. What you see on the tape is only a fraction: it took over forty minutes to cut it off, the rubber was just so tough. The whole thing was ludicrous; it took so long that people would leave me in the room and come back fifteen minutes later and I was still trying to cut it off. It was funny.

I wanted to ask you about the use of food in your performance work.

I think that comes from a mix of things. To begin with, there was a definite pop element to my use of food. In the late 60s, I would just show a series of bottles on the floor, like a row of mayonnaise jars or ketchup bottles, and sometimes I would even make these sculptural pieces where I would pour ketchup onto a

sheet of glass and then sandwich it between another sheet and call it a ketchup sandwich. I would also display various store shirts and photographs of shop windows. So there was always this fascination with stores, shelf arrangements, food on display, consumerism. At that time, I was doing a lot of painting with my hands, painting with motor oil. So the idea of food, liquids, painting being liquid and then using my body to paint with, using my hands or my penis as a paint brush, all those things were playing themselves out in my work.

And the symbolic connection between food and the body?

Well, there was that whole thing that ketchup

*Clockwise from
top right*
Tomato Head, *1994*
Tokyo Santa, *1997*
The Saloon *(detail),
1995–1996*

resembles blood; that it was somewhere
between the concreteness of it as ketchup and
the fantasy of it as blood, the image of blood.
And my use of mayonnaise and ketchup as
resembling body fluids as well as being food –
hamburger meat... it's interesting, but there
is this sort of repulsion about putting food on
the body. But then it's like the blood is inside
the body, the meat is inside the body. The mix
between ketchup and meat and the body.
A penis is a hot dog, a hot dog is a penis.

**How has living and working in LA affected
your work over the years?**

Well, I originally came to Los Angeles to go to
film school. I have always had this fascination

with film and television, but I never wanted
to become a part of the industry: my interests
are more directed towards a parody or mockery
of it. I've always been more captivated by
horror movies, B-movies or independently
produced movies rather than the mainstream;
work that lies at the edge of the film industry.
So there is an element in my recent work where
I've started to use what Hollywood uses. In
The Garden, the sculpture that I made in 1991,
the trees were taken from the set of *Bonanza*
and the heads of the robotic figures were cast
from actual heads in horror movies. It's just all
so available here.

**Such as those great masks that you wore in
Heidi with Mike Kelley, taken from *The
Texas Chainsaw Massacre* or based on pop
stars like Madonna.**

And sometimes I am Heidi and Mike is Grandpa.
[laughs] They were just the masks that were
available then. I would just buy them at the
local stores, so they all ended up being stereo-
types of people who were famous at that time,
like Michael Jackson or Clinton; horror movie
characters.

Cultural totems?

Yeah. I think it's those objects that form part of

the distinction between my work and, say, the Viennese Actions. There are similarities between what I've done in the past and some of their performances, but the fact that I live and work here in Los Angeles means my art has a different set of criteria. My interest in Disney, for instance.

Your robotic sculptures certainly maintain a sense of performance through their monstrous theatricality. There is a disturbing undercurrent, a connection between Disney, Hollywood and the abject that runs throughout your present work.
It is not only Disney but also wax figures: those inanimate objects that at first glance appear so real. In the early 1970s, I did a piece where I photographed various mannequins and their reflections in store windows. That was about not being able to tell the difference between a mannequin and a real person, and my fear of losing that ability to determine that difference. The inability to know what is real and what isn't. So those figures that Disney makes, those mechanic or robotic objects, they defy our sense of what is real. That's what I began to find really interesting, the creation of this type of virtual reality I guess, that idea transformed into sculpture.

One of my favourite pieces of your kinetic sculpture is *Colonial Teacup [a thirteen-foot diameter, two-ton pink teacup that spins on its saucer at up to seventy-five mph]*. What possessed you to make that?
That was an idea that I had had for a long time but never had the means to complete. I was waiting at this airport for a flight to London and there were these two guys from Jamaica in front of me and this little old couple behind. We had to wait in line for over an hour and I ended

up getting into a conversation with the old couple about teatime, that we were missing teatime or something. They seemed really sweet. But just when we were ready to board the plane, the older man turned to his wife and said that he hoped that we didn't have to sit next to those 'negroes'. At first, I was stunned and so were the two Jamaican guys. I thought it must have been a joke, but there was no way that it could have been. I started to think about those three things: colonial teatime, this old couple and this racism. So on the plane, I ended up drawing this spinning teacup and a black man floating in a whirlpool of tea. It wasn't until a lot later I managed to make the spinning sculpture.

How stable is it?
It can be very unstable at certain speeds, even potentially dangerous when it starts to rock on its axis. But a piece like that is an ongoing project for me: it has to do with being able to go back and change its colour if I want to, being allowed to continue to work on it whenever I need to. If possible, I would like to make it go faster. *[laughs]*

So what fantastical sculptures are you now working on for your next show at Luhring Augustine this September?
I have made these three structures: a Western saloon, a bunkhouse and a tepee. Each building has three or four robotic figures. The saloon has a bartender, a gunfighter and two dance-hall girls. The bunkhouse has three cowboys and a cowgirl. The tepee has a Western soldier, a chief and an Indian maiden. All these figures are equipped with mechanical genitals and are engaging in seduction, masturbation, sex, sleep and work. Some have human heads. Their bodies are small, but their heads are huge. It's a piece that I've been thinking about for quite a while.

Björk
and
Stock
haus
en

I went to music school from the age of five and then, when I was twelve or thirteen, I was into musicology, and this Icelandic composer and teacher at the school introduced me to Stockhausen. I remember being almost the fighter in the school, the odd kid out, with a real passion for music, but against all this retro, constant Beethoven and Bach bollocks. Most of it was this frustration with the school's obsession with the past. When I was introduced to Stockhausen, it was like, 'aaah!' Finally, somebody was speaking my language. Stockhausen has said things like, 'We should listen to "old" music one day a year and the other 364 days we should listen to "now" music. And we should do it in the same way as we look through photo albums of when we were children. If you look at old photo albums too often, they just become pointless. You start indulging in something that doesn't matter, and you stop worrying about the present.' And that's how he looked at all those people who are obsessed with old music. For a kid born of my generation, it was brilliant, because at the same time I was also being introduced to the electronic music of bands like Kraftwerk and DAF.

I think when it comes to electronic music and atonal music, Stockhausen's the best. He was the first person to make electronic music before synthesizers were even invented. I like to compare him to Picasso, because like him, he's had so many periods. There are so many musicians who've made a career out of one of his periods. He goes one step ahead, discovers something that's never been done before musically, and by the time other people have even grasped it, he's onto the next thing.

Like all scientific geniuses, Stockhausen seems obsessed with the marriage between mystery and science, although they are opposites. Normal scientists are obsessed with facts: genius scientists are obsessed with mystery. The more Stockhausen finds out about sound, the more he finds out that he doesn't know jack shit; that he's lost.

Stockhausen told me about the house he built himself in the forest and lived in for ten years. It's made from hexagonal pieces of glass and no two rooms are the same, so they are all irregular. It's built out of angles that are reflected, and it's full of spotlights. The forest becomes mirrored inside the house. He was explaining to me how, even after ten years, there would still be moments when he didn't know where he was,

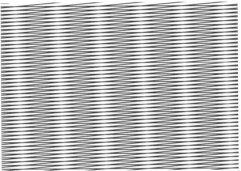

and he said it with wonder in his eyes. And I said, 'That's brilliant: you can be innocent even in your own home', and he replied, 'Not only innocent, but curious.'

Björk Gudmundsdottir | **It seems to me that your electronic music is more like your voice and your other pieces are less personal, somehow. Do you feel that too?**
Karlheinz Stockhausen | Yes, because a lot of things that I do sound like a very alien world. Then a notion like 'personal' is irrelevant. It is not important, because it is something that we don't know, but I like it, and I make it.
It seems to me that you just put your antennae out, and that is like your voice, your point of view, like from the outside. Or something like... *[pause]* I can't really explain it.
No, neither can I. The most important thing is, it is not like a personal world, but something that we don't know. We have to study it, we have to experience it. If we catch something like that, then we have had luck.
Are you sure it's not you?
Oh I am surprised myself, very often. And the more I discover something that I haven't

experienced before, then the more excited I become. Because then I think that it is important.
I've got a problem that I get very excited about music. I panic because I feel I don't have time to do it all. Does that worry you?
Yes and no, because I have learned now in my life that even the very early works made forty-six years ago are not understood by most of the people. So this is a natural process: if you find something that surprises you, then for others it's even harder to incorporate that into their being. So it would take sometimes two hundred years for a large group of people, or even individuals, to have reached the same stage that I

have reached after having spent, let's say, three years, eight hours in the studio to make something. You need as much time as I did just to hear it. Let's not even talk about understanding what it means. So that is the natural process, that certain musicians make something that needs a lot of time to be listened to many, many times, and that's very good.

Yeah, but I am also talking about the relationship between you and yourself, and the time that you have between birth and when you die – if it is enough to do all the things you want?

No, you can only do a very small portion of what you want to do. That is natural.

Yeah, maybe I'm very impatient. It's hard for me to...

Eighty or ninety years is nothing. There are a lot of very beautiful pieces of music of the past, which the majority of the people alive now will never hear. These pieces are extraordinarily precious, full of mystery and intelligence and invention. I'm thinking at this moment of certain works by Johann Sebastian Bach, or even earlier composers. There are so many fantastic compositions, five or six hundred years old, not even known to the majority of human beings. So it will take a lot of time. There are billions of precious things in the universe that we have no time to study.

You seem to be so patient, like you have all of this discipline to use time. It freaks me out. I still haven't learned how to sit in my chair; it's very hard for me. Do you always work eight hours a day?

More.

Do you think the core of your urge is more to show or record the things out there: to prove they exist, like just for scientific reasons, or is it more emotional, to create an excuse for everybody to unite? So that maybe something will happen, like your music could achieve that?

It's both.

Both?

Of course. I am like a hunter, trying to find something, and at the same time – well this is the scientific aspect – trying to discover. On the other hand, I am emotionally in high tension whenever it comes to the moment when I have to act with my fingers, with my hands and my ears, to move the sound, to shape the sound. It is then that I cannot separate thinking and acting with my senses: both are equally important to me. But the total involvement happens in both states: if I am more a thinker, or more an actor; I am totally involved; I get involved.

I used to travel with my little ghettoblaster, and have my pocket full of tapes, and always try to find the right song. I didn't care what song it was, as long as it would unite everybody in the room and get everybody together. But sometimes that can be quite a cheap trick, you know? I remember once reading that one of the reasons why you don't like regular rhythm is because of the war.

No, no, that's...

That's a misunderstanding?

Mmm, yes. When I dance, I like regular music – with syncopation, naturally. It shouldn't always be like a machine. But when I compose, I use periodic rhythms very rarely, and only at an intermediary stage, because I think there is an evolution in the language of music in Europe that leads from very simple periodic rhythms to more and more irregular rhythms. So I am careful with music that emphasizes this kind of minimalistic periodicity because that brings out the most basic feelings and most basic impulses in every person. When I say 'basic', that means the physical. But we are not only a body who walks, who runs, who makes sexual movements, who has a heartbeat which is, more or less – in a healthy body – seventy-one beats per minute, or who has certain brain pulses, so we are a whole system of periodic rhythm. But already, within the body, there are many periodicities superimposed, from very fast to very slow ones. Breathing is, in a quiet situation, about every six or seven seconds. There's periodicity. And all of these together build a very polymetric music in the body, but when I make the art music I am part of that whole evolution, and I am always looking for more and more differentiation. In form as well.

Just because it's more honest?

Yes, but what most of the people like is a regular beat – nowadays they make it even in pop music with a machine. I think that one should try to make music that is a bit more... flexible, so to speak – a bit more irregular. Irregularity is a challenge, you see. How far can we go in making music irregular? Only as far as a small moment when everything falls into synchronicity, and then goes away again into different metres and rhythms. But that's how history has been, anyway.

I think that in popular music today, people are trying to come to terms with the fact that they are living with all of these machines, and trying to combine machines and humans and trying to marry them into a happy marriage – trying to be optimistic about it. I was brought up by a mother who believed fiercely in nature and wanted me

just to be barefoot twenty-four hours a day and all of these things, so I was brought up with this big guilt complex of cars and skyscrapers, and I was taught to hate them, and then I think I'm like, in the middle. I can see this generation who are ten years younger than me making music, trying to live with it. But everything is with those regular rhythms and learning to love them, but still be human, still be all gritty and organic.

But regular rhythms are always in all cultures the basis of the structure. It's only very lately that they come to make a more complicated rhythm, so I think it is not that the machines have brought irregularity.

Yeah, I think what makes me happiest is your optimism, especially about the future. And I think here I'm also talking about my generation. We've been taught the world is going down the drain and we're all gonna die very soon, and to find someone as open as you, with optimism, is special. A lot of young people are fascinated by what you are doing. Do you think it is because of this optimism?

Also I understand that the works I have composed give a lot for studying, for learning and for experiencing. In particular, experiencing oneself, and that gives people confidence, so they see there is a lot still to do.

And also maybe because you have done so many things... I think that so many young people just have to find one per cent of its worth and they can identify with what you've done.

Maybe with different works, because they cannot know them all. I have two hundred and fifty-three individually performable works now, in scores, and about seventy or eighty CDs with different works on them, all different, so there is a lot to discover. It's like a world in a world, and there are so many different aspects. That's probably what they like: all of the pieces are very different. I don't like to repeat myself.

Do you think it's our duty to push everything to its limits – use everything that we have, like all the intelligence and all the time, and try out everything, especially if it is difficult? Or do you think it's more a question of just following one's instincts,

This page
Björk and
Stockhausen, 1996
Previous pages
Stockhausen's studio
Phil Poynter

**leaving out the things that don't turn
us on?**
I am thinking at this moment of my children.
I have six children; they are quite different. In
particular there are two, the youngest by the
way, who are still drawn into many different
directions that concern taste, or excitement and
there is one son who is a trumpeter who tried at
a certain moment a few years ago to become a
spiritual teacher – to be a Yoga teacher and help
other people who were desperate to cheer up
and to believe in a better world. But then I told
him, 'There are enough preachers, and stick to
your trumpet.' It took him a few years before he
came back to his trumpet, and now he seems to
be concentrated and leaves out most of the
things that are also possible for him. I could
have been a teacher, an architect, a philosopher,
a professor in God knows what, amid many
different faculties. I could be a gardener or a
farmer very easily: I was a farm hand for a long
time, for a year and a half of my life. I was in a
car factory for a moment, and I liked that work
as well. But I understood at the end of my studies, when I was still working on a doctorate and
as a pianist (I rehearsed four or five hours a day
at the piano, as a solo instrument, I played every

night in a bar to make a living), but since I composed the first piece and felt it sounded very different from all I know, I have concentrated on
composition and I have missed almost everything that the world offers to me – other faculties, other ways of living as you've just said,
excitement of all kind, entertainment of all kind.
I have really concentrated day and night on one
very narrow aspect: composing and performing
and correcting my scores and publishing my
scores. For me, it was the right way. I cannot
give general advice, because if one does not hear
that inner call, one doesn't do it. So you have to
hear the call and then there is no question.
Yeah, it's like where you can go furthest.
I don't know. I just think I couldn't achieve
anything that makes sense to myself if I didn't
concentrate entirely on that one thing. So I miss
a lot of what life has got to offer.
And you learnt how to sit in a chair?
You know, I conduct also – it's not just sitting in
a chair. I conduct orchestras, choirs, rehearse a
lot, and run around and set up speakers with
the technicians and arrange all the rehearsals,
so it's not just sitting on a chair, but I know
what you mean. Yes, it's concentrating on that
one vocation.

This conversation took place on the phone, as is always the case with my conversations with Alex. We have worked together for over a year on various projects and never once met. It's a beautiful Sunday afternoon and he is in the verdant hills of Gloucestershire visiting at the house of his friend, Isabella Blow. Ring-ring. Ring-ring. Ring-ring.

David Bowie | **Are you gay and do you take drugs?** *[laughter]*
Alexander McQueen | Yes, to both of them.
So what are your drugs of choice?
A man called Charlie!
Do you find that it affects the way you approach your designing?
Yeah, it makes it more erratic. That's why you get my head blown up shot. *[in reference to a Nick Knight photograph at the Florence Biennale]*
Well, I once asked you to make me a specific jacket in a certain colour and you sent me something entirely different in a tapestry fabric – quite beautiful I might add – but how would you cope in the corporate world?
I wouldn't be in the corporate world.
Even if you're going to be working for a rather large fashion house like Givenchy?
Yeah.
So how are you going to work in these circumstances? Do you feel as though you're going to have rules and parameters placed on you, or what?
Well, yeah, but, you know, I can only do it the way I do it. That's why they chose me and if they can't accept that, they'll have to get some-one else. They're going to have no choice at the end of the day because I work to my own laws and requirements, not anyone else's. I sound a bit like you!

Unlike most designers, your sense of wear seems to derive from forms other than fashion history. You take or steal quite arbitrarily from, say, the neo-Catholic macabre photographs of Joel Peter Witkin, or rave culture. Do you think fashion is art?
No I don't. But I like to break down barriers. It's not a specific way of thinking, it's just what's in my mind at the time. It could be anything – it could be a man walking down a street, or a nuclear bomb going off – it could be anything that triggers some sort of emotion in my mind. I mean, I see everything in a world of art in one way or another. How people do things. The way people kiss.
Who or what are your present influences?
Let me think... I don't know. I think that's a really hard question because in one way, one side of me is kind of really sombre and the other side of my brain is very erratic and it's always this fight, one against the other, and I choose so many different things. This is why my shows always throw people completely: one minute I see a lovely chiffon dress and the next minute I see a girl in this cage that makes her walk like a puppet and, you know, they can't understand where it's coming from because there are so many sides of me in conflict. But influences are really from my own imagination and not many come from direct sources. They usually come from a lone source of say, the way I want to perform sex, or the way I want people to perform sex, or the way I want to see people act, or what would happen if a person was like that. You know what I mean? It's not from direct sources. It's just sort of from a big subconscious, or the perverse. I don't think like the average person on the street. I think quite perversely sometimes in my own mind.
Yeah, I would say, from just looking at the way you work, that sexuality plays a very important part in the way that you design.
Well, because I think it's the worst mental attitude. Sexuality in a person confines you to such a small space and, anyway, it's such a scary process trying to define one's sexuality, finding which way you sway or what shocks you in other people and who accepts you at the end of the day when you're looking for love... You have to go through these corridors and it can be kind of mind-blowing sometimes.

There's something a lot more pagan about your work than compared, say, to Gaultier. Your things work at a more organic level.

Possibly. I gather some influence from the Marquis de Sade because I actually think of him as a great philosopher and a man of his time, where people found him just a pervert. *[laughs]* I find him sort of influential in the way he provokes people's thoughts. It kind of scares me. That's the way I think but, at the end of the day, that's the way my entity has grown and, all in all, in my life, it's the way I am.

Do you think of clothes themselves as a way of torturing society?

I don't put such an importance on clothes, anyway. I mean at the end of the day they are, after all, just clothes, and I can't cure the world of illness with clothes. I just try to make the person that's wearing them feel more confident in themselves because I am so unconfident. I'm really insecure in a lot of ways and I suppose my confidence comes out in the clothes I design. I'm very insecure as a person.

Aren't we all? Could you design a car?

Could I? It would be as flat as an envelope if I designed a car.

Could you design a house?

Yes, very easily, very easily.

Do you paint or sculpt?

No, but I just did a show the other day, I don't know if you heard, it was on water and we did this kind of cocoon for this girl made of steel rods and it was in the form of a three-dimensional star and it was covered in this glass fabric so you could see through it, and this girl was inside it, but we had all these butterflies flying around her inside it. So she was picking them out of the air and they were landing on her hand. It was just about the girl's own environment. So I was thinking about the new millennium, thinking you would carry around with you your home like a snail would. She was walking along the water in a massive star covered in glass and the butterflies and the death-faced moths were flying around her and landing on her hand and she was looking at them. It was really beautiful. It threw a lot of people completely sideways.

It's interesting how what you're talking about is somewhere between theatre and installation.

Well, I hate the theatre, I hate it. I used to work in the theatre. I used to make costumes for them and films, and it's one thing I've always detested – the theatre. I hate going to the theatre, it bores me shitless.

Well, I'm not talking about a play.

I know, but I just wanted to tell you that anyway! *[laughs]*

All right, change the word to 'ritual'.

Yeah, that's better. I like ritual. *[laughs]*

Armani says, 'Fashion is dead.'

Oh, so is he... I mean, God...

Now you sound like Versace...

He's close to dead. I mean, no one wants to wear a floppy suit in a nice wool – the man was a bloody window dresser. What does he know?

Do you think that what he is really saying is that maybe...

He's lost it.

He might still be making an observation in as much as the boundaries are coming down.

Yeah.

The way fashion is presented these days is a quantum leap from how it was presented say, five to ten years ago. It's become almost a new form, hasn't it?

Yeah, but, you know, you can't depend on fashion designers to predict the future of society. At the end of the day, they're only clothes and that never strays from my mind for one minute.

Is the 'British renaissance' a reality or a hype do you think? The world is being told that it's happening through all strata of British life, from fashion to visual arts, music, obviously, architecture. I mean there's not one aspect of culture where Brits haven't got some pretty fair leaders – English designers in French houses, you

know what I mean? It's like we're pervading the whole zeitgeist at the moment.

Being British yourself, I think you understand that Britain has always led the way in every field possible in the world from art to pop music. Even from the days of Henry VIII. It's a nation where people come and gloat at what we have as a valuable heritage, be it good or bad. But there's no place like it on earth.

But why is it we can't follow through once we've initially created something? We're far better innovators than we are manufacturers.

Yeah, exactly. But I think that's a good thing. Money's never been a big object. Well, I mean I like to live comfortably, but I've been asked by this French fashion house how I would put on a show and I said, 'Well, the sort of money these people buy these clothes for in this day and age, you don't want to flaunt your wealth in front of the average Joe Public because it's bad taste and with all the troubles in the world today, it's not a good thing to do anyway.' I'm sure these people that have this sort of money don't feel like showing their face on camera, so I said it would be more of a personal show and people with this sort of money who appreciate good art and good quality clothes and have these one-off pieces made just respect the ideal, not the actual chucking of money around. They can do that anywhere.

So when you are affluent, which I'm afraid is probably on the cards for you, how are you going to deal with that?

I'd like to buy Le Corbusier's house in France. *[sniggers]*

Here's a nice thing. What was the first thing you designed ever? Like when you were little or a kid or something?

Oh, I can't think that far back, but for my own professional career, it was the bumsters. The ones that Gail, your bass player, wears.

Was there a point where you were sort of playing around with stuff, and when you used to dress up and go to clubs when you were a kid, and all that, where you would do original things?

Actually, yeah. I would wear my sister's clothes and people wouldn't recognize it because I'd wear them in a male way. I did go round my street once in my sister's bra when I was about twelve years old and the neighbours thought I was a freaky kid; I got dirty looks and all that... and you're talking about Stepney here!

My father used to work in Stepney.

Yeah?

What age were you when you left home?

Nineteen.

Did it give you an incredible feeling of freedom? Or did you suddenly feel even more vulnerable?

I felt really vulnerable actually. I was the youngest and I was always mollycoddled by my mother, so that's why I turned out to be a big fag, probably! *[laughter]*

[laughing] Was it a clear choice?

I fancied boys when I went to Pontins at three years old!

Did you ever go on holiday to Butlins or Bognor Regis or Great Yarmouth?

No, I went to Pontins in Cambersands.

Cambersands?! I used to go there too!

Oh my God!

They had a trailer park with caravan...

Exactly.

... and next door to us we had a, at the time, very well known comedian, Arthur Hanes, who was sort of like a bit of a wide boy; that was his bit on stage, you know. And I used to go over and try to get his autograph. I went three mornings running and he told me to fuck off every day. [laughing] That was the first time I met a celebrity and I was so let down. I felt if that's what it's all about... they're just real people.

Two memories on Pontins – one, was coming round the corner and seeing my two sisters getting off with two men. *[laughter]* I thought they were getting raped and I went screaming back to my Mum and I wound up getting beat up by my sisters! The other one was turning up in Pontins when we first got there and looking out the cab window – because my family was, like, full of cabbies; it was like a gypsy caravan-load to go to these places – and I looked out the window when I got there and there was these two men with these scary masks on and I shit myself there and then in the cab! I literally just shit my pants! *[laughter]*

Which leads to, who's the shittiest designer?

Oh my God...

Who is the worst designer?

In my eyes?

Yeah, in your eyes.

Oh God, I'm open for libel here now, David...

Do you think there's more than one?

I think you've got to blame the public who buy the clothes of these people, not the designers themselves, because it turns out that they haven't got much idea about, you know, design itself. It's the people who buy the stuff. My favourite designer, though, is Rei Kawakubo. She's the only one I buy. The only other clothes I ever buy for myself as a designer are Comme des Garçons. I spent about a thousand pounds last year (I shouldn't say that) on Comme des Garçons menswear...

I've never paid, Alex! *[laughs]* **Until...**

Until you met me! *[more laughter]*

Until I met you! Yes, but I knew that you needed it!

I did at the time! But I tell you what I did do when you paid me, I paid the people that actually made the coat!

No, listen, you were so kind about the couple of things that I didn't need that you actually gave me. I thought that was very sweet of you. You work very well in a collaborative way as well. I thought the stuff...

I still haven't bloody met you yet! *[laughs]*

I know, I think it's quite extraordinary that we've done so well with the stage things that we put together. Do you enjoy collaboration?

I do, but the one thing you have to do when you collaborate is to respect the people that you work with. And people have phoned me up and asked me to collaborate with them before and I've usually turned them down.

Do your clients really know what they want and what is right for them, or do you usual-ly have to dress them from the floor up?

It can work either way and I don't resent either, at the end of the day, I'm the clothes designer and they're the public. If you want a house built you're not expected to build it yourself.

Here's a fan question: who would you like to dress more than anyone else in the world and why?

There's no one I'd like to dress any more than anyone else in the world, I'm afraid. I can't think of anyone who deserves such a privilege! *[laughs]*

The sub-headline there! *[laughs]*

Oh my God no. Because, I'm an atheist and an anti-royalist, so why would I put anyone on a pedestal?

Well it does draw one's attention back to your clothes, and what you do is actually more important than anything else.

Well, I think it would limit your lifestyle somewhat if you said your music is just for that person down the road.

You just sort of hope that there's someone out there who might like what you do.

And there's always someone. I mean, the world is such a big place.

Yeah. Prodigy or Oasis?

Prodigy. I think they're brilliant.

Well, you haven't answered this one. I have to drag you out on this one. Armani or Versace? *[laughs]*

Marks and Spencer. I'm sorry. I don't see the relevance of the two of them put together. Actually, they should have amalgamated and sort of formed one company out of both. If you can imagine the rhinestones on one of those deconstructed suits!

What do you eat?

What do I eat?

Yeah.

Well, I've just had a guinea fowl today. It was quite an occasion to come here... it's such a lovely place and I love to come here. Bryan Ferry comes here a lot. It's an amazing place and it was built in the arts and crafts movement by Isabella's husband's grandfather. It's on a hill in Gloucestershire and it overlooks Wales and everything. And my bedroom is decorated with Burne-Jones' *Primavera* tapestry – I always come here to get away.

So this is your sanctuary is it?

Yes, it is. Very much so.

Did you ever have an affair with anyone famous?

Not famous, but from a very rich family. A very rich Parisian family.

Did you find it an easy relationship, or was it filled with conflicts?

He was the most wonderful person I have ever met and I was completely honest with him. Never hushed up my background or where I came from, and this was when I was only nineteen or twenty. I went out with him and

I said to him, 'Whatever we do, we do it Dutch', and he didn't understand. He thought it was a sexual technique! Going Dutch!! *[laughs]* I said, 'It means paying for each of us separately.' He thought it was great, and he gave the best blow job ever!

How royal! Was it old money or was it industrial wealth?

Long-time industrial aristocratic wealth.

Do you go abroad very much? I mean just for yourself, not for work?

No, not really.

So you really are happy in your home-grown environment?

I like London, but I love Scotland! I'd never been to Aberdeen before and I went to see Murray's friends in Aberdeen for the first time and it was unreal because I stepped off the plane and I just felt like I belonged there. It's very rare that I do that, I've been to most places in the world, like most capital cities in Japan and America, and you feel very hostile when you step off the plane in these places. I stepped off the plane in Aberdeen and I felt like I'd lived there all my life. And it's a really weird sensation. I like the Highlands. My family originated from Skye.

Are you a good friend: a stand-up guy, or a flake?

I'm afraid I have very few friends and I think that all of the friends I have, I can depend on and they can depend on me. I don't have hangers-on, and I'm very aggressive to people that if I read through them in a second, they've usually found the wrong person to deal with. So if you've got me as a friend, you've got me for life. And I'd do anything for them, but I don't really have associates that use me or abuse me, unless I ask them to! *[laughs]*

Are you excited about taking over at Givenchy?

I am and I'm not. To me, it's sort of saving a sinking ship and not because of John Galliano, but because of the house. It doesn't really seem to know where it's going at the moment and, at the end of the day, they've got to depend on great clothes, not the great name.

Have you already formulated a kind of direction that you want to take them in?

Yeah, I have.

Is it exciting?

Yeah, it is, because the philosophy's mainly based on someone I really respected in fashion. There's a certain way fashion should go for a house of that stature. Not McQueen bumsters, I'm afraid.

Will you have time for making my clothes for next year's tour? *[laughs]*

Yeah, I will. We should get together. I mean, I want to see you this time. *[laughs]*

We could put this on the record right now: are you going to make it over here for the VH-1 fashion awards?

When is it?

October twenty-fourth or something.

My fashion show is on the twenty-second.

So you're probably not going to make it. Because, you know, I'm wearing the Union jacket on that, because millions of people deserve to see it.

You've got to say, 'This is by McQueen'! *[laughs]*

Gail will be wearing all her clobber as well.

Oh, she's fab!

She wears it so well.

I'd love to do your tour clothes again.

Oh, well that's great. I can't wait to be properly fitted up this time!

Yeah, definitely. But I've got to see you. I don't want waist measurements over the phone, because I'm sure you lie about your waist measurements as well! *[laughs]*

No, not at all...

Because, you know, some people lie about their length! *[laughs]*

I just said I'd never lie about the inside leg measurement.

What side do you dress David, left or right?

Both!

Yeah, right.

No. Yes. Well, maybe.

April 1997
Introduction and interview | Michael Sanders

*Don't fuck with Vincent Gallo. This obsessive,
neurotic, bad-boy actor, takes personal vendettas
very seriously. His inspired, intense real-life
personality seems ready to flip any film role or
personal situation into real drama.*

*He is electric in Alan Taylor's June released
Palookaville (1997), and is deathly brilliant in
Abel Ferrara's upcoming The Funeral (1997). In
the US, his tortured psyche has been sneering
from 'CK be' billboards. He has just completed
filming Roland Joffe's Goodbye Lover alongside
Patricia Arquette and has just accepted the lead
role in the Kiefer Sutherland-directed Truth &
Consequences.*

*Gallo's most personal project is the quasi-
autobiographical film Buffalo 66 (1998), a self-
written and self-starring project that takes Gallo
back to his family home. It's the story of Gallo
kidnapping a girl and forcing her to come to
dinner at his parents' house. He tells his parents
a bunch of lies about how great he is and how
great he's doing. It features his real-life mother
and father – Gallo's way at getting back at them.
His revenge was in making the film, focusing on
his own shortcomings and insecurities.*

*Thirty-four-year-old Vincent's background is
a chequerboard of swift moves and opportuni-
ties, from his youth spent interning for the local
mafia, to playing in the band Gray with Jean
Michel Basquiat at seventeen, to racing motorbikes for Yamaha; from dealing in hi-fi and vin-
tage guitars, to exhibiting his artwork alongside
Basquiat, Barbara Kruger and other art world
luminaries of the 1980s at the famous Annina
Nosei gallery. He has appeared in seventeen films
including the ill-fated tragi-comedy Arizona
Dream (Paul Leger, 1993) with Johnny Depp and
Lili Taylor. There was also a nervous breakdown
in Paris at eighteen, a five-month marriage at
twenty-three, and a few dubious tricks turned in
desperate times. No stranger, then, to the hustle,
for Vincent the art is very much in the deal,
acting being the quickest way to the 'love, money,
chicks, and freedom' he craves.*

Dazed & Confused | **You're largely unknown in
England; what would you want people to
know about you before seeing your work?**
Vincent Gallo | I would prefer if nobody knew
anything about me. I wouldn't give a shit if one
person in England or the rest of the world knew
that I was alive.
**OK. Lets talk about your feelings for
Rosemary Fergusson, the British model.**

The truth is that I'm not close to anybody. However, there's been a girl or two in my life that I've fancied and for some reason, Rosemary's been a standout. I saw her in London five years ago, briefly for a second, and I liked her, and a couple of years later I saw her in *Interview* magazine wearing these furry boots, and I had this picture of her that I carried around. And unfortunately I've had god-awful luck in pursuing her.

You must really want to fuck her.

No, no! Actually, I would be really happy holding hands and if she let me, do a lot of kissing.

Why is love horrible to you?

Because it feels bad.

And when did you first have this feeling?

A long, long time ago I realized that my love for my parents was contradictory to our actual relationship.

How old were you?

Two. I think my father had grabbed me by the throat and pulled me out of my playpen and started screaming at me for something – who knows what? – and I realized, 'Wow, it's very weird to love people who are kind of creepy and unlikeable.'

This page and overleaf
Vincent Gallo, 1997
Philippe McClelland

So what kind of relationships have you had?
There were just a couple of girls that I've had that were actual girlfriends in my life. The only time I ever really had feelings for a girl and allowed myself to have feelings without being protective was at a very early age, like nine years old. As a teenager, the only girls that I dated, I dated only for sex, so they were usually uninteresting, or unattractive, or unpleasant, but easy to manipulate into sex. I didn't know what it was like to have a sexual relationship with somebody who I had any kind of privacy with or affection for until I was in my early twenties and the first time it happened I was so shocked by those feelings that I immediately married the girl.

Have you ever sought therapy?
Yes, I've sought it out once a week for the past seven years. Going to see a psychiatrist was the smartest thing I've done. Everything got better. I know it probably sounds silly to Europeans because you guys are so stubborn in that way: you're happy to just sit and smoke and drink yourselves to death and have twisted, perverted relationships amongst yourselves. The tragedy of my life is even though I'm becoming so near to allowing myself to be intimate and loving, I've gotten so used to not being like that, that I've developed an incredible happiness within my misery and I'm so attached to it that I love it like a puppy.

When did you first want to be an artist?
I've never wanted to be an artist, I always wanted to be a professional. I just wanted the cult glory that went along with certain professions.

What was your first profession?
Selling cinnamon-flavoured toothpicks that I made, at the age of six. My first career move at the age of twelve was towards opening up a string of cleaning businesses. I then started working in the crime field a bit, doing a bunch of car thefts and robberies for some heavy and powerful Mafia gangsters in Buffalo. I was a coffee boy in a social club and would bring them stolen merchandise. So at thirteen I had my heart set at being the Godfather.

How did you not continue on that path?
Because an actual Godfather-like gangster took me aside one day and told me that I was a special kid and that it would break his heart to see me sell myself short like that. That I could have all the power and money and success that I wanted without breaking into stores. I know this sounds like a ten-cent melodrama but I got an epiphany from that conversation.

Out of all the things that you've done: painting, motorcycle racing, music, acting, trading in hi-fi, which are you best at?
Counting money. I can count ten thousand dollars in one dollar bills in thirty-two seconds. That's a record. I'm the greatest cash counter that ever lived.

Why did you do all these things and how did you come to acting?
Because you do these things and you sit back and you see what happens after you do them. You say, 'How much money did I make? How many people did I influence? How much recognition did I get? How much revenge can I execute out of this power and success? And how little time do I need to dedicate to this particular thing to get all those things?' You evaluate them with a pen and paper and I came up with acting. But don't take this as a sign of laziness because I assure you that I work fanatically till I drop and I feel guilty if I sleep more than five or six hours.

What's your greatest achievement in acting so far?

My greatest achievement as an actor were the scenes cut out of Emir Kusturica's *Arizona Dream*, the scenes that you'll never see, and that's a painful thing that I think about often.

Who have you worked with who's inspired you the most?

The most talented person that I've worked with by a million times is Patricia Arquette. She's just so pretty and loose and free and cool. To do a TV series for the next forty years with Patricia Arquette, they would be the happiest forty years of anybody's life. It's funny, in my career life, basically all I am is a failed baseball player in my mind. All I really would have wanted to be is a great New York Yankee. I've done all these things to compensate for that. In my social life, every woman I have a relationship with from this moment on will be just a consolation for the fact that I'm not married to Patricia Arquette.

When did you write the screenplay *Buffalo 66*?

The afternoon of March the eighteenth 1996.

And how did you come to the story?

It's very easy. It's the same way I do a performance. I tell it like I already wrote it. I told everybody about this script I wrote for about two years and they would say, 'So, what's it about?' And I'd make it up, and I made it up so many times to so many people that I saw in their faces, in their eyes which were the best scenes. I realized at a certain point that I was able to tell the story from the beginning to the middle to the end and keep people interested. So I tested my audience over and over and then I wrote it out over an afternoon.

So how much is actually autobiographical?

Well, most of the character himself, his feelings are true to things I've felt, and most of the situation with his family is very similar to how my mother and father are, and the concept that I would want to make someone love me, even if by force, is not that far-fetched. But it's not purely autobiographical: there's also a very clever screenplay there.

How will your father react to us turning up and making a film about his dysfunctional family?
You know, he's a very interesting guy, my father, it'll be a combination of incredible rage that I would break the family privacy to the point that he'd call me and threaten to kill me. At the same time his greed and cunning would allow him to figure out ways to make it work for himself. So it'll be interesting to watch both those things happen.

And your mother?
My mother will stay in the same kind of denial that nothing was happening as she would if I had both of my legs sawn off by a passing train and I'd say, 'Ma' and she'd say, 'Oh honey, put some ice on it.'

Why is it so important to make the documentary to go with the movie?
Because the documentary chronicles the motivation for the whole project. My inspiration for the piece: my resentments and revenge for wanting to make the piece and it also portrays my own shortcomings in a way where we see how petty someone can be in being antagonized into making a work of art like that. It's almost like you're walking down the street and someone bumps you and three years later you do thirteen movies about it, you know?

Do you have a favourite fantasy?
Listen you pervert, I like girls, I like everything. I like kissing them, touching them, sniffing them, sucking them, holding them, squeezing them, greasing them, pleasing them.

How often do you masturbate?
Let's just say that I have to sedate myself to fall asleep. So that's the minimum.

And your dream for the future?
I don't want to sound like some corny jerk you know. But my dream for the future is that I just wish that everything could stay exactly the way that it is right now. You know I just really feel happy right now.

So, more of the same?
Yeah.

June 1997
Introduction and interview | Michael Fordham

Baudrillard's writings are some of the most controversial in post-war academia. He's been (mistakenly) tagged the 'high priest of post-modernism', and berated as a heretic, or as a self-publicizing populist.

He has also become an icon for cultural studies students who hate their lecturers. His aphoristic writings of the 1980s, notably Cool Memories *(1980) and* America *(1986), introduced him to the 'it's-cool-to-be-brainy' posse in streamlined, supremely purchasable packaging. Like any controversial theorist, he's spawned an army of pretenders who think they've understood his work. Artists in particular have been quick to pick up on his reflection on the disappearance of the real, the impossibility of transgression, and the cancelling out of authenticity in the ubiquity of real time. In 1990, when he publicly posited that 'The Gulf War does not exist',* The Guardian *dutifully published his piece, prompting a flood of outraged missives.*

A clue to Baudrillard's enduring appeal is in the fact that his intellectual roots lie in the 1968 disturbances in France, when direct action and the power of the imagination finally drowned out, for many, the lumbering behemoth that was the Communist Party of France. Rioting students were urged in those fetishized May days by groups like the Situationist International – who had begun to reject Marxism in favour of a Nietzschean aesthetic terrorism – to 'be realistic, demand the impossible'. France was brought to a standstill by strikes, riots and demonstrations until, according to whom you ask, either the Communists sold out, or the students went on summer holiday.

Since his 1973 work The Mirror of Production, *an attack on Marxism that split French academia, the influence of Baudrillard's work has been like a virus, tormenting the manifestations of ideological dogma and the preconceptions of liberalism alike. In a sense, the crystallized orthodoxy of his ideas has taken hold and has dissolved into the technological realities surrounding us.*

It was Baudrillard who coined the neologism 'Simulacra', referring to the ambient play of images that is our culture – where authenticity is subsumed in an increasingly self-referential mediascape, where styles, events and destinies disappear and become fundamentally mediated chimeras. The Perfect Crime *(1995) is Baudrillard's latest major work: a beguiling meditation on the 'murder' of reality, covering subjects as diverse as the irony of technology, transsexuality, Sarajevo and the Millennium.*

While some of his ideas seem out of this world, the man himself lives in a sunny, top-floor flat in Montparnasse, rolling his own, writing with a rather archaic electric typewriter; cocooned in a fleet of weighty tomes and his own painterly, photographic still lifes. A genial disposition and the playfully ambiguous nature of his discourse betray an intellectual bob and weave; a shadow-box with reality and the imagination that liberally messes with the minds of academics, students and journalists alike. Conversing with Baudrillard, his ideas spinning over and untangling themselves as they are uttered, makes you giddy.

Dazed & Confused | **Are you surprised by the interest that a youth-culture magazine is showing in your work?**

Jean Baudrillard | Yes, pleasantly surprised, but I think that a certain number of questions that I raise are of a topical nature that could appeal to a younger generation. I think that there can be an affinity between an enquiry that is on the one hand, piercing and incisive, but which is not specialized, not professional. The young generation doesn't have too much of a historical or traditional reference and I don't either. I have always tried to take a step back, to distance myself from institutions, to go beyond the institution, beyond convention, beyond the history of ideas etc. So I think that my work can be quite easily accessed for the generations that don't necessarily have their heads full of culture.

One of your most popular works focused on America as a phenomenon. What, for you, is Europe as a phenomenon?

When I consider America, it is not in connection with Europe, in relation to Europe. I try to see it in an original, absolute light, not in relation to Cyberspace but to Hyperspace. I try to see it as apart from Europe. Seen from America, Europe is a bygone continent, a bit outdated, too loaded with meaning, too loaded with significance, too weighed down with culture. What I'm looking for in America is more of a free space, mentally and behaviourally. I'm looking for a kind of freedom that is much more linked to space, to territory, to distance and the relations between these things, more than a freedom of values, of political value, of philosophical value, etc. That's what Europe is: freedom understood in relation to history, politics, etc. While over there, it is a kind of freedom that is much more physical, biological, geological, really a completely different world. The book is not about a continual comparison between Europe and America. It's as if I've put myself in the same situation as those who discovered it. They arrived and asked themselves, 'What is it, this massive unknown land?' They discovered America almost anthropologically. It's because of this that I take America as a primitive society, which hasn't pleased the Americans! I approach America as a kind of a virgin land, not only physically, but mentally.

Do you think that Europe is becoming like America in its collective mindset?

Yes, but in a way it is like a parody: America really is modern, based on modernity or even post-modernity. I don't think that Europe can really be called 'modern'. There is always an air of nostalgia, of regret, in relation to modernity here. America is the threshold of modernity, and that's why I say that it's the primitive society of modernity. We're an older society and no longer receptive to anything other than European history. I think that we're never going to be truly modern but we are really pseudo-modern. Europe is an area of the 'simulacra' of modernity. America is the real thing. We have a sort of model, a clichéd artefact of modernity. We try hard to put ourselves on the same level as America, but we don't do it very well. You can see this by all the difficulties that they're having in forming Europe as a really modern identity. There are all sorts of difficulties and it's really because all our old political, economic and social systems are still in place. We're always defending our old values. Saying this, though, I'm not objecting, I'm not necessarily for globalization at all, but I'm saying that we want to think globally and we're not managing to.

One can detect in your most recent work an increasing moralism. Is this something you're conscious of?

I'm surprised you say that. I'm not really aware of this moralism but, yes, you could say that, because when I talk about the extermination of truth, in fact the extermination of 'reality', one could suppose that this constitutes a defence of this reality. I don't think so though, because I have never been for reality, I am more against the principles of reality and more on the side of illusion, seduction, fate and things that have nothing to do with reality. But the discourse itself is automatically moral when you expose something that has, though perhaps inaccurately, some remnants of a moral value. There exists a level of analysis that is 'beyond good and evil', if I can say that – beyond human and inhuman. Then there is a level of discourse which remains whether you're talking about truth or not. There is still the requirement of meaning that is always moral. To give meaning is a moral action. That's not a problem for me, but I resist doing it as much as possible. What I mean is that there is no moral lesson, there is no moral ideology in my work. Others, even friends like Paul Virillo, take a position that is very clearly moral, in fact almost religiously so. His analysis of the contemporary situation is very radical, while on the other hand his judgement is much more moral. Ultimately, his analysis is more radical than mine, but in contrast to mine: I don't have any judgement like that. I know, for example, that he disagreed with what I said about the Gulf War not having taken place: 'The Gulf War is real, war is real.' It is this principle of reality that I think is the true moral principle. That's where we differ. To maintain a discourse, we are forced into the morality of discourse, but that's the morality of communication. But that's all. Otherwise, I don't think that there is morality in my work. At the same time, I don't have my own ideology, personally or politically, so I'm free. Nowadays, true political morality comes from existing ideologies and that's it. But I don't follow that route, so in fact, mine is a radical immorality. That's true. I'd like that a lot, a utopia, a utopia of immorality, a discourse beyond good and evil, beyond true and false. My discourse on politics is beyond left and right, beyond distinctions, even, in a certain way, beyond morality. But I agree that we can never really achieve this.

In the light of this 'morality of communication', does the Internet represent a possible new mode of communication?

Yes, technically it's a new universe, obviously, in the world of communication. It reaches for new heights, and, in fact, attains them. It is communication. I think that it is, at the same time, an extension of determination, interrelations, connection, interaction, but I don't believe in all that. I think that perhaps we can make information by travelling through communication. But, for me, the whole area has no symbolism, has no symbolic intensity; it is such a technical abstraction. Communication is technical, it's not change. Change is perhaps something else psychologically, symbolically etc. The concept of communication is sustained, generated by technology, so, really, with the Internet we attain the highest limits of communication. But what I would ask is, 'Who is it that communicates? Who is it?' There is one terminal and then another. There are two terminals, two specific areas of abstraction that change the information. But also, all the personality changes, in fact all the charm, all these things disappear inside it. Communication is something that is factual and also artificial. In my opinion, it lifts you slightly out of simulation. You are really in the field of dissimilation. But my opinion after the last time I used the Internet is that it is not really a place that opens up communication, an area of discovery. But I haven't really had the experience; I'm not on the Internet and I don't make any use of it. However, I think it is a very powerful means of disappearance. The network is a place for disappearance and communication. Data processing, cybernetics: it is the art of disappearance. What I mean is that you can immerse yourself in the machine – digitalized, virtual reality – you can immerse yourself in it and disappear completely. There are the problems of freedom, subjectivity and many others. This is something that goes round and round and round but that's a point of view that is a little bit negative. That's true, but I have the feeling that there is at least the fantasy of communicating. It is impossible to think that it might be possible to communicate all over the world with everyone at whatever moment in 'real' time, in virtual reality... all that is too much. That's another utopia, a utopia that has been realized. But the danger is that utopia should not be realized because when that happens, it's finished. So everyone is going to vanish into thin air on the network, but what goes on inside it? Who talks to whom? I don't feel it is a place where real events happen. It's not an original place. I'd really like the Internet to be a revolution, but it's a revolution that makes us go further into 'the perfect crime'. For me, it's one of the elements of 'the perfect crime'.

Your work has tended to be viewed by academia, very often sociologists, philosophers etc., as deliberately undermining the establishment. Is this a kind of philistinism? You have mentioned your peasant heritage...

I've basically always been on the outskirts of academe, of university, of discipline, although they've treated me well. The fact that I was a little rejected by all the various disciplines is of little consequence, but it's true there was a feeling of pollution. I don't really know how to put it, but I had feelings that were 'anti-cultural', of something that was against culture.

It was perhaps the peasant heritage, but you mustn't exaggerate. I may be a peasant, but at the same time I have also become a cultivated person, an intellectual. I have always refused to profit from my stature as an intellectual, or as one who is easily recognizable. There are always those who understand nothing, those who are not cultivated, the majority – what you'd call the 'silent majority' – those who have the largest percentage of anti-cultural feelings, but not against culture in the way meant by the privileged. No. An anti-culture movement en masse has no meaning. It's the resistance to meaning, to be on the side of those who don't take any meaning, who don't see any significance, who remain removed from it. Today, there are no more peasants; the peasants have disappeared, but there is still a Third World, a Fourth World. Today, this position, outside culture, is becoming more and more occupied by those who are excluded; by exclusion, we've formed a percentage of the population that has been completely abandoned, outside culture. I've always been prejudiced – prejudiced against culture, official culture, academic culture, but it's also against intelligentsia in terms of caste – the intellectual caste, the sociological caste and all that. That is what creates a sort of privileged monopoly, and it's basically this that I resist and always have. You find yourself a little bit alone, ending up forming your own caste.

What are your thoughts on the Millennium?

I'm not a prophet. I feel that that we are already in a situation where we can't foresee the future; we can't make any predictions since we are already in a kind of 'real time'. There's no longer any history, any continuity, any future. Before, you could have a perspective. Nowadays, we are in an area of the instantaneous, of immediacy, of information, so we can't respond to the future because everything is here and now. We can see everything, and when we can see everything we can't foresee anything. I particularly have the feeling that this millennium, this 'judgement' day is not a time of communion, but more one of withdrawal. We'll arrive at the judgement day for the year 2000 with a feeling of repentance, looking backwards on everything that has happened in the twentieth century, all the violence, the wars, the corruption etc., and there's a temptation to wipe it clean, to clean the slate. We would like to have a period of purification, purification of the century gone by. It seems to me that we kind of panic more about the final judgement day happening without our having worked out our problems because the problems are even more serious than they were before. So there's a collective feeling, which is not really catastrophic. With the coming of the first millennium, people were waiting for catastrophe, though it was a catastrophic feeling that also hoped that it might be the Kingdom of Heaven arriving, so theirs was a messianic feeling. We have a much more negative opinion about the Millennium, I think. We're not able to look to the past in order to look to the future. We're much more caught up with the present, with actuality, but an actuality that is negative, pessimistic.

I haven't seen anywhere that there is any real hope for the Millennium. There is more a feeling of repentance – not a despairing repentance, but still a feeling of catastrophe, whether it be political, economic, ecological or even cognitive in some way. All these means of development, information, the Internet, all that,

can give us a sense of maximum development of humanity evolved on the back of these possibilities. It is exactly this that gives us the sense of foreboding, of upsetting everything. The image of the Millennium is exactly that: that everything will be upset, that something will happen. Because in the actual world, we have been waiting for a long time already and nothing has strictly happened. Yes, there are events that return to the past. The destruction of the Berlin Wall was an event, but not really a historical event. It is simply recycling history that has already happened, recycling the errors of history, etc. So we're here and we question ourselves: we hope that something will happen – that there is an event – but we have no control over what makes an event. But this said, this event is only for us Europeans and Americans, the Western world, because the rest of the world is not concerned at all by this Millennium. You have rather a false situation because that means that the entire world has to come into line with the Western world. That's significant. That's the consecration of globalization. In terms of time, all the continents, all the countries have to follow the Western world.

At the Pompidou centre in Paris, there was a numerical clock with a countdown to the Millennium. It's disappeared – they've taken it away! They say it's because of the work being done there, but I don't think so. I think they removed it because they started to ask themselves, 'What does this thing mean? What are we waiting for?' We don't know at all. The countdown is fascinating, like a show, but on one level it becomes dangerous; you feel that it becomes socially dangerous. I thought it would have been really effective, like a bomb going off at the end of the world and everything explodes.

The countdown is now in the Parc de la Villette. They've put it at the back of a warehouse and it continues, but in the corner of a cellar in the dark! In place of it they've put a big notice board on the Eiffel Tower, it's a countdown of days, not seconds, because that was what was worrying about the clock in front of the Pompidou centre; there you felt danger, but not with just days counting down.

I think that we're already in the year 2000, but in my opinion, it's by this anticipation that we're trying to neutralize the judgement day because it's potentially dangerous. There are no more really political events. It is the symbolic that really counts. What is clear is that all the problems that have occurred over the history of two centuries, none of them have been resolved. On the contrary, they're becoming more and more serious. Faced with all of these problems, which are potentially catastrophic, we are trying to go backwards, attempting retrospectively to clean up history, to correct all the errors, all the violence etc., thereby achieving an ideal world. A utopia. To create an ideal world of communication, it's necessary that everything is going well, so we're really entering a period of mourning. I feel we are collectively in a period of mourning, rather than having a newer, happier perspective. But that's a subjective point of view; how I feel personally. I'm not a prophet, you know!

A specific question: have you seen David Cronenberg's *Crash*?
I haven't seen the film, but I know the novel. I wrote about it for a long time and I was in contact with J G Ballard. I like him very much and he likes me, I think, but I didn't see the film because I enjoyed the book very much. I found it very complex and I don't think that you can put it into images. It's always simplified in the cinema. It's too visual outside of the text, even in a very hyper-real text like that of Ballard's. It's still complex. There are all sorts of things that you couldn't show in the cinema. I think that I prefer not to see the film.

It has been very difficult to see the film in Britain. It has caused a furore. What do you think this says about modern European culture?
Ah, so the authorities saw the violence as contaminating? Oh, that's a very simplistic idea of contamination. I don't believe that the cinema or the TV can really be contagious. What I consider serious is the actual medium itself. It is more a virus of the actual medium, the virus of TV, the corruption of images and visuals rather than the contents that are contaminating. I don't believe contents can be contagious. The real virus is that of the medium: the complete invasion of one's mental universe just by images. Everything is seen as the destiny of images. That is the true violence; that is the violence of the medium. I think that the violence of the contents are neutralized basically by the medium itself. You don't have to have

intelligence to know that it's just TV. Like people used to say, 'It's not real', 'It's cinema', 'It's theatre', that means it's not real, but people don't say that for television. I don't think that people really believe what they see: of course there are specific cases, but as a whole, if the media really was so corrupting, a virus such as that, then the whole world would be violent; there would be nothing but violence. I don't believe that. Perhaps there is even something cathartic, a cleansing through fiction like that, through the shows that are violent. However, saying that, I am able to understand censorship for other issues, not for sex or pornography – that's normal. I don't think soft pornography is censored in Britain nowadays. On the other hand, in Ballard, it is the mix of technology and sex that is specifically violent. Sex on its own isn't serious; it's the combination of the two – the 'telescopage' that, as Ballard has seen very well, is a very particular violence – and I can understand when this type of thing is banned. That seems to me a violence that is not about sex at all. It is something that is opposed to sex, something harder than sex, so it's more obscene than pure sex. It's sex mutilated by technology, which has nothing to do with the sex. I don't know, I mean we have an idea of technology in the larger sense as positive. Ultimately, technology is a good thing. There are some bad points, but it can be used well and there are good things about sex and sexual liberation etc. If you mix them together, that's not using them well. That's not good at all, that's a corruption of them both. As a result of this combination, technology becomes a bad thing and so does sex. As I said, I haven't seen the film, which is a pity, but I think it's in this way that Ballard has touched upon something very strong. In that case, I can understand censorship. It's true they should not have censored it for the reasons they said they have, but there is something very dangerous about it, that's certainly true. I see it more as a threat for sex itself as a vital function, as something everyone does, for reproduction. It is sex itself that is threatened: the sexual act, the idea of sex is replaced by artificial technology. It is the crash or the violence that takes the form of everything. There's a form of obscene pornography that sees everything as sexual and that was censored for moral reasons. What is most serious is that with this mix of technology and sex you're really starting something inhuman, no longer human. Pornography is human and therefore normal. The reasons for censorship are really very conventional, but if you take a deeper analysis, you can understand why they have to censor it. Perhaps they've realized that there is really a danger of abstract violence. The crash is the absolute danger – everything's going along very well and then suddenly CRASH. It is that dangerous.

One final question: today, what is your profession? Are you a philosopher, are you a sociologist, are you a poet, are you a prophet, are you an impressionist?
I can't really say. There really isn't a definition. I'm not a sociologist because the sociologists don't recognize me as one of them. I'm not a philosopher because I don't follow a history of ideas or maintain any inter-reference with other philosophers, so they don't recognize me either. What can I say? A worker. But what does that mean? A writer doesn't mean anything either. Thinker? But then you have the impression of Rodin's *Thinker*. No, I have no response. That's your problem!

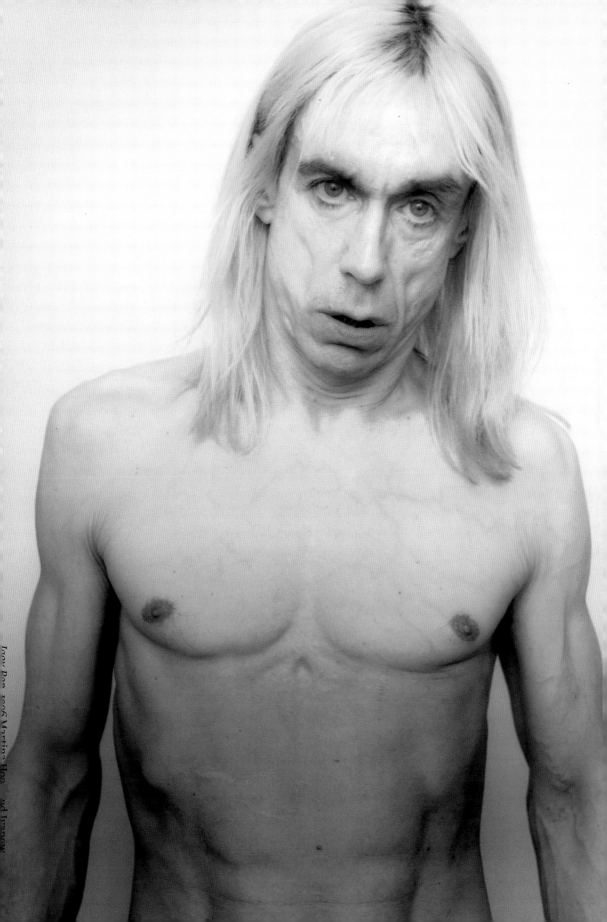

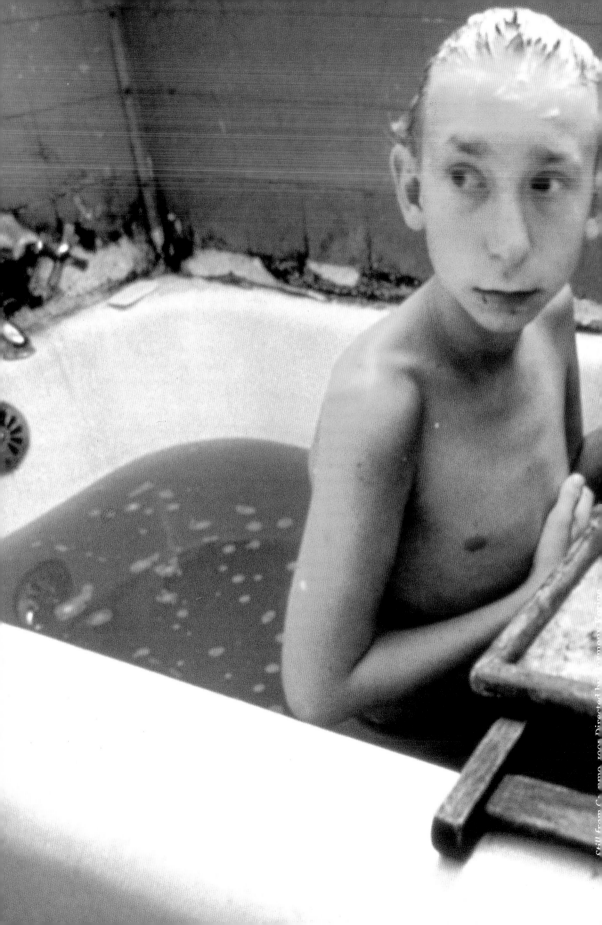

June 21, 1997

Mr. Jefferson Hack
Dazed & Confused
112-116 Old Street
London
ENGLAND
EC1V 9BD

Dear Mr. Hack:

Your letter of 20 May to Elvis Presley was forwarded to me for reply. As Mr. Presley has been deceased for some twenty years, he is presently unavailable for an interview. However, your comments regarding his stature as a role model and cultural icon, and your interest in featuring his image on the cover of your first issue of the year 2000, are greatly appreciated. We do not anticipate any change in the status of Mr. Presley's availability for an interview, but we should be in a position to provide you with updated information about his never-ending career and possibly a good photograph for your cover. When the time comes, please get back in touch.

Rumors regarding Mr. Presley's comeback as the new millennium approaches are not entirely without merit. On 16 August of this year, Mr. Presley, via video technology, will "perform" in a historic live entertainment event. "Elvis in Concert '97", staged at the Mid-South Coliseum in Memphis, will bring together the Memphis Symphony Orchestra and over thirty of Elvis' original former bandmates to perform live, with Elvis himself singing lead vocal. Among the band members will be J.D. Sumner & The Stamps, The Jordanaires, The Sweet Inspirations, The Imperials, Voice, The TCB Band, Scotty Moore, D.J. Fontana, and others. It is possible that a similar production, cast list and overall production scaled to road show size, could tour the world within a couple of years.

Your coverage of "Elvis in Concert '97", along with all of the events in Memphis that are part of Elvis Week this year, is invited. For press credentials and further information you can contact our publicity agent, David Beckwith, in Los Angeles at 213-845-9836 or Fax 213-845-9623.

Thank you very much for your interest in working with Elvis Presley and for the copy of your impressive magazine.

Sincerely,

Todd Morgan
Director of Creative Resources
Graceland/Elvis Presley Enterprises, Inc.

ST. JAMES'S PALACE
LONDON SW1A 1BS

From: The Press Secretary to H.R.H. The Prince of Wales

29th April 1997

Dear Mr Hack,

Thank you for your recent letter in which you asked for an interview with The Prince William and a photo opportunity. I am afraid I must decline your request. Both The Prince of Wales and Diana, Princess of Wales want to protect Prince William's privacy as far as is possible whilst he is so young. Whilst that is not always possible, a decision has been taken that Prince William will not give interviews.

I am sorry to send you this disappointing reply but I hope you understand why it is important that during the short time that Prince William is being educated he is protected as much as possible from the media spotlight.

Yours sincerely

Sandy Henney

Jefferson Hack

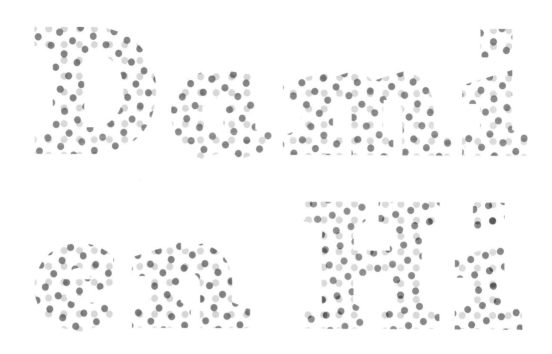

Damien Hirst

*A twelve-foot tiger shark in formaldehyde, a cow
and her calf sawn in half, preserved sheep,
black sheep, thousands of flies, butterflies, cabi-
nets full of pharmaceutical boxes and bottles,
surgical instruments, spinning canvases, spot
paintings, cigarette butts, billboards, beer bottles,
designer clothes, album covers, pop videos,
commercial advertising... Damien Hirst has caned
the art world.*

*At twenty-three Hirst kick-started British art.
At thirty-two, his name has become synonymous
with contemporary culture. Now, having recently
set up camp on a farm in Devon, surrounded by
livestock and pubs, children's toys, errant pigs
and overflowing ashtrays, he counts away the
hours, plotting his next move. But where do you
go when everything you turn your hand to is
immediately swept up by the media, to be
repackaged, resold and redefined? The answer –
for Hirst at least – is to penetrate the heart of
the media itself, by fusing two of the most potent
visual languages of the twentieth century – Art
and Advertising.*

*Contrary to popular opinion, Hirst is a
populist. At best, his art is a rendition of art and
life combined: a beautiful sore embedded in the
core of our consciousness.*

*But exactly what is it that makes Damien
Hirst tick? A desire to get under our skins? A
need to question and confirm the everyday
through every and any available medium that
comes to hand? 'My mother once asked me if I
had any regrets,' he smiles. "'Nothing," I replied,
"except that you never let me watch* The Sweeney
*when I was a kid." I'm a visual artist
for fuck's sake, and I was never allowed to
watch* The Sweeney! *That's terrible!' Welcome to
the world of Damien Hirst: media logic and
advertising.*

Damien Hirst | My first question, OK?
Dazed & Confused | **Go on then.**
What are you afraid of?
Difficult question. Nothing really...
Do you know what I'm afraid of?
What?
First of all, my girlfriend leaving me, then
maybe death, after that, nothing.
**I've managed not to think about death
so much.**
I'm also scared of finding out that art is not
worth doing because if I did I would have to
stop. But having said that, I'm fucking on for it.
I'm not going to hang around after the party
is over. I mean, what happens if you get
everything that you have always wanted and
it's everything that everyone you have ever
known has always wanted and then suddenly
you realize you don't want it anymore? Dad
happens, that's what. *[Hirst has a two-year-old
son]* You get to the top, you grow up and you
grow out of the classroom. You suddenly start
to think, 'What is it I actually do want? Not
what I think I want.' But the energy to keep
going is always there.
What do you want?
When I think about it, my whole understanding
of art has been based on images. I spent more
time in the art library and watching TV than
I ever did in galleries. I used to go into the art
library and say to myself, 'I wish I could be like
these guys, these are the guys, these are the
dons.' Sitting there looking at five-by-four
images of paintings, that was the world that I
grew up in. At the same time though, I spent a
hell of a lot of time talking about commercials
when I was at art school, conversations like, 'My
God, did you see the Coalite advert where the
dog kisses the cat and then the cat kisses the

mouse? – Fantastic!' That's one that Tony Kaye
did a few years back where the theme tune
plays *[singing]* 'Will you still love me tomorrow?' Just a brilliant advert. I didn't realize at
the time, but that was where the real art was
coming from. The rest of the time I was in the
art library going, 'Shit, I wish I could understand all this stuff.' In retrospect, my work
was always a fusion of the two.

**Have you ever thought of doing a
commercial yourself?**

A few years back I got signed up by Tony Kaye.

**Did you end up shooting a commercial
with him?**

Yeah. It was called *Walking the Bird*.

Who was it for?

The brief was from TNT, Turner Network
Television. They do all these weird B-movies, all
this shit that nobody wants to see. They needed
a commercial to advertise this series that was
going to be called *100% Weird*, a series that was
scheduled to run after midnight all over Europe.
So my brief was to produce an advert that captured the title – *100% Weird*. Initially, I had
loads of ideas, but then I thought, 'Hang on:
none of these will work, they're only ninety per
cent weird. What the fuck is one hundred per
cent weird?' Eventually I came up with the idea
of having a bloke that I had seen a few months
before walking down the street in Whitechapel
with a hanky on his shoulder and a budgie on
top. Originally, when I saw him I thought, 'Oh
look, there's a guy taking his bird for a walk',
and that was it, but when it came to making
this commercial, his image just popped up again.
That hanky instead of a lead, that's weird! So
that was the kick-off point for the whole thing.

**Is this the advert that caused such
controversy a couple of years ago?**

This page from top
Away from the Flock,
Second Version, *1994*
The Physical
Impossibility of
Death in the Mind of
Someone Living, *1991*
Opposite page
Love, Love, Love,
1994–95

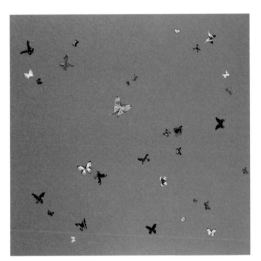

Yeah, I shot it, screened it and then it was immediately banned.

Why was it banned?

Because it was too weird. Fantastic! Can you believe that? Who in their right mind would ban a commercial for being too weird when the original brief was 'one hundred per cent weird'? Who would give me forty thousand pounds and then back out? Superb!

Tell me the whole script?

Well, the basis of the whole film is just this bloke who gets up in the morning, takes his bird Nigel for a walk to the butchers, buys a sausage and then goes home, but en route all these things happen, like he passes a hole in the wall and sees these three men with no eyes, playing cards round a barrel. They are making all these weird noises, and one of them has a pair of cow's eyes, which he holds up to his face while he makes this vomiting noise. After a few seconds, he chucks the eyes at the other guys, who are still playing cards and then this dead cow falls from the ceiling and breaks its fucking neck, *Crack!* Then this hand opens up, with these maggots in it, an anamorphic shot. The next thing is, you leap to another bloke fishing next to a pond, and he has a pile of maggots in his hand that he's throwing into the water. You see the maggots hitting the surface until the moment that he heaves his rod out to find an eyeball dangling on the end. Fucking brilliant: totally insane, the whole thing. But that's not all. The action cuts to a newsreader talking into the camera and as the shot pans back, you see that he's sitting on an eighteen-foot-high chair next to an eighteen-foot-high table with his pants around his ankles. Suddenly, it zooms in on a close-up of his arsehole – well actually my arsehole because we couldn't afford a stunt

Party Time, 1995

double – and it shits out this kidney bean: massive close-up, this time filling the whole screen, one kidney bean going 'plop' with a fart noise cut over the top. The bean falls through open space and lands in the centre of a little gold frame, whereupon we cut back to the bloke with the budgie at the beginning, walking into a butcher's full of girls in meat bikinis. The butcher behind the counter slowly leans forward and proffers a sausage, which our man takes and then heads for home. Oh yeah, I forgot: somewhere in the midst of all this there is a shot of a woman laden with suitcases, trying to walk up some stairs to her front door. She staggers to her house and accidentally drops her keys. As she leans down to pick them up, a hand appears from beneath her skirt and gets there first. *[laughs]* Completely bonkers! The whole thing runs for just sixty seconds. When I first showed it to Tony Kaye he pissed his pants laughing.

[laughs] That sounds fantastic. Why was it eventually rejected?

It was the agency that I was working with who fucked up. I said to them at the time that we didn't want any publicity, everything was in place and everybody was really happy with the final edit. Then the agency and The *Independent* turned it into front page news: 'dead cow falls from ceiling, severed eyeballs, maggots, arsehole shits out kidney bean… ', you can imagine. So when Ted Turner of TNT – who is totally environmental and married to Jane Fonda – finds out, he just freaks. You can picture the scenario: one day he's reading the international news in the bath, probably with Jane, and he stumbles across some headline like, 'TNT, Shock Horror Madness, Ted Gone Crazy.' So that was it. It all kicked off. I had to have a meeting with the marketing director who said, 'Damien, look,

I have to go and see Ted over this commercial', and I said, 'What are you going to say to him?' He took me aside and said, 'Don't worry, I can sort it out. I've seen the commercial and I think the newspapers have over-done it; it is really straightforward. I will go over there and put my job on the line because I believe in it a hundred per cent. It is "one hundred per cent weird".' So I said, 'Good on you, mate.' I never saw him again: he was sacked! *[laughs]* Lost his fucking job and everything. I can't even get copies for myself: TNT are so embarrassed about the whole thing, they're denying that they had anything to do with it. Can you imagine, my first job, forty thousand pounds? Amazing.

Chris Burden once bought a twenty-five-second advertising slot on TV in the early 1970s and he used it to screen himself crawling across broken glass. A direct media intervention. Have you ever thought about buying advertising space wholesale like that?

I know the piece, but I never knew he did it on TV. I would love to buy advertising space like that, but it's fucking expensive. I have been thinking of putting together a whole series of fake commercials and airing them, maybe on the BBC because they don't have advertising as such. Possibly even inserting them in between real adverts. I'm definitely going to give it a go. In particular, I want to do a commercial for a laxative liquid that doesn't exist. The text would read: 'Problem Stools? Difficult Movements? Complicated Jobs? Buy Anatard the new anal laxative.' Inspired.

[*laughs*] So which do you think has more integrity, advertising or the art market?
Advertising, because there's no bollocks attached to it. It goes straight to the point, it doesn't lie, it tells the truth, makes money, has a laugh – it is the truth, because it sells a product.

Is it advertising's mass market that appeals to you? Being able to talk to millions of people simultaneously?
Maybe. But what I really love about advertising in this country is that the general public are so visually educated because of the billions of pounds that multinationals spend on advertising every year. I love that: the fact that there is just far too much effort put into commercials just to sell a product.

Do you consider advertising to be the prime visual language of the twentieth century?
People can always understand an advert, however strange it is, because it's attached to a product, and that's OK. But when it comes to art, they can't get their minds around it. It has always been like that. If you say, 'Buy Radion!', they say, 'Oh yeah I get it.' But what's so ironic is that art and advertising are the same visual language. You know what I mean? You get a black screen for twenty minutes and people say, 'What's this, then? Benson & Hedges? Can't be… Is it Coalite?' But if it happens to be art, then all of a sudden it doesn't make sense any more.

It's a double-edged sword. Take Silk Cut billboard advertising: they fetishize their product, transmute it into high art and abstract minimalism. There is one particular Silk Cut ad. that always reminds me of Fontana's blank canvases in the late 1950s, the one with the slit cut down it. You've used billboards in your work before, haven't you? At the show at the Gagosian gallery in New York.
I've been asked to do billboards quite a few times before. I originally did that billboard piece for the BBC, but it didn't work out very well.

Initially, I got really excited about it, but the whole thing ended up being more about the programme than the work. The sites they set up weren't very good. When they set up my piece they didn't even print the work, they just used photographs, so within ten minutes the machine was totally fucked. I think it was up for three weeks and it only worked for ten minutes. Eventually, I decided to have it made properly as an artwork, because I knew that the gallery in New York was big enough to take it. With hindsight, I wish I had also had piped music playing at the same time: that would have finished it off perfectly.

Give it that authentic supermarket feel.
Exactly. Equally, I like the idea of it working outdoors. I've just been talking to this guy who runs a site in Times Square. He has a billboard that is eight thousand square feet and I may end up using that. One thing I do love though, is the advertising on London buses. The way they all have that big fucking round thing in the middle, like an air vent on the side of the bus or something, that the photographer has to try and incorporate into their work. I love that because if you do the photograph and ignore the vent then you have this big round mole on the woman's face.

What about Jenny Holzer's political interventions in similar commercial sites in New York?
I think she's kind of up her own arse; just trying too hard to turn the whole thing into an artwork. I much prefer the idea of using a big photograph of, say, Sarah Lucas smoking – it would just make such a great billboard without any tampering. I like the idea of direct communication with people on the street. You could even have a slogan that said 'Go home!

Your wife loves you.' [laughs] That's much more honest. Advertising is fantastic when it's used as a way to sell something that somebody has already got inside themselves. A feeling that exists within, rather than a product that you have to go to a shop and buy.

The Surrealists picked up on that: mannequins in shop windows...

Yeah. I think it was Malcolm McLaren who once said to me that he was planning to make a series on TV about all the adverts that the Surrealists made. They all made commercials – Dalí, Max Ernst, Man Ray – they all did it.

What do you think of Benetton's advertising campaign?

I think it is what I get accused of all the time.

Sensationalism?

Yeah, shock value for the sake of it, but I don't think that's true. Definitely not as obvious as Benetton. I mean, it is a successful campaign, but sometimes it can be just too easy: too easy to have a picture of a bloke with his fucking head blown off and then add the line 'Just use Tampax.' You know that everybody is going to talk about it, that all the media are going to buy into it. In fact, thinking about it, that's a great idea, maybe I should do it! But that's what I love about advertising.

But on the whole, do you think an advertising director has as much freedom as an artist?

There are an infinite number of ways to get to the same point. I think it all comes down to painting.

Painting?

Yeah, I'm sure there was a time when you would do a painting of a landscape and put it on the wall and someone would walk past and say, 'Nice window, mate' and then on closer inspection say; 'Fuck me. It's not a window! I can't believe it! Where did you get that mate? It's amazing, fantastic, had me fooled: great!' But now paintings have become exactly like advertising. Pollock fucked it with his drip paintings – that distance between him and the brush – drip, drip, drip – he fucked it.

You mean that painting became so self-referential that it dug its own grave.

But it is still alive.

Entombed?

And now, it has transformed itself into an artistic logo. That's what my spot paintings are all about: at one level they point to the death of painting, but at the same time they are the most celebratory logo for an artist: *Infinite Variety Alive; The Action of the World on Things* – fantastic! I mean they just look great on the wall. I don't even have to make any decisions anymore. I don't even have to paint them myself.

Like the cigarette butts.

Yeah. Someone once said to me that a photograph that I had taken of this cigarette butt was like a self portrait. I suppose it is, but only in the same way that wiping your arse is a self portrait. But I have to say, all those butts are very personal. I've smoked every one.

I heard recently that one of your signed cigarette butts you did last year for *The Idler* magazine sold for a couple of hundred pounds at auction.

Well, that was a very important cigarette in my life, that one. [laughs] But I like the idea that I'm playing with the companies in a subliminal way; that cigarette companies are glorifying and sexualizing all these images of cigarettes and I'm glorifying the dirty end of it and using all their techniques. If you can do it fast enough and well enough you can beat them at their own game, maybe.

Exactly.

Yeah. I did a whole book on cigarettes for my show with Bruno Bischofberger in Switzerland; it was essential that they were photographed only when they had died out. None of them are lit, none of them are smoking, they have all reached their final conclusion – five hundred and twenty pages of actual-sized cigarettes on white backgrounds. There is no text but you can read it if you look hard enough. Every cigarette

The Problems with
Relationships, *1995*

has a story to tell, it's own indelible mark.
**That reminds me of the hands-off
detachment of Warhol, Koons, even Dalí.
They subsumed themselves into consumer
culture to such an extent that they
actually became it. Do you see yourself in
that category?**
All of those artists gave up their own idea
of themselves, which is perfect, but I like other
people too much. In New York last year I made
an eight-foot-diameter ashtray filled with
normal-sized cigarette butts. I shipped them all
as art freight, fifteen bin bags full of butts from
the Groucho club in London. Just before the
final date for the shipment, the gallery in New
York phoned me and asked if we could save
some money by getting cigarette butts from
surrounding restaurants in New York, but I
refused because, for me, art should always be
made from the objects that surround you. Then,
after the show had closed, I got another phone
call from a museum that had bought the piece
and were in the process of installing it. They
wanted to know whether they had to install the
fag butts in exactly the same way as they were
laid out in the accompanying transparency. I
was so tempted to say 'yes' but, because I used to
work in a gallery myself, I knew that some poor
cunt would be made to go through thousands of
butts saying, 'Not that one, is it that one?' They
would do it! It's completely insane.
**Most art institutions are still hung up on
this notion of individual genius.**
But then again, genius is such a great idea. I'm
thirty-two and I'm in this position, and you take
a step back and say to yourself, 'I've got two
choices: I've caned the art world, fuck it, I've got
to the top.' But then you go, 'Hmmmm, I've got
two choices...'

Hmmmm *[laughs]*

… that's what you do, you go 'Hmmmm, I've got two ways of looking at this. I am either a genius – hmmmm, fantastic – or the art world is incapable of dealing with the kind of art that is going on today.' My answer is the art world is fucked. I'm not a genius. I definitely believe in freedom but not genius. I'm thirty-two and I'm enjoying myself. I was listening to pop music and watching TV before I ever went into an art gallery. Galleries are just boring shops.

Are you planning to do any more films in the near future?

I would really like to, but I have to say, film is a very difficult thing. When I did *Hanging Around*, it started from the script up. I mean, it's the same as making art, you've got to have a story you want to tell and I just didn't have a specific enough idea in mind when I started. I only had a rough idea of the story and a rough idea of the people that I wanted to work with. When I did it, I didn't direct properly, in fact it was a bit like when I curated 'Freeze', but then the artists I was working with were all incredibly talented so it was easy. When it came to the film, it was more difficult to manoeuvre. At the crunch, I was more into people having a good time. It's not so much that I want to make a film. I just want to know that I can because it is such a massive visual thing in our lives.

What about the TV sculpture for Channel 4? That was a great piece.

In the end, that worked out perfectly but took a long time to get right. To begin with, I got an old TV set and put all these flies in it. Channel 4 wanted to create this feel of your TV being an artwork but because we are all so used to looking at a screen, it didn't seem to work. It just looked like the bridge on the Starship

Beautiful fuck the psycho's wife, and the psycho finds out painting, *1996*

Enterprise or something. At that point, I didn't have any effects on it at all, so I went and got an old bike light, one of those flashing red ones, to give it a bit of drama. That meant that you could watch it for about twenty seconds until you became bored. Then I got a couple of cigarettes and threw them in the back so that it was constantly smoking, but it was still not working; perhaps you could watch it for a minute and a half before getting bored. Finally, in post production I hit upon the idea of adding these blue flashes that killed the flies randomly. That was boring after about three minutes, so I was just about ready to discard the whole thing when Jarvis Cocker saw it with Ant and they asked to do the music. They came back a week later with a version of 'Flight of the Bumble Bee' that ran all the way through the piece, slowly building up to this crescendo – a Neil Diamond disco version with loads of channel-surfing over the top. It evolved slowly into being ninety per cent sound, an audio monster that I eventually titled *No God*. The whole thing was a happy accident and a true collaboration.

It's like the beginning of *Doctor Who*... blurring the boundaries. Is it music? Is it art? Is it TV? I'm very happy with it.

That seems to be the basis of the British art scene, cross-collaborations, breaking down those boundaries. Sometimes it works, sometimes it's self-congratulatory shit, but those crossovers often define the work. Where you are now is a unique position not seen in this country since Hockney. You could break out and go in whatever direction you want right now.

But anyone can. Jeremy Paxman asked me that question in an interview and I just replied that I have always been in that position. I'm lucky, I've always gone, 'Fuck off: this is what I think.'

Do you think you have changed the way people in this country look at artists?

Yes. You have to step over the boundaries to know where they are. I think that I'm doing what any artist from the past would be doing if he were alive today. You make art from what is around you – you can make art about anything. There is just an incredible amount of visual stuff around and if you're not using it, you're kind of missing something.

Does fame restrict you?

No, it gets easy at the top because you have all the keys; you have freedom.

What about the question of assimilation. Do you not fear that your own work will, in the end, become repackaged, stripped of its meaning?

Not at all, because it's not about assimilation; there are no boundaries – all the boundaries are in our own heads. I mean if I walk around a corner in the summer and suddenly become confronted by a massive bunch of flowers, they just go 'Blahhhhhhh, Nenenenenene, Wooooo, Wahhhhh, Wooooo, Wahhhhh, Tick... tick... tick...' You know what I mean? They scream at you, scream at everybody. Call me an old-fashioned colourist, *[laughs]* but when I walk around that corner I say to myself, 'Shit, there should at least be a sign up that says "Warning: Flowers in Sunlight".' Then people could say, 'Oh flowers, I better prepare myself.' *[laughs]* I mean, does everybody get that or is it just me? Daffodils in sunlight – or are they just being shocking for the sake of it? OK, you might not get it from daffodils, but you must get it from cherry blossom?

I'm with you there: sensory overload.

I mean, how ridiculous is that, blossom? One minute they are there, next minute they're not. It's like, fucking hell, it's a monster, it's a visual monster!

I never knew you were such a naturalist.

It's just over the top. Outrageous. That's why we need public warning signs. I'm certain that everybody gets that feeling and I see it as my job to remind them because so often they all walk around as if they've somehow forgotten.

That's what made your severed cow so powerful: veal calves, BSE, severed cow... it all seems to fit together somehow.

You can get it with anything, though. It's the same with tulips. I mean what a fucking stupid shape! Who decided they should be red? Magnolia or fawn, fine, but *red*?

They are but prostitutes for the bees.

Exactly. Sluts. People often say to me, 'Your work's just sensational.' If they said, 'You are sensational', I would say, 'Thanks – so are you.' But when they say it about your art, you begin to think it's a problem, but is it fuck a problem. The world is sensational.

People often like to be shocked, though, because it provides them with a yardstick against which to judge their own moral standing. There is a definite double standard at work in the media.

As my friend Ant said, 'It all comes down to the X-factor.'

What's that?

The X-factor is a bloke who has tons of money, big boat, houses everywhere but he's having a shit life, and then a guy selling *The Big Issue* who is having a laugh, enjoying his life. That's the X-factor: it's the bits you miss.

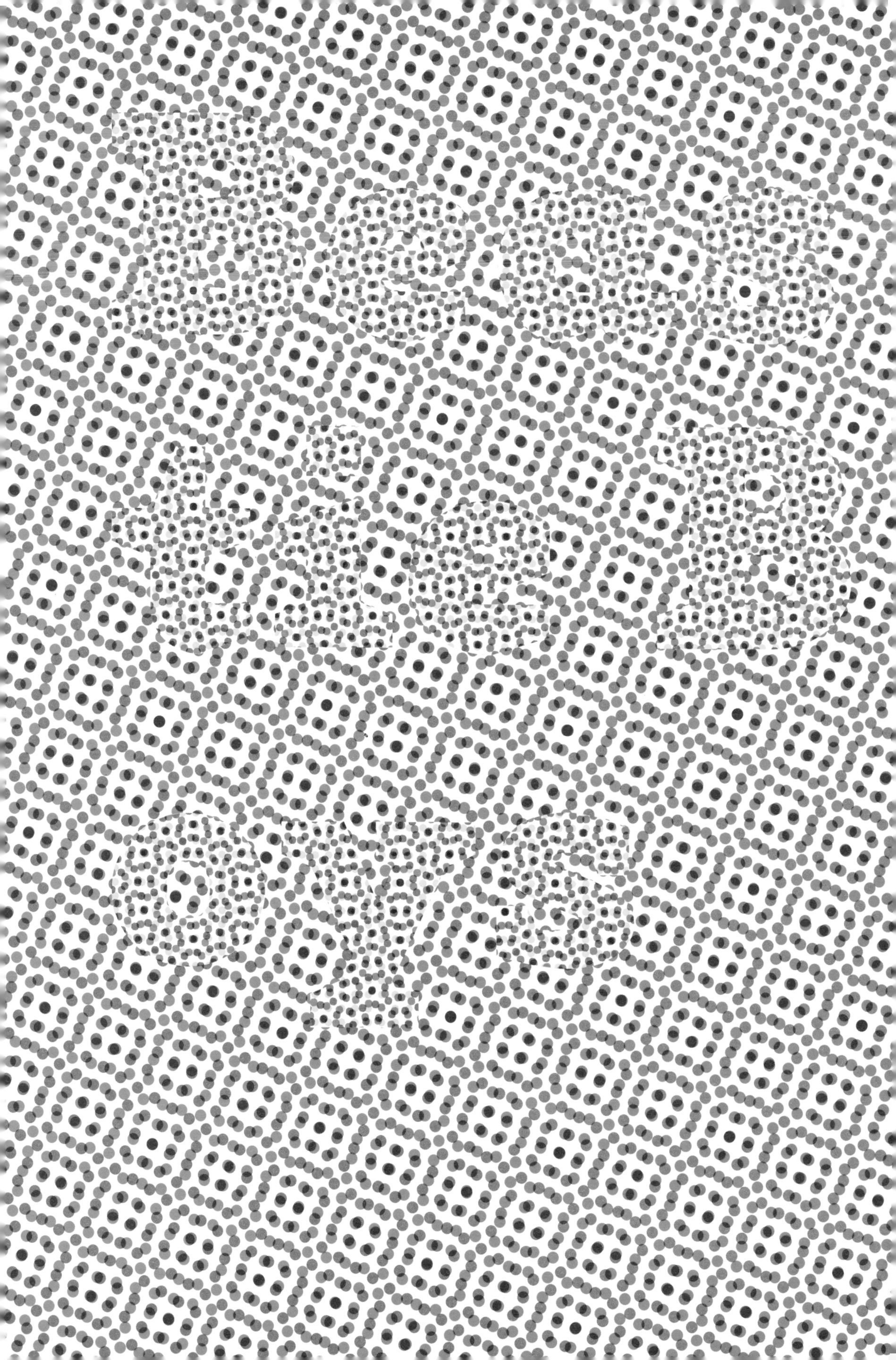

December 1997
Introduction and interview | Simon Price

Back in 1986, when they were still The! Bea! Stie! Boys!, Mike D, MCA and Ad Rock were three Bud-swillin', gun-totin', porn-collectin', spastic-tauntin', parent-annoyin', New York Jewish wiggas with the ethics of Tasmanian devils on crack. As 1998 dawns, Mike Diamond, Adam Yauch and Adam Horowitz (well, maybe not Adam Horowitz) are paragons of moral rectitude, penitently disavowing their sexist excesses and patiently campaigning for the liberation of the Tibetan people from Chinese oppression. They've stopped fighting for their right to party and started fighting for human rights. On their debut, Licensed to Ill, it was: 'I got money and juice, twin sisters in my bed/Their father had an eppy, so I shot him in the head.' By their last record, Ill Communication, it is: 'I want to say a little something that's long overdue/The disrespect to women has got to be through/To all the mothers and the sisters and the wives and friends/I want to offer my love and respect to the end.' Diamond and Yauch are born-again style gurus and moral crusaders. It isn't just one of the biggest transformations in pop-cultural history, but two of them.

According to Yauch, there was no Road to Damascus moment of revelation. 'If anything, it was probably more subconscious than anything else. It was never a decision. But the way we used to be was somehow intended to be more rebellious against the stiffness of society, the rigidity of certain ways of thinking, like "Oh, that's not proper", and thumbing your nose at what you're not supposed to do. But I think that somewhere over the years, we realized that some of that stuff was destructive. That's where the difference came: when we started to have more awareness of how it was affecting other people.'

Diamond agrees: 'If you put what we were

then and what we are now next to each other, that's two different extremes, and the juxtaposition can appear weird. The flipside is that people respond to us, people come to us and say, "It's weird, because when you were into that, I was into that, and now you're into this, I'm into this." We're changing all the time. It's the nature of things . On the other hand, we do get people going, "Hey, when you coming out with another 'Brass Monkey' joint?"'

Sartorially, too, The Beasties have reformed themselves from 1986's fashion outlaws, sporting their crass, vulgar, white-trash take on B-boy style – a Day-Glo explosion of Kangols, chains and stolen VW badges – into the epitome of understated skate cool (a dress code that, if they didn't invent it, they've certainly done more than anyone else to popularize).

Yauch and Diamond have left Adam Horowitz in New York working on beats for the new album while they promote the extra-curricular activities that make up the Beastie Boys' empire. Yauch is in London to publicize the film and CD of the Concert for Tibet he organized in the summer. Diamond is here to promote the latest flurry of activities around his Grand Royal corporation. Grand Royal is two things: an indifferent record label (Luscious Jackson... but on the other hand, Bis), and a glossy periodical, one of the coolest magazines in the known universe.

The genius of Grand Royal lies in its wit, its infectious in-jokes, but above all its obsessiveness. Recent issues have dwelt in startling detail on Beastie fixations such as Lee 'Scratch' Perry, Polaroid cameras, Bruce Lee, how to swim for free in Los Angeles hotels and a nine-page illustrated study of the meaning of popular American hairdon't, the 'mullet' (a word that has since entered the language). The most recent issue sees

Yauch interviewing the Dalai Lama. The joy of reading Grand Royal *is in knowing that someone who thinks like you do can gain the power and wherewithal to do this kind of thing.*

Diamond and Yauch represent a dichotomy within The Beastie Boys. Diamond, no longer the chubby, overgrown bleach-blond B-boy who can't believe he's been allowed into the corporate boardroom, has slimmed down, grown a Wildean mane, and bought a suit. He's every bit the high-flying music biz executive. Even his initials are 'MD'. Yauch, the soft-spoken Buddhist, with his big soft-brown cow eyes and woolly Kangol ski sweater, is as cuddly and placid as a koala. It's like having Gordon Gecko and Mahatma Gandhi in the same band. (Third member, Bart Simpson, has stayed behind in NYC.)

So what, in their heart of hearts, do they actually care about: good causes, or good clothes? Trainers, or Tibetans? Do The Beastie Boys really give a fuck? Torches in the eyes, guns to necks, time for some answers.

The businessman: Mike Diamond

Dazed & Confused | **Sum up the Grand Royal aesthetic in one neat soundbite.**
Mike Diamond | Impossible! No, I'll say... planetary intergalactic, intergalactic planetary. That's my answer.
It's a very old skool aesthetic. The Beasties dig Biz Markie, Space Invaders and Bruce Lee. They do not dig Puff Daddy, Sony Playstations or Jean Claude Van Damme.
I know what you mean, but that's probably just a generational thing. I'm sure *Dazed & Confused* is probably the same. To a degree, we're all showing the influences that we grew up on. Just taking things that are integral, and putting them out there.
Is anything beyond rehabilitation for ever? Where's the cut-off point? Would you have serious worries about endorsing something, say, from the year 1991, or 1987?
I'm sure that'll come around. Maybe not necessarily from us, but from somebody.
When you came back in 92, wearing 70s Adidas, no one else was doing it.
The 70s gear came with the 'Hey Ladies' video. I don't think we were the only people doing that. I dunno, maybe I'm being delusional, but a lot of

things came from our friends, who are equally passionate and into the same things at the same moment. We just have access to the bigger platform. Just because we've done them doesn't mean someone else wouldn't have. If we hadn't gotten on the mic as white kids, MC-ing about that stuff, I'm sure other white kids would have filled that role. Maybe some other band would have come through wearing, I dunno, Puma Clydes instead of Adidas Sambas.
Presumably the reason you can't rehabilitate anything too recent is that people might think you haven't stopped wearing it from first time round – you just don't know any better.
I was joking with Eli from X-Large, that we should have held onto our first run of X-Large baggies, below-the-knee shorts, because probably by next summer they'll be back.
And you'll be there in your stolen VW badge...
Yeeeeeeeahhh.
Retro – being fetishist about cool shit from the past – is a very white thing. For instance, if Isaac Hayes played a gig tomorrow, you wouldn't see many black people there.
It boggles my mind, but I know that does go on. Hip-hop culture, or R&B culture has always been engineered to be constantly in the present. Although if Isaac Hayes played the Apollo tomorrow, he'd sell it out, not just Manhattan. The older black audience grew up on his shit. Unfortunately, he wouldn't be relevant to the kids who grew up on Blackstreet.
You once defined the concept of the Fashion Risk (wearing something no one else considers cool, in the hope that you can carry it off and make it ultra-cool). What was the last FR you took? And did you carry it off?
It's all about the Fashion Risk. The people who really come up in this world are the ones who take the Fashion Risk. That's the heart of B-boy fashion. Like the guy who first wore a sheepskin hat or a sheepskin coat, if we're talking old skool terminology, or the first guy who wore Helly Hansen, if we're talking newer skool. I mean, Helly Hansen was made for people who boat – rich people on boats. Like the first B-boy to wear Helly Hansen was taking a risk, co-opting this look that was meant for white people

on their huge yachts. And it worked, he made it fly. Those are the risk-takers. The movement-makers. The feet-breakers. I think you're looking at a walking fuckin' Fashion Risk right now! And as for whether I've carried it off, that's for you to judge! Actually, that's the subject of great controversy. The hair, the suit, the whole shit.

The hair's quite Oscar Wilde. Very topical.

Really? I had no idea. I don't even know what he looks like.

Like all great bands, you've created a self-sufficient, hermetic, private universe around yourselves. Do you find it possible to shut out contemporary mainstream culture altogether and exist completely in your invented world?

I think people think that we do! I guess that's the perception. Yeah, what we do is, we actually have horse blinkers on and we go from our apartments filled with eight million pairs of sneakers and covered in Bruce Lee posters, to the studio with Lee Perry records lying everywhere... No, there is part of that, otherwise we wouldn't express it, but there is a lot else there too.

The Beastie aesthetic has almost been too successful. You can buy instant Beastie cool off the rail now: wear the clothes, listen to the records, read the magazine... Doesn't that defeat the whole point (to invent your own definition of cool)?

Actually, yeah. You see, that's really not the intention. And if that's what it's become, we'll have to stop doing it. And that's why we have to slow a few of those things down. However, I think people like Levi's are trying to sell ready-made cool much more than us.

On the other hand, how would you react to the accusation of elitism?

It's hard, because in part I think that's fair. The purpose isn't just to be like other people by saying 'You're excluded, fuck you, you're worthless.' That's the negative side of elitism. The other part is the element of, when we started the band, it was just like an inside joke to us: 'Wouldn't it be funny if, like, we had no idea what we were doing. We'll make a punk rock band, we'll try MC-ing.' It was never, like, 'We're gonna be the best MCs ever.' Each endeavour along the way has been similar in approach. It starts on a modest scale and gets bigger. Like, even with the Concert for Tibet, we'd done a couple of songs with Tibetan monk samples on, and it was, like, 'Let's do something more appropriate.' There are in-jokes, on the records and in the magazine, but hopefully it's... an inclusive elitism.

When Adam converted to Buddhism, did the rest of you think 'uh-oh!'?

I think the word 'convert' is wrong because he never had any other religion. I'd have to check the dictionary, but I think convert implies to transform from one to the other. Our reaction was 'The guy's a freak! You freak motherfucker!' Nah, it wasn't like he came into the studio one day and said 'Guys, it's like this, things have changed.' It was a very gradual process. And it's not like it conflicts with the band. Part of our job is to figure out how to evolve as a band, and incorporate different things that we learn and become involved with along the way.

The philosopher: Adam Yauch

Dazed & Confused | **You recently said that one of the lessons of Buddhism is to develop the mind and soul, and not be attached to material things. But The Beastie Boys are one of the most materialistic bands I can think of. You're obsessed with cool things, cool stuff...**

Adam Yauch | Mmm-hmm. Yeah. I think we do put forward a lot of stuff as being important that isn't really, necessarily, and people should probably take what we say in that realm with a grain of salt. It doesn't really matter what sneakers you're wearing. The thing that is really significant is how one affects other people. If I meet somebody who has some really cool sneakers, I'm really not going to be that impressed, and if somebody has some sneakers that are doofy-looking, then it's really not going to bug me too much. What I'm going to notice is whether that person is a kind person or not. You know, we talk about that stuff for fun sometimes, but that's just talkin' shit. It's OK to pick out clothes that you think are cool, but it's important not to get attached to that stuff.

Are you sick of being condemned forever to be those three guys who bounce around on stage and shout a lot?

Usually when it's expected of us is exactly when we stop. Like we did another interview earlier where I think the guy wanted us to be really silly, and I immediately didn't feel like it. But in the right atmosphere, it's fun to be that way.

It takes a certain maturity to really know how to enjoy being childish.

I think there's a big, big difference between 'childish' and 'childlike'. I think the word 'childlike' represents the positive aspects of being a child, and 'childish' is the negative aspects. I think the one is very important to reap and cultivate, and the other is very important to get beyond and grow out of. When you look at somebody like the Dalai Lama, he's very childlike in that he laughs in this completely innocent way with no negative intentions towards anyone else. You see this often with monks: because they are not caught up in the entanglements of the world, their motivation is very pure. Like when a baby really looks at you and smiles, the smile comes from the kid's heart. It's often harder for older people to have that. I think 'childish' is a whole other thing. That has to do with selfishness, and being upset if you don't get your way.

Mike D once said you were all dissatisfied with your secular Jewish backgrounds, that you were almost too devoid of any spirituality. Was that part of the attraction of Buddhism?

Mmm, that doesn't sound strictly accurate. I beg to differ, sir! I think in a sense I was raised on some very good principles, similar principles to what's within most religions. Things like, my mom would say: 'Do unto others as you'd have them do unto you.' Basic principles of respect for other people. For me personally, with a good teacher, with a religion I feel comfortable with, there are things that I can gain, especially from a teacher like the Dalai Lama, which are on a much higher level of clarity than I could achieve otherwise. It's not necessarily for everybody.

The way you chose the Tibetan cause seems almost random: you happened to be holidaying there. If you'd been backpacking in Central America, it could have been Nicaragua.

I spent a number of years studying different religions, from 1988, just after *Licensed to Ill*, up to 1992. I took a trip to India, Bali and Nepal because I was already interested in the philosophies that came from that part of the world. Then I met Tibetan people, and became very interested in Tibetan Buddhism specifically, because many of the principles that made sense to me in other religions, like karma and reincarnation, were very solidly put within that religion. So I continued to study that for four years before I made the decision to actually become a Buddhist. But I don't think that's a decision anyone should take lightly. It's a really serious decision; a life decision, like getting married, that one should not mess around with.

So you weren't just in the Himalayas for the snow-boarding season?

No. It wasn't just like meeting someone on the street and becoming interested in it. The reason I went to that part of the world was to be in a place where religion was more natural, more synonymous with the culture.

Buddhism is one of the three main destinations for bewildered rock stars. The other two are rehab and psychiatric treatment (some try them all).

Ha ha! What about Christianity? Don't a lot of them get into that? A lot of them get into Hindu also. Or is that jazz musicians, do you think?!

If it wasn't for the religious aspect, if the

Tibetan people were just another race being oppressed by the Chinese (like, for instance, the East Mongolians), would you care as much?

If the Tibetan struggle were a violent struggle, I would not care as much as I do. I would care somewhat, that they were suffering, but in the same way that I care about the Chinese who are torturing the Tibetans. Because in a sense, the Chinese are causing their own suffering, generating their own karma, so I feel sorry for them. But the reason that I think the Tibetan struggle is so significant is because it's based on compassion and on non-violence, and that's why it has something to offer the rest of the world.

On the Tibetan Freedom Concert film, a monk says, 'If you throw a stone in the air...' and a group of American teens sagely answer '... it falls back down on you.' They're wrong. If you throw a stone in the air, it usually comes down on someone else's head. Crime does pay. The meek don't inherit the earth, the rich do. Those clichés are meant to keep us passive, keep us in our place. Like The Temptations said, you make your own heaven and hell right here on earth.

I don't believe that's true. I don't believe in reality that those things are in fact the case. On an immediate basis it may pay. You may rob someone and get some money, go spend it and be happy for a minute, but I think ultimately you'll wind up feeling extreme unhappiness from that. And you can test those principles if you don't believe it, see if it makes you happy. But chances are, if you do things that you know are destructive to other people, other beings, even other animals, whatever, you will feel that same energy coming back at you. It's a good principle to test, though. Test it in your own time...

Why hasn't the American government backed the Tibetan cause? You'd think they'd be grateful for any stick with which to beat Communism?

There were so many Tibetans who did want to fight the Chinese, early on in the struggle, after Tibet was invaded, and Nixon's CIA was helping to train them. But for the last twenty years, the struggle has been non-violent. Nowadays, American business stands to make a fortune out of China, and unfortunately that has now overridden any other consideration. Corporations are making contributions to our elected officials, and our officials are doing what the corporations want them to do. That's what this cause is about: putting pressure on our government to act responsibly.

Violence seems to work. In Ireland, in South Africa, in the Holy Land, former so-called 'terrorist leaders' have been welcomed as mainstream statesmen.

Uh... They succeed in getting into power, but I don't know that they succeed in changing the negative momentum in that society. It's just maybe a shift of power from one negatively motivated set of hands to another. And I think that sometimes, through using violence, it changes the goals. The goals are destroyed.

What do you think the proper reaction should have been to the beating of Rodney King?

Non-violent protest. Speaking out. Demonstrations, letter-writing campaigns. Non-violence does not mean passivity. It means doing very specific things, speaking out to raise people's awareness, or to block certain things by sitting in a place to stop somebody from moving somewhere. It means trying to change what is going on without harming anyone.

So if the American army did what they did in Kuwait, and tried to liberate Tibet, you wouldn't support that?

No. I would not support that. I think there may have been times in history when violence has somehow helped. But I think that as humanity has evolved, becoming more and more techno-logically advanced, as the world is becoming smaller and our weapons are becoming more and more powerful – chemical weapons, nuclear weapons – the potential for destruction is so high that humanity has to transform itself into a non-violent society in order to survive. We need to do away with these old, animalistic motivations of greed and selfishness because our technology is too advanced for us to be running around like these childish beings that we've been for so long. That's why this struggle is so symbolic.

Sorry for cross-examining you like that, it's just...

That's OK. I think it's best. Let's shake hands.

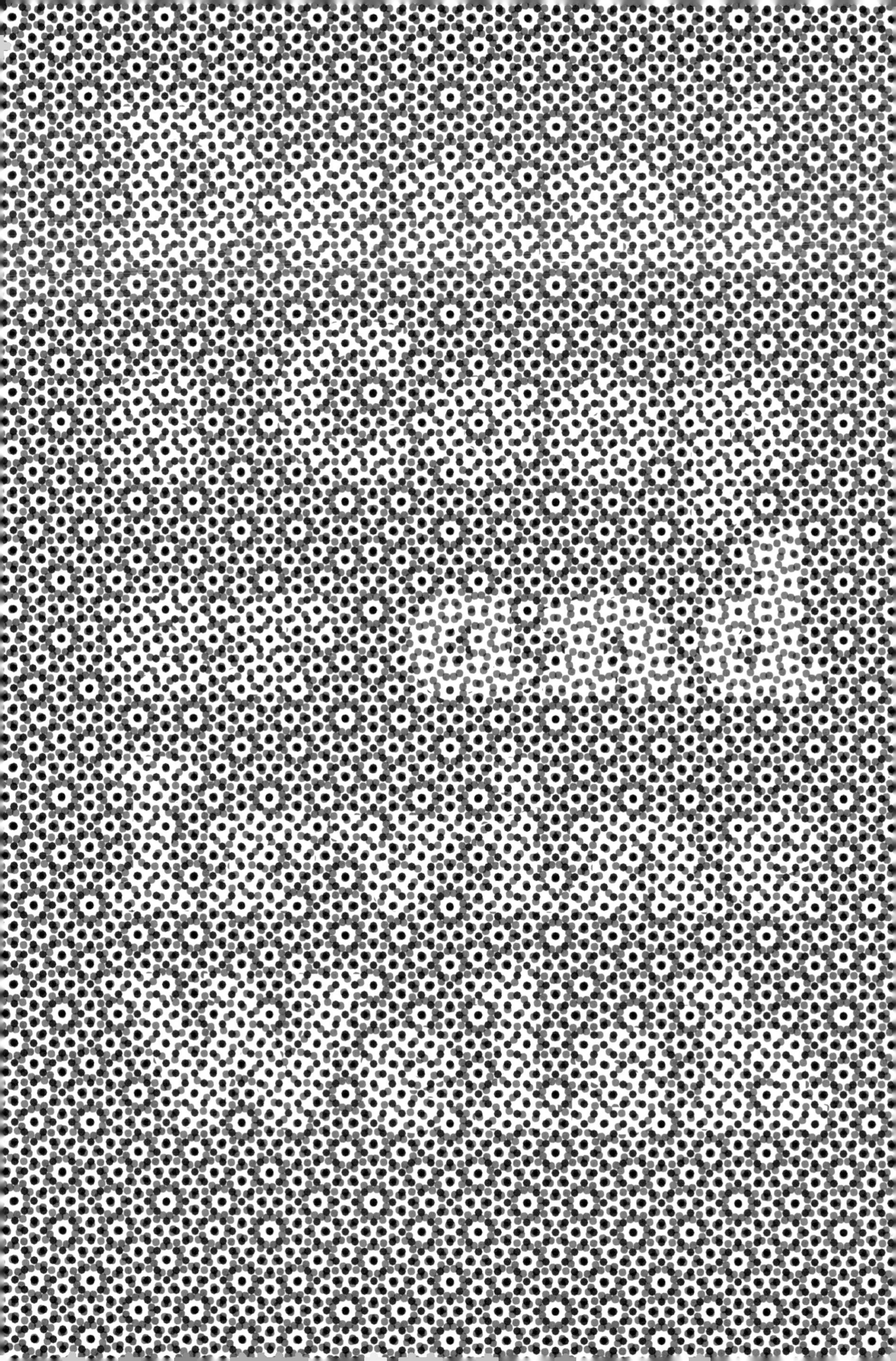

Los Angeles writer Dennis Cooper is often
indolently tagged to such figures as William
Burroughs or Jean Genet. The only real
resemblance he bears to these antecedents is
that he is a true original. He is also one of the
few cutting-edge artists today still, thankfully,
persevering with that most beautiful and
challenging medium: the novel.

I first came across Cooper's writing a few
years back, and checked out one of his readings
in Edinburgh. The one thing that struck me was
the audience: firstly, how small it was; secondly,
how everyone there seemed to be a writer, or a
musician, or artist of some sort. It was
reminiscent of Brian Eno's comment about
the Velvet Underground's first album: hardly
anybody bought it, but all those who did tended
to go out and make records of their own. In the
same manner, Cooper's writings have a powerful
cult influence, which stretches way beyond their
sales profile.

As is the general nature of such scenarios,
there has been no shortage of voices suggesting
that this is a far from positive influence. It's true
to say that Cooper pushes the limits of liberal
tolerance as far as they can go; obsession, disen-
gagement and mental collapse invariably
manifest themselves in torture, murder and
paedophilia. Some would argue that this is one of
the key functions of art. Personally, I've always
inclined to the view that anything can, and
should, go onto the blank page, if the intent is
honest. I also think that most people can distin-
guish between genuine artistic intent and crass
exploitation. Powerful figures in politics, business, and the media are fond of hamming up the
extent to which art forms can exert a (negative)
influence on people, usually in order to smoke-
screen their own dirty deeds and shortcomings.

I found Dennis Cooper's new book, Guide,
his most unsettling, not due to its content, but
because I felt that the writer employed a stylistic
device that served to blur the lines between
selective internal biography (i.e. personal fantasy
and obsession) and fiction. In Guide, the author
attributes his own name, 'Dennis', to the central
protagonist and narrative voice. This was also
the case in his earlier novel, Frisk. This character
then obsesses over real people like the guitarist
from Menswear, the actor Leonardo DiCaprio,
and most chillingly, the bassist Alex James from
Blur (or, more accurately, the media construction
of those people), with the standard Dennis
Cooper results. By taking this route, I felt the
writer had introduced an unsettling and perhaps
unnecessary element to his fiction and could
even be guilty of 'stalking through the page'.
I couldn't really see what the point of doing this
was, outside of unsettling or confusing the
people in question. This was one of the major
themes I wanted to explore with Cooper. What
follows is a discussion that took place in a North
London pub. (Incidentally, in person Dennis
Cooper was humorous, relaxed and playful, far
removed from the intense, tortured predators
who are the protagonists of his novels.)

Irvine Welsh | **Maybe the best thing to do is
for me to pick out some themes from the
book. One thing is that you use your own
name for the narrator. And you've got
characters who can be identified as real
people, various Britpop stars. Do you see
that as a literary mechanism? Can you
explain why you've changed your approach?**
Dennis Cooper | I guess I have to say that all
the books are part of the same project. It's like
the same book written five times. In this case,
mostly I was interested in just exposing the
mind creating the novel. It was a device. I had
this idea about making this book sort of
'architectural'. I was thinking a lot about
building this sculptural thing, out of words...
so that it was somewhere in between the spaces.
I wanted to have the mind working, which is
like the depth, the bottom of it, and then
I wanted the pop-cultural references to give
it this real, light, recognizable surface, but
hopefully for it not to be about either one.
It's kind of like a film. You can see these

major representations of rock stars. It's like their media stereotype characters that come out.

Yeah, they're totally cartoons. Everything they say is, like, the most clichéd.

That's what I found most unsettling about the book – that you're rushing between 'fact' and fiction. It's quite a dangerous, subversive device because it breaks down the division between the two. I've never met Alex James but I know Damon Albarn quite well. To see them popping up as characters in a work of fiction is quite strange. What was the effect?

It brought the excesses of fiction and made them more real. It brought together these two worlds, the real world and the created world.

The Blur characters and the other characters are so falsified. Ostensibly, all the thought processes, all the nuances, the apologizing and the confessions and all that – they're not true. I wanted the Blur thing to kind of meet with 'the other'. One of the characters says that what he really wants is to be at that moment when he is about to die and know what that's like. I was thinking about that for the whole book. And acid was a great device for creating that space. The book's doing that on every level.

Have you felt that kind of frustration, when you're tripping on acid, and you're in this world where you're seeing things in a different way, and when you come back, it's like waking up from a dream, and it's all slipped through your hands? You think – is there a way I can access that, and take it back. You get the idea that there's so much here. You can break through the barriers but there's no terms of reference to bring it back.

Yes. That's what the book's really about. And how you isolate? There are things in the book where everything just goes completely haywire... but it's all in a language of sanity.

Yeah, I was totally trying for that. I mean, that whole thing in the book is true... about how I took acid every day for a month and had a nervous breakdown. At the end of it, I couldn't talk for about six months, I was so wiped out. That was my big attempt to... bring it back. I thought if you took enough of it, you would just stay there. My mind had been in that state so long that I thought it would always be in that state. Of course, that's the kind of thing you think when you're on acid!

You think to yourself – why is there this sort of inhibition? Is it a way of maintaining your sanity, is it something that evolution has given to us in degrees? Or have we not developed in an intellectual way, and in a social way, to be able to process that information?

Language is so inadequate to get it out. It's so tough. Also, sex is such an un-acid thing. It's so weird to bring that into the equation – what would happen to sex if you were on acid? When I took acid I was never horny.

There's too much going on to construct a sexual scenario.

There's no, like, sensuality when you're on acid. When I've had sex on acid it's been like, Jesus Christ – nipples, they're so weird...! How did you manage to write about acid? Because I ended up not describing the trip. Just doing the before and the come-down. I couldn't figure out a way to do it right. I thought if maybe I just suggested it by its absence that would work. But you did it – did you find it easy?

I think I went about it kind of backwards.

I used that empty, tired, brittle feeling and that sense of loss, of not being able to put something back. And then I thought about that kind of overwhelming period – even on your first acid trip – you always feel that it's not new, you've done it before somehow. Maybe it's a childlike thing – seeing the world afresh. As weird as it is, you feel that you've been here before, but you can't think how or why. All your reference points have been wiped out, but there's a sense of recognition. I think I started off with that sense of recognition to construct it. Basically, it was almost as it happened – the mood swings, and then feeling comfortable within a certain space. Then suddenly your vision of that space becomes affected and you'll want to move somewhere else... but also that total lack of ability to move: trying to go two blocks from one pub to the next can take about eight months.

The only way I could do it was formally, with all the spaces and separations. That was the only way I could get a sense of things being missing.

I like the bit where you have the response to letters of the alphabet – you start to look at things in that acid kind of way. You don't know whether you're being really profound or really silly. You look at it and think it's just a set of symbols: it's the meaning that's attached to it that's important. Language isn't. What you eventually do when you start talking about acid is you simulate a trip in a way. You move into that state of consciousness. Is it profound or useful? Or is it there just to give us a good time? To forget about... is this reality, is this the higher state? Is this really important, or is it just a lot of shit?

I know that when you're on acid, you try to note down the thought, and then when you come down, it just says something like 'orange'. I mean, it's amazing how beyond language it is. It's so hard to write about.

Within that 'orange' are so many textures and moods, emotions and twists...

But it felt like enough to write 'orange'. I was trying to figure out how to write *about* acid, reading all this stuff from the 60s – Thomas McGwain, Terry Southern. And then a friend of mine started to read Ivy Compton Burnett – and that was so terrific because that was the complete opposite, it was so fucking anal. And I thought, that's great, I'll write about acid in that way. It was the only way I could think about doing it – do the exact wrong thing.

You say that you're trying to write the same book in different ways – did you see a progression in the novels?

Absolutely. There's this guy I used to know, and he's sort of my muse – George Miles – I've written about him tons of times. He's like the main character in *Closer*, and I mention him in *Guide*, too. He's been the poet type of all the characters I've written about in a way. I lost track of him a long time ago, and earlier this year I found out that he killed himself ten years ago, so this book ends up being about that, because I had to write about it. So it's sort of a weird conclusion. It's kind of a memorial.

It's like there are things that you *have* to write and things that you *want* to write. They can be different things. The first thing I did was what I had to write, and the others have been what I wanted to write.

All these books for me have been things I've just obsessively written. That's what scares me a little. I've never really written about anything else since I was a kid. I don't know if that's why I write. I'm a really laborious writer. I rewrite so much. I don't even think I'm a natural writer at all – it's really hard for me. So I'm really curious to see if I really give a shit to write... to find out what happens, because they have written themselves. It's like I knew exactly what I wanted to write and then it was just a matter of toying with the language forever.

Do you feel a sense of completion?

It feels like it. And if I do anything after this it

will be just repetition. But I'd like to try something else. I really believe in this work, but I get really tired of people finding it difficult to read my books because of what the subject matter is. I don't have to write about it – I'd rather not. I'm tired of people saying I'm, like, a monster, so if I can do something I'm pleased with, that isn't about murder and pornography and child sex and stuff... I'd like to see what I can do.

Do you think there's a difference between the way gay people and straight people perceive your stuff?

This is a really strange thing to say, but I think straight people understand it better. That's not to say that a lot of gay people don't like it too, but it just seems people who read it who aren't gay, they feel slightly distanced from the subject matter and they're able to understand the books.

Do you think there's still a bit of that subconscious demonization – 'That's how homosexuals behave, it's nothing to do with us'? Maybe the gay community feel more threatened? Like, say, people have become aware of defining Scottishness in a way that they have to have this composite of images of 'Scottishness' all the time. Do you feel like you're forced to work at the gay tourist marketing board?!

I'm not interested in being gay. It's one of the least interesting things about me. A lot of women like my work, and that surprises me, because they're hardly in the books. The thing about it being with two men, is it gives you all this freedom to explore all this weird stuff, without baggage, because it's these two beings that are the same. I'm aware of that – that you can erase the homosexuality... If I was straight, I don't know if I could do this.

If you were writing about a male protagonist and a woman in the same way, it would be very difficult. But you've got a kind of freedom and it perhaps has to do with the way we condition male sexuality to be aggressive. Whether it's culturally or genetically determined, I don't know, but because it's seen in that way, it has given you a freedom.

Have you found that you've had to stop yourself writing certain things?

I've written mainly about heterosexual

relationships. But there was a gay psychopath shagging a captive guy in the play *Maribou Stork Nightmares*. That was strange to do. But it's weird – you become detached from it. But to me, what was quite shocking was seeing the actors going for it and playing the role. In some ways, I was so involved in expressing the landscape in writing terms, I became detached from it. Then you hear it read back and you don't necessarily get what you've written. When I was writing the rape scene in *Maribou Stork Nightmares*... it becomes like a technical thing you're doing... a technical exercise...

But you didn't stop yourself. You can trust it, right?

You know the effect you're trying to achieve and the way to achieve it. You just have to trust yourself and your motives: I think when people write books – this sounds a bit strange – I think they actually want to do good. You go to different extremes of behaviour, but you want to do something that's – maybe not good – but quite helpful. I know it's fashionable for people to wrap themselves in this cloak of badness – you know, 'I'm bad and enigmatic, all nasty and subversive.' I think it's all bollocks.

The way I think about the novel, I can't think of another art form where the reader has so much power. Not just in terms of what they read and how fast, but also in how they take responsibility, because they create the picture in their head. I feel I can do more with a novel because of that. It's such a great relationship. It's almost like a script for a film that's in their head.

It's really strange when you're on the tube and you see someone reading one of your

own books. You wonder what's going on in their head. What are they seeing? It's so great that everybody sees different things. It's funny though, you have this line in your head where you know it's going to communicate, where it's not self indulgent, so it's kind of, like, *finesse*. But it's not about a particular person you're trying to address. It's really magical and tricky. And when you find that you've finished, you have really just been pleasing yourself. But how would you know to be so objective? It's so curious.

After *Acid House*, I stopped reading reviews. The publishers send a big pack, and I just stick them in the bin. With my stuff, I've found there's been a big division between the critics and the people who are reading it. It's a whole different cultural thing. I don't want the perception of how I write to be formed by other people.

Yeah, it's a public thing.

With *Trainspotting*, some people said I was just doing that to make lots of money – because drugs were cool and all that. But it was about a lot of Scottish schemies banging up on smack – what's cool about that? It's gone through this process of appropriation, through this commercial thing, and now it's, like, Richard Branson's book rather than mine.

But every time a kid reads the book, it comes alive again.

It's quite a patronizing, middle-class/liberal thing to think everybody else is thick and easily led and 'we're the only ones with any critical antennae'. One of the great things about the working-class kids in Scotland who've read the book is that they know what's bullshit about it, what's crap about it as well, rather than just gushing praise. In Britain, it started with this class/ imperialist thing, like you've got to keep back all this referential knowledge for yourself and you deny that other people can come to it in that critical sense. I got some men saying, 'Oh, the books are misogynistic.' Most of the people who read the books are women!

On the drugs thing, I get people saying, 'Oh, you're glorifying heroin by writing about it.' I hate heroin. What are they talking about?

I don't know anyone who would read *Trainspotting* or one of your books and say heroin is a positive thing. You can't write a book that says 'drugs are great. Take drugs' – that's bollocks. But you can't just say 'Drugs are terrible, they kill you.' It's nonsense.

Getting back to your books, the same characters seem to reappear. There's this kind of intellectual, cerebral guy who lives in his own head and is quite predatory in an exploratory way. And then there's always his counterpart: a quite passive young guy. Where do these characters come from?

I guess it's a combination of things. The younger characters are people I'm interested in: some are my friends, some are boyfriends. And then the other character is, I suppose, what I'm afraid of about myself.

It's like a *doppelgänger*. You've got it out there to put your fears into it.

But there's a chemistry there and I have faith in it. And having the same kinds of relationships and the same kinds of set-ups keeps everything together, because formally, I tend to go all over the place. Especially in *Guide*, where it goes off in all directions. The relationships are the grounding... or the spine of it.

You say *Guide* goes off in all directions, but actually I found it one of the easiest of your books. I recognized a lot of your themes and concerns, and was able to lock into it a lot faster.

That's cool because, especially at the beginning of it, I wanted it to flicker. I wanted to disorientate. And then you get used to the shape of it, although it throws new shapes at you all the time. But it's like being high. You get used to it. And then I guess it kind of comes together at the end. And then there's the non-fiction stuff: what was supposed to be the truth. Like, I included an interview I did from *Spin* and it was a real interview, although I added all the sex! I wanted to see, if I fictionalized that and used the same voice that I would in the article, if I could mimic the truth with fiction and make it seamless. I was trying to do that all through the book.

Do you like doing journalism?

I think it's really interesting and it has affected my writing. I think I'm crap at it, to be honest with you. I'm really amazed they give me jobs. I have decided I'm not going to be a great journalist. I haven't got the brain to do it.

Switching from fiction to journalism, you'd probably think, 'I don't want to write about what happened; I want to write about all the possible things that might happen.' Do you feel that?

They give me leeway because I'm a fiction writer. They basically hired me because of my novels. But at the same time, it's like writing a sonnet – I know what they want and then I just fiddle with it a little bit. But I love doing interviews. Editing's great. Playing with the way the voices intertwine. I liked interviewing people like Pavement or Leonardo DiCaprio.

Has Leonardo DiCaprio seen the reference in the book?

Yeah. He lives down the street from me. I talked to him a few times since then. He was so cool. He's so straight, so normal. He's seen it and he was fine. He had read the work already. And I didn't think that Blur would mind, because I knew they liked the work. One time, Graham called me and said, 'Do you want to come over?' So I knew from that they liked the work. Or at least, he did. I just hoped they wouldn't think,

'Oh, this is a bit funny.' Do you think that was wrong? A really tricky thing to do to someone like that?

Yeah, I've always felt uncomfortable writing about real people, but with that Madonna/Kylie/Victoria Principal thing I did ('Where the Debris Meets the Sea' from *The Acid House*), I had no conception of their existence as real people. Now I've got to know some famous people, I can envisage the rest of them as being real. I always try to keep real people out of my work and do composites as much as possible. With 'Where the Debris Meets the Sea' I made it appear, implicitly at least, that it was not the real people and their characteristics. It's done in a constructed way. I shy away from interviews because what always strikes me about them is that the people that I've actually met, I've never really recognized them from their interviews. Like, I don't know Alex James, but I imagine that he's very different from his media construction. And I know Damon Albarn and he is very different from what you read in the *NME* or whatever. And Noel Gallagher – he's very different as well.

Yeah, it's true. That's why I thought that Alex James would just understand me. There was a bunch of us and we got sort of obsessive about him and that's what I ended up writing about. There were two artists and me doing work about him and there was this collective insanity. I mean, I don't know. I've never met him. I like the way he holds a cigarette in his mouth when he's on stage... But the closest I've ever come to him is across a concert hall.

I think it could be like stalking culture, where these people are taking so many references from the media. I think some famous people would find it very uncomfortable – the idea that someone was obsessed about them. It might get into that person's head that if you're obsessing about him, then loads of people might be – and one of them might be a nutter.

I guess that's the danger – people find it hard to separate fact from fiction. I mean, it's not like I sit around jacking up thinking about killing him or anything. I just thought he was interesting and cute. And then I thought 'I can

From top
Dennis Cooper and
Irvine Welsh, 1998
Donald Christie

use this' – and really make it really insane in the book.

[laughs] **Not all the time then! But there is generally something weird going on: there's this whole confessional culture that's growing up now. Like, you have to confess your sins to your personal priest.**

I was trying to fuck with that. People would think that it was my biography, but it wasn't. It was getting totally twisted on me all the time. Rather than pastiche. I saw that you have *The Ricky Lake Show* and all that over here now.

Yeah, great... all these fat people from Louisiana shouting at each other. It's just fucking boring. You're not giving people a voice to really say something, you're just setting them up. They're being made to make fools of themselves. I just think it's time for culture to start moving on. It's been stagnating in its post-modern hole for too long.

Are you feeling that when you're working on stuff? Are you trying to go there? I don't think you've ever been a post-modernist.

When I started I had this base/superstructure thing, where the base is the culture then the other stuff was built on that. I'm getting tired of the decorative 'other stuff'. I'd like to go back to the real thing – back to the pure: *Trainspotting*-type social realism. I was looking again at the *Ecstasy* trilogy. Two are quite 'fantasy', but the middle one, *Fortune's Always Hiding*, is quite realistic and it's the one I enjoyed the most. One of the films I enjoyed last year was *Nil By Mouth*. It's not a film that's comfortable to watch, but there just seems to be something so real about it. I think I've got a similar preference for *Fortune's Always Hiding*, so I think I should get back to that.

I know what you mean. I don't know if you have this, but there's a part of me that has a real fear of the conventional. And there are such conventions in the novel and I guess I'm really afraid to write a novel. Do you ever get that? I don't know if you're like me, maybe it's just because I did a lot of acid, but for me it all happens in flashes.

Yeah, it's like you've always got to do something to fuck it up a bit. When you go into Waterstones, there are so many novels, all with the same voice – white, middle class, male, heterosexual – particularly British novels. They're practically all written with the very same narrative voice.

English fiction's so strange, anyway, all that Martin Amis stuff. It's so witty.

I think that's like a lot of 'classical' English fiction. Because it has that elitist feel to it. A lot of it's an in-joke for the salons. The salon of interaction is very important. I think the London/metropolitan novel suffers from that. But there is also a lot of really strong writing coming out of England and it comes from a really different place from all that. It's blowing a lot of that crap away. I think America is real because it hasn't got that imperialist/class tradition – there are so many different voices. There shouldn't be just one tradition.

But most people in America read genre fiction, like Grisham or Stephen King. Ninety per cent of what sells is genre. I don't know if that's the same here. And then once in a while, something will break through like David Foster-Wallace... something interesting. But generally, it's all self-help books, detective or law novels.

I think I can see myself writing a suburban

novel. It really appeals to me: doing something else. The characters that I write about are generally ten years younger than me. But I think that's the way with writing. I only started in my thirties. I couldn't have done it in my twenties. You're a bit too involved to stand back.

I write about people a lot younger than me too. Even when I put myself in the books, I can't quite bring myself to make myself forty-five. I make myself thirty-something.

Nah, it's not an age thing at all.

I work with some bands and clubs because... well, I don't know why, I guess it's because that's where I come from – rock. But it's really mixed ages. I wonder if people think I'm from the record company or something when I go there.

I guess there's no reason not to go to clubs. If I stopped enjoying it, maybe... But there's no reason to stop other than social conditioning. But that's the whole point of writing – to challenge those kinds of conventions.

People forget that. I don't think people go to fiction for an adventurous experience. It seems like it's changed so much since the 60s, when I was a kid.

The novel has become far too important to be appropriated in that kind of way: the pedestrian clubbing sort of way. It needs to be pumped up again, away from the control and the commercialization. It's got to be part of people's life and part of people's culture again.

Well, there's good writing around – here and in the States.

Yeah, but there's too much to the whole culture of being a writer. People want to be a writer rather than write. They want to immerse themselves in what they see as the trimmings that go along with being part of something. In Scotland, they're really into celebrating writers. There's this bad balance where you've got too many critics and too many celebrators – not enough people actually being creative.

In the States though, there's this establishment. I never even considered I would get to this place where the people who get reviews in *The New York Times* are, or where you get dubbed as being part of the 'canon' of American writing – it's so foreign, so far away. It's so impossible. I wish there was a different superstructure.

Absolutely. Unless you're fortunate enough to just sell loads of books, it's really hard – there's this infrastructure, this bureaucracy. It's class-based and appearance-based.

It makes it really difficult. When Burroughs died, he realized he was still considered a freak. How long had he been writing? But he still wasn't accepted. He never will be. That was a real shock to me. Also, when Kathy Acker died. It's never going to happen – there are always going to be these weird, outsider, cult people. And I guess you just have to revel in it. I sort of like that.

There's a tendency to embrace anything that is thrust on you, but it's self-defeating as well. If you feel an outsider or a deviant, then there must be some sort of mainstream. But there isn't a legitimate mainstream. It's a multi-cultural society that we live in. There shouldn't be a mainstream – writers should all be treated and accepted in the same way.

At least, the way it is, some people get my books thinking, 'This is cool, nobody's ever heard of this guy.' They're outsiders, so they gravitate to the work for that reason – because it isn't mainstream. It's strange though, Alexander Trocchi, for instance: he's still considered out there.

Yeah, not in Scotland though. He's seen as a bad boy but also a godfather. But a lot of writers are compared to him, like me, or Barry Graham, which in a way gives him the credit he's due. But we are seen as badboy disciples. Which is bullshit. There are-

loads of writers I like, but they haven't had the credit they're due in their time.

Yeah, if one more person says I'm the new Burroughs, I'm going to kill them! Or the new Genet. Jesus. They weren't even major influences on me. It's insane.

Again, it's that imperialist literary tradition. The idea that all your influences must be from literature rather than from some other medium, like rock-'n'-roll.

Yeah, like, then you're not serious! You say that's not true to interviewers and you see them go, 'Yeah, right, right...'

Either that, or they think you're saying this to try and be hip. But you grow up in an era of film, magazines and television. Unless you come from a really bookish family – which is generally a kind of upper-middle-class family in this country – you just don't have literary references.

I guess it's because they're not writers – they don't think that you can transpose ideas from film and music into fiction. They don't think that's possible. Music is so far ahead of fiction.

Yeah, you take a piece of music and you can visualize so much from that.

Absolutely. Music is a source of ideas.

It's so personal as well. You interpret it in a completely different way from anyone else. Whereas in literature, you're guided down a path.

I get most of my influences from outside of literature, but every now and again I'll read a book – and it's more like I feel I've found... a comrade. That's a great feeling too, but it's not like it influences you. It's more that there's another person out there who makes you feel less alone as a writer.

Acclaimed screenwriter, award-winning first-time director, neophyte artist, pending author, comedic bit-part actor, twenty-three-year-old instigator of controversial ideas, Harmony Korine is attempting the near impossible: to infiltrate his pure non-commercial and uncompromising vision into the mainstream. He seems to be succeeding in one thing at least, and that's getting people talking about him.

Ext: Mercer Street, Lower East side – midday

Outside some shops, a young girl is standing alone. She is dressed like a gypsy princess. She has the body of a thirteen-year-old, but the face of a beautiful woman. Korine spots her from a distance and immediately begins talking, asking her name, age and where she's from. Her mother exits the shop holding a violin. She looks nervous that a strange man is talking to her daughter. The girl's father follows and recognizing Korine says, 'I shoot for Screw *magazine, I shoot real hardcore. You want to see real New York, I'll show you real New York. None of that fucking* Kids *stuff, I'll show you hookers, the youngest girls, and rent boys. I do real reportage.'*

His daughter stands next to him, looking unfazed. Korine asks her for her telephone number and she asks him why he wants it. 'So I can call you, I'd like you to be in a film,' he explains. She looks him up and down, and with a completely straight face says, 'No, gimmie your number. I'll call you.'

Gummo *(1997), Korine's debut film, has been championed by directors Gus Van Sant, Jean-Luc Godard and Larry Clark, and has earned the congratulations of Werner Herzog, Lars Von Trier and Abel Ferrara. They are far older than*

Korine, yet all unconventional directors in their own right. Perhaps what they see in Gummo *is a pure and daring singular vision, something that is almost impossible to achieve let alone maintain in the commodified world of popular culture. With so many careerists, crowd pleasers, recyclers and fame-for-the-sake-of-fame seekers, insurrection in the mainstream, especially in an original and new voice, is not only to be celebrated, but practically revered.*

Gummo *has won both an International Critics' prize at the Venice Film Festival and, more recently, the Grand Jury prize at the Rotterdam Film Festival. Yet it also has its detractors and has been denounced in some sections of the US media as 'boring, redundant and sick', as well as 'the worst film of the year'. 'When it comes to boy wonders exploring the cutting edge of independent cinema,' wrote Janet Maslin in* The New York Times, *'the buck stops cold right here.'*

Two-dimensional media analysis paints Korine as a genius wunderkind on the one hand and a cause-célèbre opportunist on the other. Perhaps he is both, but more likely he is neither. Truly original voices are rarely understood and nearly always marginalized by those who control the status quo. The laws of our mainstream media landscape are there either to mock or to scapegoat those who attempt to do new things. Korine's a three-dimensional rebel, the real thing. That's why the mainstream media in America have done their best to try and discourage him.

So who is Harmony Korine? The portrait of an artist as a slightly younger man shows 'Harmful' Korine, the teenage skateboarder, and the Mohican-sporting photographer Larry Clark meeting in Central Park. Korine told Clark about a short script he had written. It was the story of a boy who is taken by his estranged father on his thirteenth birthday to a prostitute for his first sexual experience. It wasn't until almost a year later that Clark, remembering Korine's script, talked him through a brief outline for a film. Three weeks later, the then nineteen-year-old Korine finished the first draft of Kids. *With the help of executive producer Gus Van Sant, the film began shooting in the summer of 1994.*

Although he is an avid cinephile, Korine never studied film or scriptwriting, yet Kids *showed a natural ear for dialogue and cinematic* structure. Korine then teamed up with Cary Woods, the producer of Kids and subsequently Scream (1996) and Cop Land (1997), to make Gummo. Woods' protective style suited Korine's creative independence and although Gummo was eventually made with Fine Line, a mini-major for approximately one million dollars, it was virtually uninfluenced by corporate strategy. In fact, given the increasingly commercial climate in the US film industry, it's incredible that Gummo was even funded.

Ext: A sidewalk in front of a music shop – late afternoon

'You've dropped your pocket.' Korine walks past a couple shopping, and taps the man on the shoulder, repeating the line, 'You've dropped your pocket.' The man looks down at the ground, confused, searching for nothing he has lost. 'Watch this, he'll be there for half an hour. We'll get to the end of the street and he'll still be there.' We walk further into the distance and I turn round as we reach the end of the street. The man and wife are now both on their hands and knees, arguing with each other, and looking for the nothing they've lost. 'You see, it works every time,' says Korine.

Welcome to the world of Gummo; a film in which you're never quite sure what's going to happen next; a cinema of unpredictability, where conventional structure and plot are discarded in favour of a different approach to storytelling. Welcome to Xhenia, a tornado-devastated town in Ohio.

Where Kids exposed us to a compelling portrayal of twenty-four hours in the life of a group of New York teenagers, their attitudes to underage sex, drugs, street fashion, and AIDS, Gummo transports us to smalltown, run-down, rural America, where handicapped sex, breast cancer, teenage transvestitism, paedophilia and racism are exposed. Korine takes no moral stance, leaving it up to us to work out whether we should laugh or cry, feel embarrassed or afraid at this mirage of truth, closeness and access. This is what more cinema should be about – not a fast-food, pop-cult-fiction package, where we all consensually laugh and cry in syncopated rhythm.

These subtexts are brought to you through a vortex of original ideas, stunningly shot imagery, and an ear-bending, death-metal soundtrack. It's imagery that keeps popping back into your mind weeks after you've seen it, and a film whose unresolved dilemmas are left scratching away under the surface of the skin: a Down's syndrome girl shaves her eyebrows because she thinks it makes her look more beautiful; a midget arm-wrestles a big bear of a man and wins; a deaf couple argue through intense hand gesticulation; teenage boys kill cats to sell so they can buy glue to get high; an albino waitress in a car park describes what she finds attractive about men; three extremely young, white-trash sisters get touched up by a middle-aged man. It's part poetry, part nonsense, part youth-culture rhetoric and in Korine's own words a 'complete genre-fuck'.

There's no cynicism here, no irony or post-modern mask. Korine's observed sense of realism verges on social anthropology. Shot mainly in Nashville, Ohio, Korine's home town, Gummo features only four actors: Chloë Sevigny (Kids), Linda Manz (Days of Heaven), Max Perlich (Beautiful Girls, Drugstore Cowboy) and Jacob Solomon (The Road to Wellville) in an ensemble cast of over forty speaking parts. The lives of the local people, old schoolfriends and acquaintances are seen through the hypnotic and beautifully inventive cinematography of Jean Yves Escoffier, who has also worked with Leox Carax on classic films such as Les Amants du Pont Neuf and Trois Hommes et un Couffin as well as Martin Scorsese's short film 100 Years of American Cinema.

Int: Korine's apartment – late afternoon

Korine puts on a video cassette to show me a scene from Gummo cut by the censors:

Int: Apartment in Xhenia, Ohio – afternoon

The sound of a Bach cello concerto

A small child begins by taking the pictures off the living-room wall. Behind the framed prints, spiders, cockroaches and woodlice crawl. He squashes them with the edge of the picture frame and gets off his stool to return to the

couch, where a couple are inhaling aerosol
fumes. The TV is on, but the sound is switched
off. The house is a mess. The young child climbs
into his mother's lap and in framing reminiscent
of the Madonna and Child, she holds his head and
offers him the aerosol. He cups its flute with both
hands as if it were a baby bottle and takes a
deep, inhalatory breath.

Korine's unprecious yet precise mixed-media
approach to collaging Gummo sees Polaroids,
home-movie footage (shot by many of the kids)
as well as sampled TV clips cut into Escoffier's
fluid filming. There is a rhythm and layering
not far removed from the looping and sampling
process of drum-'n'-bass. Korine brings to the
cinema a contemporary vernacular and a street
suss; a new beauty, a new way of seeing and
thinking, and in the process, a big 'fuck you' to
everyone else.

Korine's debut novel A Crack Up at the Race
Riots will be published in America in April. He is
also represented as an artist by two prestigious
galleries: the Andrea Rosen Gallery in New York,
where he recently exhibited a collection of fake
suicide notes, and the Patrick Painter Gallery in
Los Angeles (which also represents Mike Kelley,

Richard Prince, Larry Clark and Douglas Gordon),
where he exhibited video installation pieces. (The
installation was sold to the San Francisco
Museum of Modern Art.) This month, Korine
tears up the big screen in a hilarious, but very
brief part as a convict in Gus Van Sant's Oscar-
nominated film Goodwill Hunting (1997).

Korine looks like a schoolboy; a blur of
unkempt hair and undone K Mart shoes, hip-hop
stances and heavy metal T-shirts, but maybe he's
really fifty-three years old – he's just got one of
those rare anti-aging diseases that makes him
look permanently eighteen. He was an authorita-
tive documentarian in the 60s and now he's busy
reinventing himself as a renaissance man, thinly
disguised as a cheeky adolescent filmmaker with
the concentration span of an art star on coke.

The urban mythology of Korine: he pretends
to be drunk on The David Letterman Show, his
on-off relationship with long-term partner and
prominent actress Chloë Sevigny is peppered
with alleged supermodel affairs; he has been
banned from a New York hotel bar after starting
a fight, and has slagged off big films like Boogie
Nights (Paul Anderson, 1997). Although it
seems to have calmed down in recent months,
his reputation as both auteur and raconteur
precedes him. In a medium where everything is
autobiographical and fictional at the same time,
Korine's fiction is ultimately a branch of his
truth, and being one stage removed, it's hard not
to see him as the main character in the movie
adaptation of the story of his life.

**Ext: SoHo. Busy street corner by a bar – early
evening**

Leonardo DiCaprio and Korine are walking
together. They approach a group of bikers who

are busy drinking outside the bar. Korine
accidentally knocks into the biggest biker as he
walks past. He is enormous; his hair hangs in a
ponytail, his fists bandaged in black leather,
fingerless gloves. He partially spills his drink and
begins screaming at Korine, 'Come here you little
punk, you fucker.' DiCaprio stands behind Korine,
taunting the biker with a highly animated gorilla
impression. DiCaprio's arms are swinging from
side to side as Korine walks towards the biker
and instinctively pulls a switchblade from his
back pocket, the street lights reflecting off the
steel blade. The biker backs off, and Korine avoid-
ing a prolonged stand-off, starts walking down
the road. With the sound of the cursing biker
fading in the distance, Korine turns to DiCaprio,
they put their arms around each other and piss
themselves laughing at the ridiculousness of the
situation.

Dazed & Confused | **Did you ever have an
attention deficit disorder when you were
younger?**
Harmony Korine | I'm sure I had it. When I
was a kid, my parents didn't take me to the type
of people that would know what that was. I
should have been on Ritalin. I was a total Ritalin
kid. But I guess my parents weren't into that.
You know, instead I would like, light the yard
on fire.
You lit the yard on fire?
Yeah, I remember my parents went to see *The
Outsiders* at the shopping mall a hundred miles
away from our house and I stayed home and lit
the yard on fire. The fire trucks came and there
I was trying to put it out with a wet towel. The
fire trucks were there for hours, but my parents
were at the shopping mall. When they came
back, the yard was all burnt and there was still

smoke. So knowing my father's penchant for
violence, I took a chair and I pulled my pants
down, exposing my ass and I said, 'I lit the yard
on fire; you can beat me', and he didn't say
anything. He went outside and got a yellow bat
and he smashed me, without saying anything.
That's what I remember most, that he wasn't
saying anything. He wasn't even out of breath.
It was amazing.
**Most kids would try to run away, to escape
what was going to happen. But you just
decided to face the music.**
I guess, I never thought about it like that.
**Are you interested in making any
documentaries?**
This is what I talked about with Werner. I feel
documentary always falls short. I think cinema
vérité is a fallacy, that the documentary is
manipulated; there's no such thing as truth in
film. Godard's idea about twenty-four frames of
truth was always for me the ultimate lie. It's
just twenty-four frames of lies. But the best
cinema, to me, works on a kind of theoretical
level, where it's twenty-four frames of sort of
truth. For me, being a writer and an artist and
a viewer, the only thing I'm interested in is
realism. If it's not presented to me in a way
that's real, with real consequences, real
characters, I have no desire to see it, because
then it's fake. It's a cartoon, and I just don't care
about that stuff. But at the same time, in this
ultimate search for truth, for realism, I know
it's impossible to attain, so what do you do, it's
like *Gummo*. People say, 'Oh my god, it's got no
script.' And there's a total script. But what it is,
is a trick. Everything is presented as if it's real,
but I'm manipulating everything.
**One of the things I found were these
philosophical statements. There were simple
one-liners of the 'I'm going to kill myself
and will anyone care when I'm gone'
variety. The 'life is great, without it we'd be
dead' rhetoric.**
'Life is great, without it we'd be dead': it was an
old vaudeville joke.
**Or, America would be nothing without
wood! I assume what you're doing is just
punching people with ideas, images,
sequences, and then hopefully they will
extract their own truth from it.**
I'm also interested in the whole kind of beauty

of nonsense and in fully trying to make all the connections. A lot of times I come up short and I'm saying things that aren't really the intention.

What would you say to someone who said, 'Well it's not realism, it's just as stylized as MTV'?

I wouldn't understand that. I never feel the need to defend my work at all. I sometimes will, but it's either gotten or it's forgotten and that's fine.

I remember talking to you when you were very worried that the film might not get a rating. And that was the time that you were maybe at your lowest point after the film had been made. What happened?

I'm a hundred per cent commercial filmmaker. I have nothing to do with independent directors, alternative cinema, I make Harmony movies. It's a cinema of obsession and passion. But at the same time, I can't differentiate between notions of underground. Underground film, underground music, alternative culture, to me it doesn't exist. To me, the future is either good or bad and it's kind of making sense of both those things. Like the film – I involve scenes and situations that are the scenes that I love. It's only scenes and images that I wanted to see, with no real explanation, nothing coming before it. So getting back to the question, I was basically free to make this movie this way, which is a miracle. Because what's on screen is a pure vision.

The way things were structured is that people leave me alone. I have nothing to do with anyone. I have no idea about how other people make their movies. I don't make very much money. I don't concern myself with others. I don't fraternize with the enemy. I just work, and I love and I fight and just do my own thing. So I'm making this film and I finish editing and it has to go before the ratings board. The only stipulation in my contract with the studio, Fine Line, is that I had to turn in an R-rated film. Basically in America, few studios will distribute NC-17. NC-17 in the States, is a kind of word for X. Basically that's because seventy-five per cent of the theatres in America won't accept the film. Ninety-five per cent of the video chains, like Blockbuster, where you make half your money, won't accept it. You can't advertise on MTV. You can't advertise in ninety

per cent of magazines or newspapers. So right there, you're limited to ten per cent of the funds.

So there was this point where you were being told it was going to be given an NC-17.

We gave it to the NPA, who are these people who have these really vague guidelines. There's nothing really to follow. It's more like 'how do you feel?'

What did they find particularly outrageous or shocking about *Gummo*?

They would say 'You're lingering on these boys huffing glue out of their sacks. You're lingering on it for too long.' So we'd cut it, but it wouldn't be enough. And then basically, after the seventh time and I'd cut a few more minutes out of the film, and I was going to cut no more...

You probably could have cut those sequences shorter. But instead of lingering on the kids taking drugs, the image would have been less exploratory and far more punchy and perhaps even more destructive.

That was their whole point. They were saying that if it were more MTV, if I cut it, if it was really rapid, if I stripped the film of any type of content, if I made it totally void of any kind of meaning, if I made it like what *Trainspotting* was, if I made it heightened and I made it kind of cartoonish, and something that was much more over the top and much more satirical that you could laugh off, then you would realize that it was a movie, and it would be OK.

So you must have wanted to punch their heads in.

I went nuts.

Did you go in front of the board? Did they summon you or did you ask for the meeting?

After the seventh time, you're allowed to – it's kind of like going to court – you're allowed to call the jury. And then you're allowed to make a speech, and there's supposed to be a certain number of representatives from the ratings board, and I swear to you every single person was over sixty-five years old; they all looked like Barbara Bush. There's only one woman; they're all men. I made my speech. I said, 'If you look at the film, you're seeing almost no nudity; there's no real violence except violence toward animals.' I went into this whole speech and I hated myself for having to explain to these fuckers, but I knew I had to do it, and it took

them forty-five seconds to vote me down. Forty-five seconds to say 'NC-17'. They didn't care. So the next day, I called. I told them that what they were doing was illegal: 'I'm calling all the newspapers, I am going to expose you'...
Who?
Someone on the board. And I meant it. It was someone that was a liaison between the ratings board and the studio, who I felt was lying to me. I told him without any hesitation that I'd take the next flight over and I'd stab him in the fucking throat. I said, 'I'll cut your fucking head off 'cause I didn't grow up as a rich kid playing that whole game. I'm not a part of that and the work means so much more and if I can't show it, it's not only a betrayal to me, it's a betrayal to all those people in the film because these are people that gave themselves to the film.' The next morning, I got a phone call from my agent and he's freaked out that I threatened someone's life, but the rating was reversed.
That's amazing. Absolutely amazing. Do you think it took them forty-five seconds to reverse it?
I wish we could have timed it.
Do you think all films should be R-rated or can you see some reasons for a ratings system?
I think it's fine... I think ratings systems are fine. Some Disney films should be PG.
Did you ever apply to film school? Were you ever interested in learning the art of cinematography, or studying the art of film-making on that level?
I feel really strongly about that, because I'm not making movies for the same reasons that most people make films. I grew up in the cinema. Buster Keaton changed my life. When I saw Buster Keaton, I realized that there was something so pure, there was a kind of pure tragic beauty that I had never seen before, and it was so moving and so big. What could be more amazing than what I was seeing? So for me, there was almost something holy about the cinema. My life is always fifty per cent watching movies and fifty per cent living life. Living life is always more interesting than films. I find life is more exciting than films, because it's limitless. Films can only imitate life. They can only go to a certain point and then life begins. Watching films, I started to realize that they are

all starting to seem the same. That they all have the same kind of humour, the same kind of actors, the same kind of characteristics. Why is that? And I started to realize that everybody is going to these film schools and these are all people who fifteen years ago would have gone to doctor's school and now they want to make movies. None of these people have any kind of stories to tell. All of their films are about this kind of process, about this kind of generic storytelling. More than anything, the great films are about life. There was once a day when cinema had glory: when John Ford was making movies, and Fassbinder was making movies, and Cassavetes; when there was glory 'cause films once had the essence of life to them. And then something happened. I felt that film school was a place that was teaching people to be technicians, and to think the same, have the same sense of humour and the same stories. And I realized that all you ever need to be a filmmaker is to see films. I understood this at a young age.
Would you have made *Gummo* if you only had twenty thousand dollars and one camera or would you have waited until you got a million?
Yeah, I would have waited.

And what if it never came?

I would have walked away.

You wouldn't have made the film?

No.

Isn't that bullshit? If you're that passionate about it, if it meant that much to you to tell that story and not be a technician?

I might have made another film. The thing is this, it's like, the reason I never did music videos and all these other things that came along, is because I only wanted to make *Gummo*. I only wanted it to be this way. It either had to be perfectly this vision or it fell short.

***Gummo* does not obviously reference any other film; if it does, it's very hidden. And what's interesting is that right now, everyone is being ironic, everyone is using parody or heavily quoting their influences. All the young- and maybe middle-generation filmmakers seem more influenced by the past than the future.**

I was only interested in inventing a new film, like the way I wanted to watch movies, with images coming from all the right places. A 'mistakist' art form.

Can you explain that term?

What I mean by mistakist – and I think it's important sometimes to give a kind of aesthetic or form a name, just because it's easier for people to reference – what I mean by mistakist is almost like anti-Hitchcock. When Hitchcock would make a film, before he made it, it was finished. When I make a film, the script is the script and that's the bare bones and it's dead. All the accidents, all the life that comes to it, that's the film. It's by juxtaposing certain, say...

There are moments you could never direct; they're undirectable, like the chair smashing scene.

Jean Escoffier, the cinematographer, and I talked before we shot about what films we might reference and we both decided to reference nothing. We decided to let the situation dictate the way it's filmed. And so what we did was, I set up chaos. Everything around me was chaos.

You mean behind the scenes there was chaos?

Both behind the scenes and in front of the camera, a lot of the time, mixed. And I was setting up situations where a chaotic event

would happen and I knew it would happen. And I would give everybody a camera. I would give my little sister a camera. I would give Escoffier a camera. I would give someone a video camera, or a Super-8 camera and everyone would be filming.

So there's a large element of collaboration with the subjects of the film, the actors, the non-actors. They were collaborating in the sense that they were helping you make the film. This is what negates any sense of exploitation for me.

It's all about life; that's what's interesting to me.

You're working from the inside out, in a sense?

Because art for too long has been from a distance. It's been coming from the wrong directions. It's about artists trying to solve problems and then go inside.

Like maths problems?

Exactly. That's what it's become. Post-modern art to me is like math problems.

So your book, the film, the scripts at the moment are a random collection of your obsessions and thoughts. What's the spirit of what you're trying to say through all of it?

I would never answer you as far as what I'm trying to say. Because, for one, I don't even really know, and for another, I do the work and I would never take on the responsibility of answering. The one connection would be what Charles Eames said about 'a unified aesthetic'. I could design a chair, I could do a tap dance, or I could write an opera, or hang glide...

You don't feel precious about any particular medium?

... or I could go in my bathroom and hang myself and die, but it would all be part of the same person and the ideas. There would be this unified thought. This unified aesthetic.

There was a thing that you mentioned last night. You said, 'There are people who want to hurt me. They really want to hurt me and I won't let them', and that was a reaction to the people that want to maintain the status quo.

The people complaining about my nihilism. Like that guy from *Vogue* magazine who was screaming that I was a nihilist and I was the reason that the world was bad.

People need scapegoats to blame for the reason that things are the way they are. You're a twenty-three-year-old director working to bring new images and new ideas into the mass arena where they don't already exist. In a sense this makes you a flag carrier. These people want to maintain the status quo, that power. Have you thought about how you're going to have to fortify yourself against them? Are you worried about that or does it excite you?

What excites me is that these people are old and I want to destroy these dinosaurs. I feel that they're ruining the air that I breathe, killing the films that I watch and the way that I live. I want to get them out of the way. In another ten or fifteen years, the people that understand and appreciate *Gummo,* or my other work, will be in positions of power, but for right now, the bourgeois fuckers, they must die. *Vive La France!*

That's exactly what I was hoping you were going to say.

But it's true. It's time for youth culture to take over, I know it sounds silly, but it's true and I am not even saying that I have this great belief in the youth, because I don't. I have a great belief in certain individuals. Certain talented individuals. I don't have a great belief in a group of people, but at the same time, many of them aren't getting the attention that they deserve and maybe it's time for them to step up.

Tell me about the final day of filming.

We shot the entire film in twenty days. There's a scene in the movie where the girls are in the swimming pool, in the rain. I had this picture, this image, and we could never get it to coincide with the rain, and at the same time, I wanted it raining at the finale. Every day it was supposed to rain; it wouldn't rain. And these were the really important shots, and I kept putting it back and putting it back. And people kept saying, 'You're nuts. There is no way we'll ever finish this movie.' I knew not to worry. I always have. So on the final day, we had a storm. That day, out of twenty days of sunshine, we had a storm. We shot the swimming-pool scene and we shot the finale with the rabbit. We shot the entire arm-wrestling scene and we shot my scene, last of all, with the black dwarf.

All in one day?

All in one day.

Were you drunk when you shot the scene with you and the dwarf?

I never work when intoxicated or under the influence, but I knew for the scene I wanted something special so I got very drunk. I did that scene and I was totally out of it and it was two in the morning and that was the end of the film. It was dead quiet and everyone was shaking because here I am trying to make love with a black dwarf and I'm being rejected. And the dwarf was in his tight, white underwear and I'm whispering in his ear that I'll give him a hundred dollars if he takes off his underwear and he won't do it for me. So I stand up, it's two in the morning and I stand up and scream, 'We made a movie, we finished the film. We made an original movie!' I'm screaming and I'm totally out of my mind. And everyone starts clapping and is happy, but I don't really know what's going on. My younger sister, who's nineteen, who worked on the film, runs up to give me a hug and I throw her through the door. Then I take a painting that's lying in the house and I start running and smashing the windows through the house. And Chloë and a few people start crying. Everyone starts flipping out; my sister's bleeding and I'm just smashing up the windows. Then this huge grip, this bald guy that looks like Mister Clean, takes me by the neck and just throws me in a car. He drove me back to my apartment and then we all kind of had a party afterward. I tried to walk home and someone gave me a cigar on the street and I took some scissors and I started cutting my pubic hair, with my pants down, and I just fainted into a plastic bucket.

Let's talk about all these other directors. There's this whole list that is generally prefixed before you in articles. Godard, Cassavetes, Fellini, etc. Which of these are truly your favourites and which are just critics sticking them in to make themselves sound important?

The idea of being a pragmatist or being a worker doesn't appeal to me. It's only about great artists. For me, it's certain directors, or maybe certain films that have influenced me. Of course, the most interesting career is Fassbinder's career because he was working at such a rate, such an intense level... One year, he

made nine feature films. He worked without stopping, and he never worried about making the single, great film. It was more about films where it was about scenes; where he would be judged on all the films that he made, and at the end of the day, he wouldn't be judged on his masterpiece. He was famous for saying that his films were like a house: some were the floors, some were the walls, some were the chimney. At the end of his life, the whole idea was that he could live in this house of his work, and I love that idea. The two things I remember about films are its characters and certain scenes. I never remember plots; I never remember the whole thing, I only remember specifics, and Fassbinder was so great because there are certain scenes that he would show you that no one else would give you.

How did you come across Alan Clarke [Scum, Billy the Kid and Green Baize Vampire], because he's quite obscure in America?
If someone said to me, who is the greatest director, or my favourite, I would say Alan Clarke without hesitation. His stories, without ever being derivative, and without ever having a simple ABC narrative, are totally organic, precious and amazing. It was nothing but him. In a strange way, I don't even like talking about him in the press or to people, because he's the last filmmaker or artist who is truly sacred. But especially in America, no one knows who he is, even in England, there's very little attention.

How did it feel to win the critics' award at Venice?
It's good that people liked the movie. There's someone that likes it and someone that hates it and I just got to keep truckin' baby.

You are getting your ass licked by the whole of young, avant-garde New York. It must be quite strange. Do you feel how temporal all of that is?
Because my ass is all slippery? To be honest with you, I'm working, so I don't deal with it, but I guess now that the film is over and I'm doing all this promotional stuff... I just deal with it. I was a little bit more prepared for it because of *Kids*. When *Kids* came out, I'd just turned nineteen, and all that stuff happened and that was almost traumatic. I was almost having nervous breakdowns. I was going from living at my grandmother's house with no money to...

... being around supermodels and film stars...
Right, which to me was really unfulfilling.

Is that the kind of world that you feel quite comfortable in now?
Obviously not. The only time I have anything to do with them is when I'm approached by them. I have the same friends I've always had. And it doesn't really matter to me. You know, I have nothing to do with any of them, except when they bother me.

Do you think that you would work again with Chloë Sevigny in a movie? Would you cast her again? Or do you think when she started to work with other directors your period of working together was over?
In the future, the more she works with other directors, the less interested in her I become.

Do you really mean that?
I totally mean that. And that's not to say that she shouldn't be working with other directors. If she likes the script, she should do what she wants to do. I mean that for almost anyone.

Do you think she's one of the best actresses of her generation? Or has the potential to be?
Definitely. I don't even think she has any competition. Because I think she's not scared of taking on characters. I don't think of Chloë as a leading woman. I think of her more as a character actor, which is the only kind of actor I would ever be interested in. But at the same time, the more films she does with other directors, the less interested in working with her I am.

The final question is that everyone must think that you're absolutely loaded, that you must be a very wealthy young man...?
It's a lie!! It's a fucking lie!

Noel Godin, alias Georges Le Gloupier, is a true
veteran of May 68. Author of Cream and
Punishment *(1996) and an 800-page* Anthology
of Subversion *(1988) he has, since his early days
as a film critic in Brussels, been the leader of the
infamous Entarter Movement; that pie-flinging
band of self-styled revolutionaries who stop at
nothing in their quest for freedom and personal
liberty.*

*Formed in the late 1960s as a response to
the growing complacency of the rich and famous,
the Entarter have since grown in stature.
Advocating what they politely term 'a symbolic
pastry assassination of the image', they stalk
the would-be darlings of the media ready to
plant a well-placed* bombe surprise *at but a
moment's notice.*

*No one can escape their wrath. Novelist
Marguerite Duras, film director Jean-Luc Godard
(for turning Catholic and kissing the Pope), the
Bishop of Nante (while delivering the Eucharist),
the French Minister of Culture (on his first-ever
official engagement), five Swiss MPs and the
reviled right-wing French philosopher Bernard-
Henri Lévy who, holding a special place in
Monsieur Godin's heart, has been pied five
times in as many years. Their latest victim,
Microsoft chief and the richest man in the world,
Bill Gates, is still recovering from his multi-
layered chocolate gateau onslaught, which took
place earlier this year, prompting* BodyGuard
Weekly *to ask 'IS ANYONE SAFE?'*

*But, as the controversy thickens, Godin
remains oblivious to any danger that might
threaten him. In a quiet suburb of Brussels,
surrounded by thousands of stolen books on
subversion and thousands more pirated video
tapes of slapstick comedies, he plans his next
move. 'We are only just beginning,' he grins*

*mischievously. 'We feel ready now. We are strong
in numbers. A genuine International Brigade
Patissière has been born, and I firmly believe that
we are capable of achieving even greater things
in the near future. For instance, I believe we can
eventually flan the Pope.'*

Dazed & Confused | **The first person you ever
flanned was the novelist Marguerite Duras
in November 1969. Your latest, Bill Gates in
1998. That's almost thirty years of constant
flanning.**
Noel Godin | It started all that time ago and I
just never stopped. I will never stop. For the
first time, it was like an orgasm, the coitus.
There's something so sexual about flanning
someone: you feel so gratified.
**Do you consider a pie in the face an act of
subversion in the spirit of the late 1960s?**
Of course! I have always remained true to the
spirit of May 68. I still live for that time and
have always advocated direct sabotage; the
sabotage of the professions; the sabotage of the
roles into which we are trapped by our day-
to-day boredom. I propose to all workers to
sabotage their work, to sabotage their
production and their employers, and so, in
accordance with that philosophy, I myself
sabotage my own position as a proletarian
intellectual. That's how I started in the first
place, working as a cinema critic for a magazine
published by the Belgian Catholic League. There,
I sabotaged everything that I ever wrote.
In true Situationist style.
Indeed: the systematic sabotage of life. During
my time as a cinema critic, I printed complete
falsehoods. I would invent non-existing films
that I illustrated with snapshots of my relatives.
I wrote well over two hundred interviews with-

out ever leaving my desk, asking questions
and then writing the answers immediately.
Everything in my short celebrity news column
was faked: breakfast with Robert Mitchum,
aperitifs with Jack Lemmon – none of it ever
happened. I only got away with it because I was
a credible editor and no one would ever see the
copy outside of Belgium.

Poetic misinformation?

Exactly. A methodical form of private and
public subversion. It lasted for twelve years and
I never got into trouble.

Who was your most popular creation?

I once created a blind director from Thailand
named Viviane Pei. I wrote this glowing review
stating that hers were the most beautiful films
in the history of cinema, although she couldn't
see a thing. Masterpieces such as *The Lotus
Flower Will No Longer Grow on the Shores of
Your Island* dripped off my pen. In fact, she
was so convincing as a character that an Asian
cinema critic named Pierre Dial actually went to
Thailand to find her. Once he discovered that
she didn't actually exist, he went ballistic!

And your personal favourite?

That has to be Georges Le Gloupier, leader of the
Entarter Movement. I made up this story that he

was on a crusade, flanning film directors around the world. His first fictitious victim was Robert Bresson, but when I learnt that Marguerite Duras was coming to Belgium, I decided to cross over from the realm of fantasy into the world of reality.

And that was your first venture into the world of flanning. Were you alone on that fateful day?

No. I had a girlfriend who, in accordance with tradition, handed me a pie at the moment of delivery. There was also a cameraman and two photographers, but as usual, the cameraman missed the shot and only the photographers were successful. We were on the front cover of all the Belgian newspapers and have never looked back since.

And now, Georges Le Gloupier has become the official disguise of all would-be Entarters.

As soon as one flans a victim, one instantly becomes Georges Le Gloupier. That's why anyone involved in a hit should wear the Le Gloupier disguise: a false beard, thick spectacles and a bow tie.

Even women?

Especially women!

And now the Entarter movement stretches across the world.

There are cells everywhere, ready for action. We have received well over a thousand letters giving us support. Wherever I go, people want to fight for me. I take down the addresses but I never get round to calling everyone. We could be over ten thousand strong by now, a huge organization, but we operate in a complete mess all the time so we recruit from the street instead. When I was last at the Cannes Film Festival, we were building up a *safari patissier*, but I was only with one other friend. But by the time we flanned Tuscan du Plantier, Bernard-Henri Lévy and Arielle Dombasle, we numbered at least thirty. Many people volunteer, so I just choose them at the last minute.

As you did recently with Bill Gates.

With that particular hit, we numbered thirty-two. We had twenty-five pies in all. We were very cautious, even scared. We were careful to make sure that on the morning of the proposed flanning, two thirds of those involved still didn't know who the target was, because we didn't want people giving the game away by talking to their friends, who would then undoubtedly repeat the information and destroy our cover.

You plan these hits to absolutely the last detail. How do you find out where a potential victim is going to be at a particular time or date?

For the last five operations, the victims have been betrayed by their own entourage. We have informers who come to us with a precise plan of action. That's what happened with Bill Gates. We announced in the press that we were targeting him and within nine days, someone high up in the Belgian headquarters in Microsoft contacted us with a full itinerary of his forthcoming trip to Belgium. His reasons were simple enough. Although he had always admired Bill Gates, he felt that he had become unbearably arrogant and needed to be brought down a peg or two. From that moment on, he never stopped faxing us inside information, including a map of the hotel where Gates was going to be staying.

You had his every move pinned down?

Exactly. The day before he arrived in Belgium, friends of ours in Paris managed to get hold of special press passes and so were able to inform us that he had a bodyguard of five armed men who never left him alone for a second. Our informant at Microsoft also told us that on his journey to Belgium, he would be accompanied by four motorcycle policeman and that wasn't even taking into account the interior security that would undoubtedly be in place in all the sites that he was to visit. But we had numbers on our side. Bodyguards are trained to stop a conspiracy of say, two or three terrorists, but against thirty-two people armed with custard pies they are useless as a defence.

Did you have to stalk him further?
On the actual day of the hit, we had to wait all afternoon. We congregated at the pub and drank Monks beer to give us all courage. Finally, we left the bar singing old anarchist songs to keep our spirits up. When we arrived at the scene, we divided into small elite groups of three people called Unitées Gloupinesque or 'Gloup Gloup Units'. We hid our ammunition in shopping bags and waited. Then suddenly, Bill Gates arrived with all these sirens screaming. At that moment, all the 'Gloup Gloup Units' gathered together to form a pastry whirl and then fell on him in a hurricane of flying pies.

[laughs] And what was his reaction?
At first, he attempted an advertising smile but it soon shrivelled up and changed into a grimace. We shouted the war cry, 'Let us flan, let us flan the tainted money!' and then went into action. In total, he received three pies outside and a further one straight in the face when he entered the hotel lobby. He was so annoyed, he fired his bodyguards the next day.

Other victims have been even less fortunate though. The pretentious French pseudo philosopher Bernard-Henri Lévy has become a regular target of yours hasn't he?
Bernard-Henri Lévy has been flanned five times so far and we are currently planning the sixth operation. He has become so paranoid about being flanned that he now lives in a complete psychosis. When he was in Belgium recently to talk about his latest film production, he would only be interviewed if the journalist agreed to be picked up in a car and driven to a secret location. It got so ridiculous that many Belgian journalists wrote that he was turning totally insane.

So which pie is best suited for assassinations?
It has to be very simple and slapstick: the more orthodox the better – very soft dough with mountains of cream so we don't have to throw the pies, but instead we can lay them directly onto the victim's face. This way, our hit rate is ninety-five per cent. I am almost embarrassed to say that we hardly ever miss our target.

How do you choose your preferred victims?
Our main principle is only to flan people when they are in a very powerful position. In Lévy's case, he uses his position to encourage either war, as he did in Bosnia, or his own profile, as he is presently doing with the Algerian conflict. But we shall carry on flanning him until he learns his lesson. We have the access code to his flat that was given to us by an English journalist. But Lévy always has the option of ceasing hostilities. If on the next pie that he receives he sings the old French song 'Avez-vous le beau chapeau de Zozo', we will sign a peace accord.

You've written that a pie in the face is a good barometer of character. Is that always true?
A pastry assassination always reveals the true colours of its victim. When we hit Jean-Luc Godard in 1985, he showed himself to be elegant in defeat, whilst most other victims are quick tempered. Godard was the great exception. When, after the attack, he heard that I had been banned from the Cannes Film Festival, he called from Switzerland to demand that my pass was given back to me. In contrast, Bernard-Henri Lévy after his fifth flanning in Cannes, demanded that I be banned for life.

Do you consider your pastry assassinations to be assassinations of the image then? A media assassination?
Exactly. On the one hand, it is real terrorism, but it is also a burlesque terrorism. It's very violent, but only symbolically violent; a violence that can be found in Bugs Bunny cartoons or Monty Python. If anyone is wounded, it is only in their self esteem. A pie in the face is a great leveller.

As in the spirit of Dadaist abusive letters sent to celebrities at the turn of the century. [laughs]
I'm a great partisan of those abusive letters

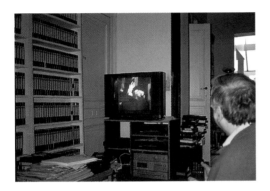

[laughs] sent by the Dadaists, and those sent by the Surrealists, and the Situationists; in fact, a pastry assassination is the perfect materialization of the classic abusive letter. It's an abuse that becomes a reality, that explodes in your face.

The subversive power of humour...
We kill our victims with ridicule...

A cream pie transformed into a bomb!
I believe that we have to use the principal weapon of the enemy and that is the media. The Yippies and Hoffman understood that, they would accept an invitation to appear on television in order to mess around with water guns. That was a major force in amplifying the counterculture movement. They may not be terrorists per se – they didn't kill – but they were extremists. Once, the Yippies managed to get one of their organization inside the Pentagon and put a massive dose of LSD in the drinking water reserve. Other members burned dollar bills in Wall Street.

In contrast to the activities of the more hard-core combat groups such as the Black Panthers or Weathermen.
All those groups were sympathetic, but they lacked of humour. They took themselves far too seriously: righteous Marxists who were very austere. There are a few groups that I felt sympathy for at that time. In particular, the English outfit called The Angry Brigade.

Who's your next target?
I've written a note to Bill Gates saying that we will flan him again before the end of the summer unless he gives the equivalent of one day's salary to the Zapatist Commandant Marcos in the Chiapas.

And your main objective?
To declare Chattily war on all heads of state. We vow to get Chirac within the next year, to cover Clinton from head to toe in chocolate gateau; also Tony Blair, Fidel Castro and the Pope. That is the thing of real importance. I don't consider it a negative act to prostitute myself if it helps me to reach my goal. I know that some so-called 'pure' revolutionaries say that you should never compromise in order to reach revolution, but they always seem to be saying that while drinking in bars. They want to rebuild the world sat on their arses. I've nothing to lose by playing games. It can be dangerous of course, but I trust myself. Nothing will make me recant. I say, 'Let them all eat cake!'

Dazed & Confused | **Are you the tenth richest woman in Britain?**
Kate Moss | Yeah I read that as well. *[laughs]*
Where did they get that from?
I don't know.
Do you ever need to work again?
It depends on the lifestyle I want.
What would your porn name be? What's your middle name?
I haven't got one. Your stage name is your middle name and the street you grew up on and then your porn name is your first pet's name and your mum's maiden name. Isn't it? What was your first pet's name?
Olga.
And your mum's maiden name?
Pearman.
Olga Pearman. *[laughs]*
I thought it was your first toy and your mum's maiden name.
I would have been Bonnie Shepherd.
What part were you in the school play? In the Nativity?
I was an angel. Of course. *[laughs]*
Are you good at lying?
Yeah really good. I did a really good trick on my friend. We were on holiday and my boyfriend had gone away. I was left and everyone else was all couples and I was sitting up by myself and everyone else was in their bedrooms shagging and my friend walked out of the bedroom and I was like, 'Fuck!' and she was like, 'What?' And I was like, 'You cow, it's not fucking fair.' So I followed her down to the mosquito net and pretended to cry for about fifteen minutes, really hysterically. 'You fucking bastard. You just don't care, you're just so selfish.' And she was like, 'What's wrong with you?' She was really freaked out and I went WAARRRERRR!

and she was like, 'I'll get you for that, I'll get you!' It was a funny one, she was really pissed off. I like it when you can get people.
If you were doing a compilation tape, what would be on it?
'Melody' by The Rolling Stones and 'Sympathy for the Devil' and 'White Horses Warm Gun' by The Beatles and 'Ticket to Ride' and 'Unfinished Symphony' by Massive Attack and 'Heart of Glass' and 'Rapture' by Blondie. 'Lust for Life' and 'I Wanna Be Your Dog' by Iggy Pop. Snoop Doggy Dog and Packetman and Donna Summer 'Love to Love You Baby'.
What's your favourite film?
Abigail's Party.
Is it?
Oh I don't know. It's got to be in there, I've watched it so many times.
Who would you most like to meet who you haven't met already?
I don't know. I'd like to meet Lucien Freud. I heard he was really cool. Like, for eighty years old, he's really hip and cool apparently.
Favourite sexual position?
Nosey cow. What's yours?
[laughs]
Exactly. Can I have a light?
Can you recite a poem please? Or write a poem, even if it's only three lines long.
Hang on... We'll come back to that one.
What are you taking on holiday?
Oh, I've remembered one. Hang on. Oh no, it's a bit heavy though, it's a sad shepherd poem.
That's OK.
It goes something like: The thrill has gone, the thrill has gone, I can see it in your eyes, I can hear it in your sighs... No, what is it? Oh, it's a really good one... I can't remember, but that's three lines though.

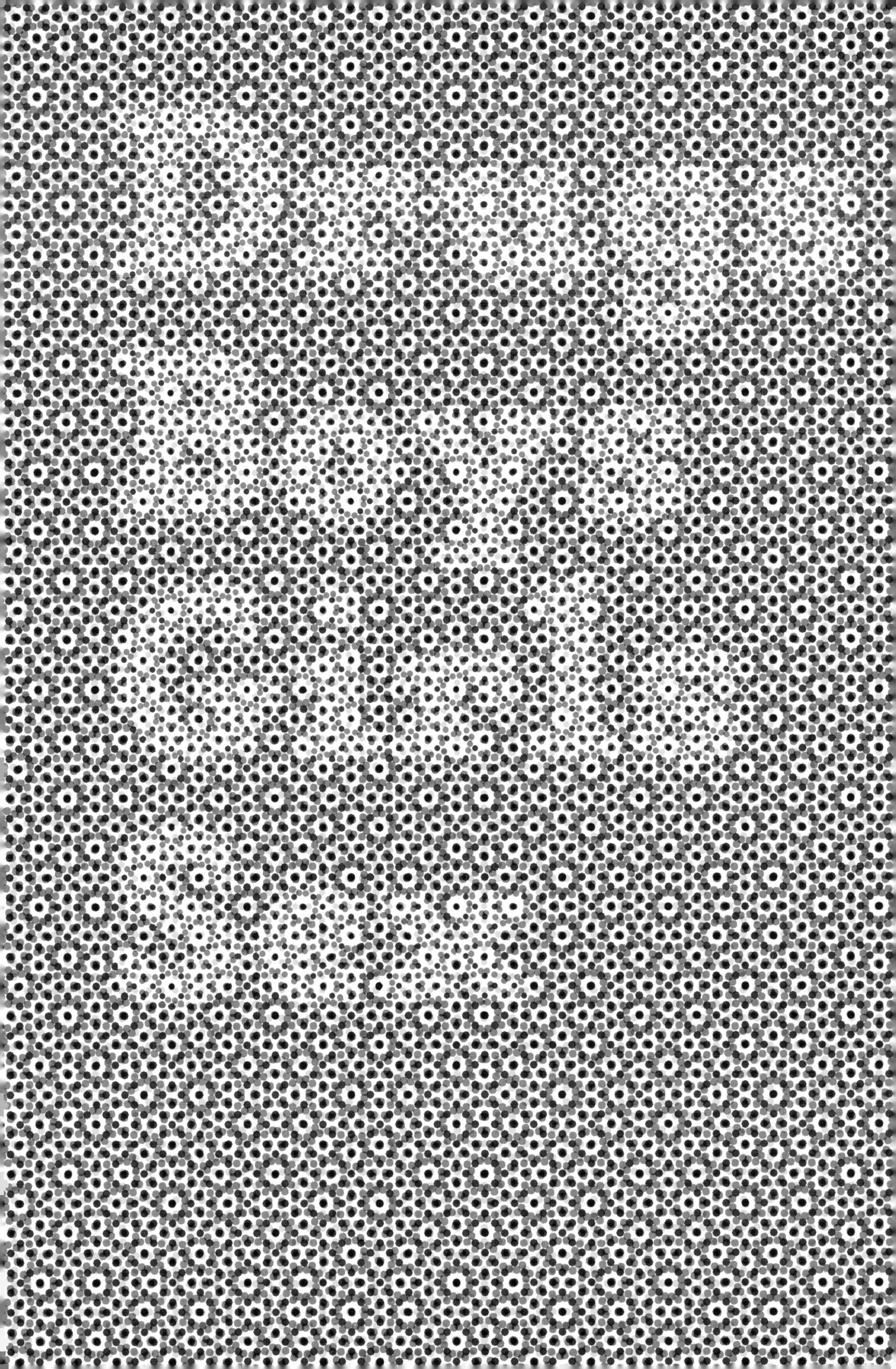

Kate Moss, 1999
Rankin

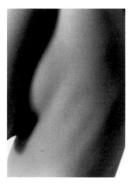

Have you ever been dumped?
My first boyfriend finished with me.
Why?
He went back to his first girlfriend. They're getting engaged now. They've been together since they were about thirteen.
What's your favourite drinks recipe?
Sea Breeze or Martini. Sea Breeze is always good.
What's the key to a good Martini?
A shot of vermouth on ice in a shaker poured over five seconds' worth of Belvedere vodka over ice and then stirred slowly and then poured into a Martini glass over two olives.
Do you like tequila? Do you know what's fantastic? Tequila shot and lemon and then on one side you put ground coffee and on the other side you put sugar. And you do the Tequila and then bite on that and it's fantastic.
Wow! I can't do tequila shots. It makes me go mad. I lose the plot. I get that excitement thing in the bottom of my spine and I start to go like this... squirming around. It has to be Belvedere vodka.
Let's play word association.
I don't know how to play that.
First word that comes into your head. Sex.

[laughs] Dick.
Cock.
Screw.
Driver.
Mercedes.
Diana.
Crash/Dodi.
Chariots of Fire.
Ben Hur.
Cleopatra.
Cow.
Bath.
Chartreuse???? It's really pure: it's like cotton wool.
Decadence.
Drugs.
Boys.
Girls.
Tits/Sex.
Vibrators.
Do you own one?
Yes. Every 90s girl does.
What colour is it?
Silver bullet. I couldn't really go in and buy it for myself, so it was kind of a gift. My friend got it for me. Do you own one?
I was bought one once and I threw it out.
I don't actually use it that much. I'm not really into them. My friend had one and I thought they were fantastic. I thought it was really good and thought 'wow! I'll have to get one of these' and then when I got one I didn't really get on that well with it...
What's your favourite picture that anyone's ever taken of you?
I suppose it's Corrine Day's. Steven Sproust did a gun-metal silver one of Iggy Pop on a cross, and he gave me one for my birthday and now I've painted it white.

Dissent in America is practically unknown. This is because, as Ralph Nader noted recently, Americans are 'growing up corporate'. While the rest of the world seem happy merely sporting corporate brands on their T-shirts, Americans must live the brand with high schools, athletic teams and entire communities pledging contractual allegiance to Coke, Pepsi or Nike. Grossly emblematic of our times, the corporate-spun hyper-consumption teeming across America is imprinting itself literally onto our DNA.

Humans may someday have diseases with brand names such as 'Dow' Syndrome, GE/PCB Condition, or DuPontitis. Since 250,000 new chemicals are released into the environment every year – with virtually no testing for their long-term health effects – it's no wonder that the most toxic substance we ingest in our lifetime is mother's milk. As Nader says, 'This is a situation beyond satire.'

In the US, where news and entertainment are indistinguishable, Nader is heaven-sent. Besides his massive network of lawyers for social justice and a website umbrella of citizen-action coalitions (www.essential.org), the giant clerkish attorney has the big-picture lasso to pull US resistance together. He was ranked by Time magazine as being among the hundred most influential Americans in the US, and the recent federal anti-trust suits launched against Microsoft and Intel are proving big-time the power of his persuasion.

'Do you know what happens to a biological organism that spends most of its day entertaining itself?' he asks. 'Do you have any idea what happens to a society that spends more of its time tending to its pleasures, and in this case corporate-shaped pleasures, and less and less of its time on serious grappling with its problems?

The issue is where do each of us stand in challenging and participating in the future. If you don't turn on the politics, the politics will turn on you – corporate-style.'

Most Americans, their critical faculties fading and eroded from decades of corporate-image pummelling, automatically link progressive movements, labour unions and government regulations with Stalin, Jimmy Hendrix or the Mafia, and find it surprising that a political 'activist' like Nader actually believes in America and the democratic process.

His master-plan is to enable citizens to monitor and influence how their tax-dollars are spent by linking them with statewide tribes of consumers. 'I can assure you that a handful of watchdogs can save billions of dollars just in the last week of the congressional budget, by throwing a spotlight on, and exposing these arcane provisions in the tax laws that give business X $5 billion a year or Y-industry $6 billion of forgiven debts, etc.'

Nader's question-and-answer sessions are often longer than his speeches, as he is known to field questions and comments until the lines behind the microphones are sapped – presumably hoping to find someone in possession of a leaked document, or a smoking corporate gun.

Ralph Nader | Thomas Jefferson said that the purpose of representative government was 'to counteract the excesses of monied interests'. They felt it was so important, that every time someone wanted to start a company, they had to get a bill in the state legislature: a charter. And it was chartered for a public purpose. And then the companies got bigger and said, 'We can't go through the Legislature, let's just do it by the State corporation commission', and their criteria loosened, and they could produce anything, and the rigours began being weakened. And in the nineteenth century, there were big debates on what was being unleashed. For a century, corporations have been getting all the rights that we human beings have, and an avalanche of privileges and immunities that we don't have.

Dazed & Confused | **What is happening to working people today?**

The greatest power of the corporate State is not their power: it is the widespread feeling among millions of Americans that they don't count, they don't matter, and 'why try'. 'Why try' because the powers that be will decide for them: whether they get laid off or not from their work, whether they grow up in toxic chemical exposures, whether they're sent off to foreign adventures, whether they're bled dry in taxes that go into unproductive investments, through Washington and State capitals – they just seem to have lost control – and you can see that everywhere. It doesn't matter if they're liberals or conservatives, moderates or anarchists, libertarians, whatever. They feel they have lost control over everything that affects them; whether it's the marketplace, the workplace, the government, the streets, the environment, their own children. And it's that recovery that spells the future of democracy as a problem-solver, as a fulfiller of human possibilities in our country.

What kind of privileges?

In the late 1940s there was a lawsuit brought by the Justice department of the Chicago Federal District court against General Motors tyre companies and oil companies. What these companies did was to buy up the mass-transit systems, including the biggest electrified trolley system in the world – in Southern California –

rip up the tracks in twenty-eight metropolitan areas, and push for more highways, so they could sell more buses, more vehicles, more oil, more tyres. And the result was the devastation of public transport development in the United States, and the enormous accident, economic and other tolls that people are going through, and the billions of hours lost every year. You know what fine General Motors paid for what some scholars think is the economic crime of the century? Five thousand dollars. And they were off back to Detroit to design Corvairs.

Is Gen X being supplanted by Gen Rich?

Corporations can now have patents on life forms in genetic engineering. They're going to be producing humanoids in thirty to forty years. A microbiologist from Princeton wrote a book called *Remaking Eden* and he said that we are heading into a society where people who can afford it will enhance their physical and mental ability, and most of the people who can't afford it will stay natural. And, increasingly, the gap will grow, the experience level will grow, they'll live in different communities, and by the year 2350 they will have as much appeal to one another as a chimpanzee and a human being have today. But the most chilling part of this prediction is that the global economy will determine this situation. In other words, genetic engineering policy and practice is shaped by the market – by commercial imperatives – and there won't be countervailing values with any power behind them to counteract the problem of a restrictive view of the gene pool.

Americans seem content to pay companies to poison them – like Martin Marietta, who dumped military waste into local drinking water, or Superfund clean-up contractors (and the EPA) turning toxic sludge, some of it radioactive, into food. These are the shadow corporations whose logos are not promoted on any sweatshirts, but to whom unique endocrine and hormonal disruptions may someday be traced back.

Corporations sign contracts with the Pentagon. You know what they get reimbursed for? Their pollution and toxic dumping – and the clean up – even if it's intentional. If the Pentagon accuses them of criminal activity, they hire corporate law firms, and until recently, they sent a bill to you, the taxpayer.

When Martin Marietta and Lockheed merged and laid off thousands and thousands of workers, the Pentagon spent half a billion dollars of taxpayers' money to facilitate the merger, and thirty million went to bonuses for the top executives. And it just goes on and on!

What else goes on?

Medical malpractice is one of the leading forms of preventable violence in this country. A conservative estimate by the physicians at the Harvard School of Public Health says that in any given year, eighty thousand people in the US die in hospitals from malpractice – that's in hospitals, not including clinics. That is, more lost lives than the combined fatalities of motor-vehicle deaths, homicides and death-by-fire in the United States, and that doesn't count the injuries, which cost sixty billion dollars a year in lost economies. And guess what? The corporations are on Capitol Hill, trying to restrict the rights of victims of malpractice from having their full day in court, to hold their perpetrator responsible. And one of their ways is to make sure that the brain-damaged infant, the teenager who will never walk again, the housewife who is a paraplegic or the worker who is a quadriplegic cannot collect more than two hundred and fifty thousand dollars for a lifetime of pain and suffering, no matter what the judge and jury think they're entitled to.

Crikes!

Now to show you the inequity that even exceeds medieval comparisons, one of the executives of one of the insurance agencies pushing for these kinds of reforms is the head of the A I G insurance company – which pumped hundreds of thousands of dollars into the Republican convention. I looked up what he made in 1994. This man wants a two hundred and fifty thousand dollar cap, non-inflation adjusted, spread out over a fifty-year life expectancy for a brain-damaged infant from medical malpractice. He was making two hundred and fifty thousand dollars a week, every week, with no pain and suffering. And the top CEOs of the *Fortune* 500 companies are making one hundred and eighty times the entry-level wage. You know what it was in 1940? Twelve. You know what it was in 1980? Forty. You know what it was in 1990? A hundred and forty. It's now over one hundred and eighty.

What happened to Clinton's proposed health-care system?

Clinton came to Washington for some sort of universal health care – why should we be the only Western nation that doesn't have universal health insurance? Forty-five million people including children not covered, twenty million under-covered, the rest of us worried about falling through the cracks – pre-existing conditions, co-payments, deductibles, exclusions, cancellations and all the fine print. And in came the lobbyists to Washington: the corporate jets flew down, the political action committees animated themselves with their swollen purses to corrupt the members of Congress further. The medical lobbies, the hospital lobby, the drug/ pharmaceutical lobby and, of course, the HMO lobby. And they pretty much got their way. Now they have gag orders on doctors not to level with the patient. They give bonuses to doctors to withhold referrals and save money. In effect, they are rationing health care. You have drive-through births, drive-through mastectomies.

What is the State of the Union?

In the last twenty years we have had an extraordinary concentration of wealth in fewer and fewer global corporation hands. When you have that kind of concentration of power and wealth, you have a weakened democracy; you have a weakened public voice; you have a weakened public advocacy. We have allowed global corporations with no allegiance to our country to scour the globe for the dictatorships and the dirt-cheap labour, to exploit and export the jobs there. We have allowed them to take over our government, to take over our economy, to exploit small business, to straitjacket inventors, to shape our very culture, to replace our folk culture with commercial culture that stresses violence and addiction, to stress what kind of research is done at our universities, to decide that the ordinary people pay the taxes, to decide that they, the corporations, are not going to pay any taxes.

Don't corporations pay taxes?

In the 1950s, corporate income tax represented between twenty-five and thirty per cent of the federal outlays, today it's between six and eight per cent. Record corporate profits, record stock-market prices, record executive compensations, and they are paying a shrinking amount! Many of these corporations pay one or two per cent federal tax. Between 1981 and 1983, the giant General Electric Company – which produced six and a half billion dollars in profits and paid no taxes because of a safe harbour loophole provision – got a hundred and fifty million dollar refund, which was supposed to get GE to invest in new, productive capital equipment. Instead they bought RCA and NBC. And now, maybe you wonder why NBC isn't covering the close-down of four nuclear plants in Connecticut, three of which were closed down due to safety reasons this summer? GE's in the nuclear business! What do you expect!

Go Ralph go! Go Ralph go!

Go? We go!

For all those super-rich Pollyanna's who think America is number one: in 1980, the US was first in wages in the world. It's now eleventh and sinking. In 1980, the US was the greatest creditor in the world. It's now the biggest debtor. We're seventeenth in the world in infant-mortality, we have twenty-three per cent child poverty – almost one out of every four children in America live in dire poverty with all that means in terms of stunted human potential: health hazards, safety hazards, brutalizations and surroundings that you wouldn't want to have to describe. You know what the child poverty rate is in the Netherlands and Sweden? Three per cent Netherlands, two per cent Sweden, and they're ashamed of it! We're the only country that doesn't have universal health insurance, the last country in the world to face up to it. Over forty million Americans, many of them children, have no health insurance, twenty million are under-insured, and the rest wonder when they're going to fall through the cracks when they change jobs: pre-existing

conditions, co-payments, deductibles, exclusions, cancellations. Hey! This is the land of the free, home of the brave. What gives?

Go Ralph go! Go Ralph go!

Go? We go!

One per cent of the richest people have taken two-thirds of the financial wealth increase in the 1980s. The wealth of ninety per cent of the American people is barely equal to the wealth of the top two per cent – even one per cent – depending on which figures you rely on. That kind of concentration of wealth is greater than any country in Western Europe, greater than in Japan. We now have the biggest disparity in wealth and income between the rich and the rest of the American people of any country in the Western industrialized world. And we used to have the least inequality, because Europe was so class stratified with barons, etc. Just imagine the decline: corporations are contributing fifty per cent less to private pensions of workers who are lucky enough to have private pensions. Homelessness is up. Notice what happens: the GNP goes up in the aggregate and the yardsticks show growth, but it's decline for more and more American people. What happens is, the big guys at the top start dividing and ruling, and the middle is told, 'Hey! it's those poor people on welfare – they're eating your taxes alive!' Have you ever heard these big guys at the top say, 'Hey! It's those rich guys on welfare, they're really eating you out of house and home.'

Go Ralph go! Go Ralph go!

Go? We go!

I'm going to mention the following words: 'crime', 'violence' and 'welfare regulation'. What do you think of? Street images and government regulation? That's growing up corporate. Because, while you certainly are entitled to think of street images, more violence is preventable by corporate activity, and more welfare is disbursed to corporations than to the poor, and corporations regulate us far more than our government. Here's the propaganda: you ask the average citizen in this country, 'What percentage of federal outlay goes to means-tested poverty entitlement programmes: food stamps, AFDC, child support, child nutrition, school lunches?' Not many of them would say, 'Three-point-four per cent of entire federal outlays.' Now, when you ask them, 'How much do you think goes for corporate welfare?' Well, suddenly there's a lack of statistics! But even the Wall Street Journal estimated it at one hundred and forty billion dollars a year. If you take corporate welfare in terms of subsidies, bail-outs, inflated government contracts, tax loopholes of the grossest sort and forgiveness of corporate debt, you're up to two hundred billion dollars a year – easily! And yet, when the citizen groups go up to congress and say, 'Please, can we have fifty million more dollars for safe drinking-water systems?' – 'Sorry, no money'; 'Can we have three hundred million dollars for equal justice under law, called legal services for the poor?' – 'Oh, no! We can't afford it'; 'Can we have three hundred million dollars for public broadcasting, wholesome programming for children instead of the violence they see on TV?' – 'Oh, no! Gotta balance the budget!'

[laughs]

Yet, a few years ago, this congress funded billions of dollars for the biggest mass-transit programme in this country. You know what it was? The MX missile! What if an average family allocated its budget the way the federal government under corporate power allocates its budget? The family would be committed!

What if an average family spent twenty per cent of its budget against a non-existent enemy? *[applause]*

How about if it spent another fifteen per cent to make the people living in the mansions on the hill richer, and then wrung its hands when it came down to feeding its own children, providing them with health care, or a decent education, clothing and housing? Our federal budget has enormous money that is being misused and wasted and escalated up from the middle class to the rich and the corporate – money that could be used to produce millions of jobs in public works: building, rebuilding, repairing America.

Go we go! Go we go! Go we go!

Go we go! Go we go! Good!

Our society is being corporatized to a point where we are being turned into Pavlovian specimens. We are moving into a societal pattern where you have commercialism *über alles*, subordinating other more important value systems. Democratic processes are undermined by closed tribunals in Geneva under the World Trade Organization – health and safety subordinated and accused of being too tough and therefore trade restrictive.

Refusing hazardous waste or products of child labour could be 'market discriminatory'. Here in Colorado, we've got a Superfund site containing plutonium that a government contractor and the EPA are converting into toxic sludge to be spread over local farmlands.

They've inured Coloradans to radioactivity. You are more inured here in Colorado than almost anybody in the country. Watch out for silent violence. Toxics, irradiation, etc. The data is quite compelling in terms of the level of plutonium that is being permitted in this sludge, but of course, if you come down with cancer, the doctor isn't going to say to the morning radio show that it's due to this. The problem with silent violence is that they don't leave tracks – the way a mugger does in the street – and therefore we tend to let our guard down. Sensorially, we can't alert ourselves to it: we can't feel, see, touch or smell it – we have to do it intellectually – and if we're not given the data, the information, the risk levels, the alternatives of disposal – we'll wake up with serious problems.

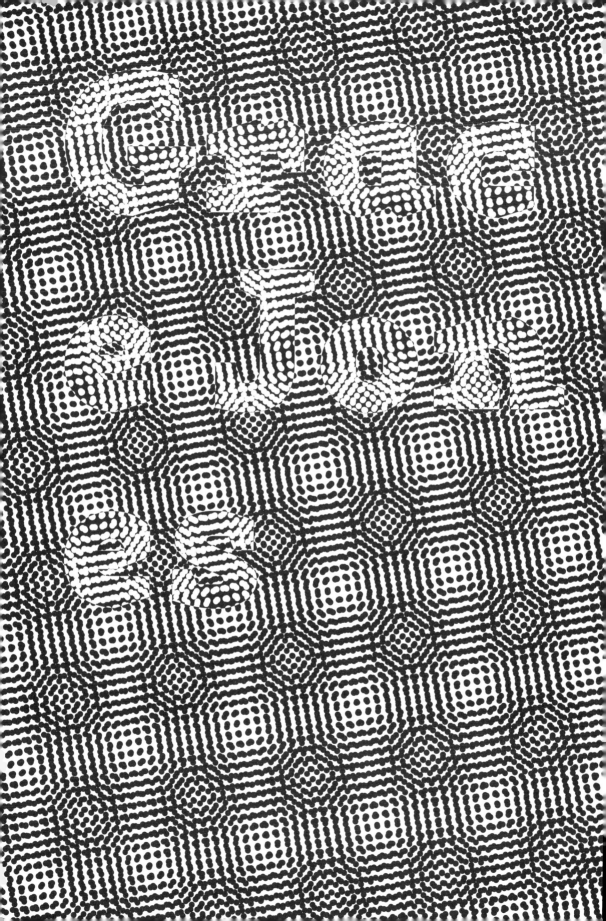

September 1998
Introduction and interview | *Alix Sharkey*

Grace Jones is the very definition of an icon, a person whose unmistakable image has come to symbolize all the incredibly diverse and often contradictory elements of her own life.

As a Jamaican-born, American-educated, Paris-based catwalk queen, Grace became the world's first supermodel a decade before the term even existed. An androgynous female who toyed with the look and sound of masculinity, a shockingly beautiful black woman who stunned weak-minded liberals by inverting racist images and selling them back as the latest word in clinical chic, a musician who combined the lazy skank of Kingston, the coke-powered sass and rumble of New York disco, and the existential alienation of the European electronic tradition... You want an icon? Take your pick.

In deliberately selecting and synthesizing the most powerful elements of a new and radically empowered emergent youth culture, Grace Jones created something that happens only once or twice in a lifetime: she invented a new definition of stardom. Madonna had Monroe, Harlow and countless other bombshell blondes, and decades of photographic and cinematic treasure troves to plunder – but Grace had to start from scratch and build herself from the ground up. Her vision has stood the test of time. Before Grace Jones, nobody looked even remotely like her. Today, her influence is everywhere. It will probably be thirty or forty years before the power of her fusion of art and artifice is fully recognized and appreciated.

Besides bringing catwalk chic to the rock stage, she gave continental finesse to the dancefloor, she took Jamaican rudeboy attitude uptown, and brought Armani to the attention of a whole generation of flea-market stylists. While the first British style magazines were struggling to articulate their new self-consciousness, Grace was already light-years ahead, toying with signifiers of gender, fashion, race and class – manipulating and distorting her image with the help of then-lover and collaborator Jean-Paul Goude, who at that time was probably the most innovative art director in the world.

So while overweight white boys paraded in pantomime costumes, feline Grace and her twelve clones goose-stepped across the stage, sleek in Mao suits and black stilettos, a cruel satire on the fascist underside of the fashion industry. While New Romantics flounced to cheesy sub-Kraftwerk rhythms, Grace was incorporating state-of-the-art studio technology with a live sound built on the bedrock of the world's most powerful and subtle rhythm section, Kingstonian reggae masters Sly Dunbar and Robbie Shakespeare.

While three-chord troglodytes babbled about breaking the conventions of the dreary rock gig, Grace toured her astonishing One Man Show in theatres across Europe, setting standards for concert production that remain unequalled even today. And while pop crooners recorded pale imitations of the Bowie sound, Grace went straight to the source, rewiring its artificial intelligence with Nightclubbing (1981), an album whose title track actually improved on the 1978 Iggy Pop/David Bowie original. How many Suedes or Blurs or Verves do you think could pull that trick off? I'll tell you – none of them.

Nightclubbing was sly, slick and shallow; it was sexy and witty and beautiful and bored, it was blasé and world-weary; in short, everything that early 80s nightlife wanted to be but couldn't quite manage. While the rest of the nightlife bratpack yearned to be featured in some glossy fashion magazine and photographed by the world's best lensmen, Grace Jones had already photography. It would have to be someone who's really in tune. It's my little baby, you know what I mean? But it doesn't have to be someone from Jamaica. I have a couple of off-the-wall directors in mind, including a Japanese guy. *[laughs]* Because it's a story that can happen anywhere, to any foreigner who leaves their country, grows up and leaves it, and returns many years later; it's a universal theme.

So it's about returning to your roots and really dealing with where you're from and what you're about. Is that a theme that's going through your life at the moment?

Oh no, it's been going my whole life. Every time I go back to Jamaica, it goes through my life, *[laughs]* through my life. *[laughs]*

Do you go back often?

Yes. I force myself to go back often, because... that's another film. That's gonna take it even higher. I've had some very... it's like Jamaica was spitting me out. Like it tried to kill me a few times. Oh yeah.

Do you know why?

No. It's something with the island, it's something with the nature. It's a spiritual thing. And I have to keep going back to resist it. To overcome it. It's like, they say you fall off the horse, you get back on it. I saw a psychic once, I was so scared to go back. Every time I went back something strange happened to me. I had near-death experiences. So that's another film.

There's not much cinema about Jamaica anyway, and though *The Harder They Come* was a great movie, it only really touched on this idea that there is a certain power in this place...

There is.

What's the native magic of Jamaica called?

Obia.

It's still practised?

Of course. It goes on, generation after generation. They pass it on. They believe in inheritance. *[laughs]*

Do you believe in God?

Yes. Oh yes, definitely.

But do you believe in a Christian God? Is it that God you believe in?

Um... yes. Not necessarily the way it's written, you know. But the writings are inspirations; a lot of them are written in parables and inspirations and visions and over the years,

---

been there, seen it and done much, much more. Her adult life is virtually a history of the last thirty years of pop culture, involving friendships and collaborations with Andy Warhol, Keith Haring, Jean-Michel Basquiat, Jerry Hall, Mick Jagger, Michael Jackson, Halston and dozens of others. She was at every club that meant any-thing over the last two decades and plenty more besides. Even now, she's working on the cutting edge, recording new tracks with Tricky and Lil' Kim with a view to a new album, and writing a movie about Jamaican life with the backing of Chris Blackwell. She is still one of the most jaw-droppingly beautiful women in the world. She lives large, loves Roederer Crystal champagne, she won't give in and she won't feel guilty, from the nipple to the bottle never satisfied... Ladies and gentlemen, Miss Grace Jones...

Dazed & Confused | **So this movie you're writing, are you going to star in it?**

Grace Jones | I'm playing a lead role, but I'm not going to play myself, you know? I don't want to give out the story just yet, though, because someone might decide to take it. But it's about a family that's moved away and we all have to go back to Jamaica – something brings us all together again... and it's family and secrets, things that come out, because it's a very emotional time – the reason that brings us back there and just throws us all together. It's a very simple movie, but it's gonna be great. The dialogue and the story will make it.

Any ideas who's going to direct it?

I've been thinking a lot about that. A couple of guys have said I should just do it myself.

Could you handle that?

Yeah, if I had the right support, back-up. Either an assistant director or a good director of

This page and overleaf
Grace Jones, 1998
Juergen Teller

things get changed, whereas we know it's a history book as well. I don't take every single thing that's written in the way some of my family will take it. I still sit down and have conversations with my family about, 'Come on, really now, tell me there were no people before Adam and Eve.' I think that's kinda hard to believe. It means something, but I don't take it as absolute truth. Do you know what I'm saying? If you really read the Bible, and believe me we had to read it a lot... every time we got whipped we had to read, you know, a part of it.

You were whipped?
Yeah, of course. We got whipped in school, caned. Same thing, it's a stick. Mmm.

In the limo

A legend has started to build around Studio 54, so how do you see that period now?
I just did this thing about it, a couple of TV interviews, actually. There's this whole explosion of interest: two films being made, it's unbelievable. I guess there's just still so much mystery, stories... there's probably stories I've never even heard of, I'm sure... you couldn't be everywhere at the same time, and it was a big club, so... No, it was great – very airy, very breezy – the music was great, you know, obviously the music is what everybody is still sampling and rapping over. It was a magical place. I think that a lot of magic has to do with... starts with the place, before the people even go inside, you know. It had its vibe already, you know? Like we were talking before about Jamaica already having its own thing, without... And when I walked into Studio 54, they'd just found the building, and it had such a great feeling.

You went down there with Steve Rubell when he'd just found it?

Not with Steve, no. I went down there with Carmen D'Alessio, who was the press person hired to make things happen. And we were very good friends then, we were hanging out all the time together. So she took me in there to show me, and said, 'Oh, I think it would be great for you to do a concert.' So she dragged me along, and we went in. There was nobody there, it hadn't been fixed up or anything, and I started going 'ahh, ahh', making sounds, and the sound was... you could give a concert without any PA system.

So you performed there?

I opened it. I did the opening night. And I think I did what, maybe three or four concerts there. Yeah, I mean we're talking authentic disco. *[laughs]* And people didn't think that disco would have any effect on record sales at that time. It was just like, aaahhhh, people dancing, and you know, whatever.

Is Studio 54 where you met Andy Warhol?

No, I knew Andy way before that. I don't know how I actually met Andy. Probably with Richard Bernstein, who did all the *Interview* covers. Yeah, I went to The Factory with Richard, and met Andy there.

And was it through Andy that you met Keith Haring, which then led to him doing that amazing body painting on you?

Oh, Keith and I worked together all the time, even before we did pictures or anything. I probably met Keith at the Garage.

Paradise Garage, you used to go dancing there, too?

Oh, of course. Yeah, I'm sure I met Keith at the Garage.

Grace, the thing is, you represent a *line*

right through the culture, right up to this present day, like, what you haven't been involved in really doesn't matter. This is such an astonishing life story. How did this happen?

It just happened. There was no plan. There's always been a magnet that would pull me together with like, crazy artists, unusual people. Even though I wasn't looking for that, somehow it was just predestined that we would cross each other's paths and share time on this earth, y'know, in a way that was unique.

You also shared a flat with Jerry Hall in the 70s.

Yes, we shared a small hotel room, in a model

hotel in Paris – you're all models in the hotel. We had this tiny room and this little mirror where we were both bumping our faces, trying to put our make-up on, to go out. I think they wanted to encourage the models to go out, because it was too small a space to live in. It was just big enough to sleep in and do your make-up – no closet space, and we were just clothes freaks. We were crazy about dressing up, making up, painting ourselves, inventing looks. I mean, designers used to love to watch us walk in, to give them ideas for their next collection. Jerry turned me on to this place called The Rag Queen, which sold antique clothing, stuff from the 40s, and Liz, the owner, would go hunting for antique clothes just for us. It was an amazing time, and we created a whole style from the antique clothing. I'm sure there are still a lot of passionate people out there still doing it, but you have to be a passionate historian about it. I mean, then, fashion was really about style, not just throwing on something really quick. I mean, we spent time and we thought about how we were gonna look before we stepped outside. We weren't denim girls, who would just throw on a pair of jeans. I guess that was still what one would call the hippie days, where you would just throw on some jeans and tie your shirt like this. And I guess that's more what we're coming into now.

I think we're back at that point on the historical cycle just before disco, before punk, when the hippie thing had gone as far as it could go, had become completely mainstream and tired and used up, and now we're waiting for something to happen, do you not think?

I know what you mean. And you know *why*? We're going through a period without the emo-tions, without the convictions, without the revolution. And when you don't have all that to go with it, you're in limbo, because it's just about repeating the look without the spirit behind it.

It's about sampling, about recycling the sound but not the feeling, right?

Thank you, *[laughs]* thank you! It's true, you know.

OK, let's do tabloid. Tell me about the time you were performing in New York and the guy jumped on stage and handcuffed himself to your ankle.

Oh, there was a double page picture of him in the papers and the magazines with the black hood, the mask on.

One of those leather rapist masks? With the zip across the mouth?

I don't know, I was scared, I didn't look. I just beat him in the head. I got so upset I started pounding on his head. When I realized what he did, I was beating him. *[laughs]*

How did you get him off?

Oh, man. The bouncers were very evil, actually. They just broke three of his fingers apparently, he had to go to hospital, and they just said, 'Right you give us the keys or you're a dead man.' Three or four of them jumped him and they had a good time, pounding on him. They wait all night for some shit like that to happen.

And when it does, it's 'OK, showtime!'

And the next thing you know, my publicist's called me and told me the kid's in the hospital with three fingers broken. I mean really, I don't like to hear that he got hurt, but he came there with this in mind, it was planned.

Right, so what did he expect, an invitation to dinner? Next question: what's the thing you least like about yourself?

Oh, my skinny legs. *[laughs]* My calves, to be exact. I have this huge – what do you call it – complex, this major complex about my calves. So that's physically...

And apart from physically?

Well, I shouldn't say that I don't like it because it actually saves me a lot, sometimes, but, I have a bad temper. *[laughs]* I put my foot in my mouth a lot. *[laughs]* I just say what I... woaaaaaagggggghhhhh! You know what I mean? But then if you know me well, you know I'm just blowing off steam, like a bull. I've got that Taurean thing, that can really hurt me in the long run, by not thinking. So I try to learn to count to ten, and if I'm not on my period, and I haven't got a toothache... *[Grace's manager John Pelosi interrupts at this point, saying, 'Which leaves, what... two weeks a month?' at which both collapse laughing]* Oh John, fuck you! *[laughs]* You're so... So, anyway, I should be locked away at least a week every month. Otherwise... The other night something upset me and steam, I swear to God, steam was literally coming out of my ears, my hair, my head, and I got really, really nervous because I thought I was spontaneously combusting. Yes! It never happened to me before, but I was upset about something... and I was freaking out. You could see it! Like, steam! Rising out of my body, my ears, and going up... I kept seeing this blur, and then I realized I was steaming! I thought I was just going to burst into flames! *[laughs]* Oh, yes, it was at the airport in Buenos Aires.

Upstairs in the hotel room

I'm so upset that this jacket doesn't fit me... *[holds up a scarlet leather backless jacket by Alexander McQueen]* and this piece... *[holds up a McQueen corset-skirt]* it's beautiful, but it's for someone anorexic... though you can always order it in any size.

I noticed when you were talking about fashion earlier on that you know a lot about the way clothes are constructed.

Yes, well we all had to sew; my mother made us sew and crochet. The whole family sews – the boys, the girls, everybody. We learned to embroider, we learned tailoring, dress-making, the whole thing, because my mother was a seamstress. And we had to stay up when my mum was doing weddings. So we had church and all that, then you'd come home, sewing all night. So late night, going to bed when the sun came up, was a natural thing for us. Because we were helping mum out, you know, because Jamaican weddings are big! And there's a lot of handwork, you know what I'm saying? We had to go hunt for patterns; we had to cut them, sew them, you know? So I was staying up all night sewing Givenchy patterns to wear to school. Yeah! You know, you wanna new dress, you buy the pattern and you make it. All the *haute couture* pattern books. So if I buy something expensive and see a stitch out of place, I get really upset!

So what's the trait in yourself you like the most?

Oh dear, it's patience. Yeah, I think I've really understood what patience means. *[laughs]* That takes a while... it does...Yeah, but... it makes me relax. Patience is stress free, it's kinda watching everything go by, without feeling that you're missing out on something. Feeling that yours is out there. It may not be passing at the same time, with everything else that you see moving... that you can't just jump on that because, you know, you're feeling, 'Oh, I should be here', you know? Where I am is where I should be?

I know you're Jamaican and all, but this reminds me of the Fitzgerald quote about American lives not having third acts. And so many legendary figures just burn up, they're over and finished very quickly, but you are a survivor and you are definitely going to have a third act. I guess what I mean is, I find it strange that there is no biography of your life, and very little real appreciation of the course that you've pursued through culture, and your importance in its development, and I wonder if it's, like... *[lowers voice]* because you didn't die, Grace.

Ahhhhhhhhhhhhhhhhhhhh-haaaaaaaaaaaa *[shrieks with laughter]* Aaaooooooooooowww!

You know what I mean, though? If you'd died, we'd all be elbowing each other away from your gravestone in order to prove who loved you and appreciated you the most. We'd be bowing and falling down in front of your tombstone, like, I loved her, she was so precious, she was so wonderful! I've seen that kind of behaviour a lot recently here in England and frankly it disgusts me.

Yes, it's strange that we've moved into that kind of culture; it wasn't always like that, but things are changing. And I'm like wine. So it depends on, do you like wine, do you even want to taste it? It's not for everybody and I'm OK with that. I don't want to please everybody. Actually there's certain people I definitely don't want to please. *[laughs]* There's some people I'm like, 'Oh no! Puh-leeeeze don't like me!' I remember, one of my biggest spiritual problems was that I wanted to be understood, desperately. I'd be very upset if someone didn't understand me. I was obstinate about it. Why don't you understand me, know what I mean? *[laughs]*

But actually, with patience, I realized it's not about everybody understanding me. And with that realization, I found a certain freedom. Why did she cut her hair like that? Why doesn't she wear a wig? Why did she shave her eyebrows? Why, why, why! Like, why do I have to explain everything, you know? I am grossly misunderstood. And it's funny – what was my worst phobia is now my mystery. And I like it. I've grown with patience, into that. I know my whys, I've figured them out, some of them. And I'm time-tested. I never thought I'd live past thirty-five because I was so vain, I didn't want to. I didn't want to be old. I had this thing about going to die before I was thirty-five. And now I think I'm going to live for ever.

You got married recently and there were newspaper stories that you married your bodyguard.

Oh, people love bodyguard stories, don't they? But no... Atilla was a marketing student when I married him, plain and simple. It's just because he's big. And very protective around me. It must be a very romantic idea or something.

You know what I think? I think it's because they're scared of you, and they would like to think you need protection, that you can't quite look after yourself. That kind of story is reassuring for certain men.

Oh, like it puts the female in her place. *[laughs]* You know what, I think you're right. *[laughs]* ... Yeah.

Finally, do you still have an 'Unlimited Capacity For Love'?

Yes. Of course. Yeah. Real love is unlimited, unconditional, it's in the air, you can't deny it to anybody who needs it. How can you measure love? You can't buy mine, that's for sure. *[laughs]*

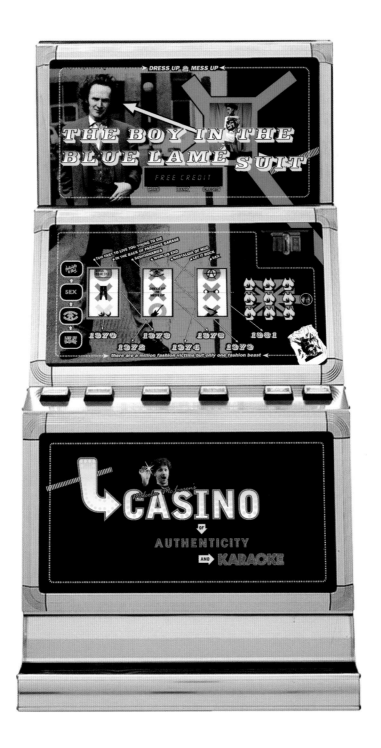

Living quarters at Hingkstrasse, Frankfurt, July 1969. Astrid Proll fourth from left, Andreas Baader first from right

Still from Kids, 1996 Directed by Larry Clark

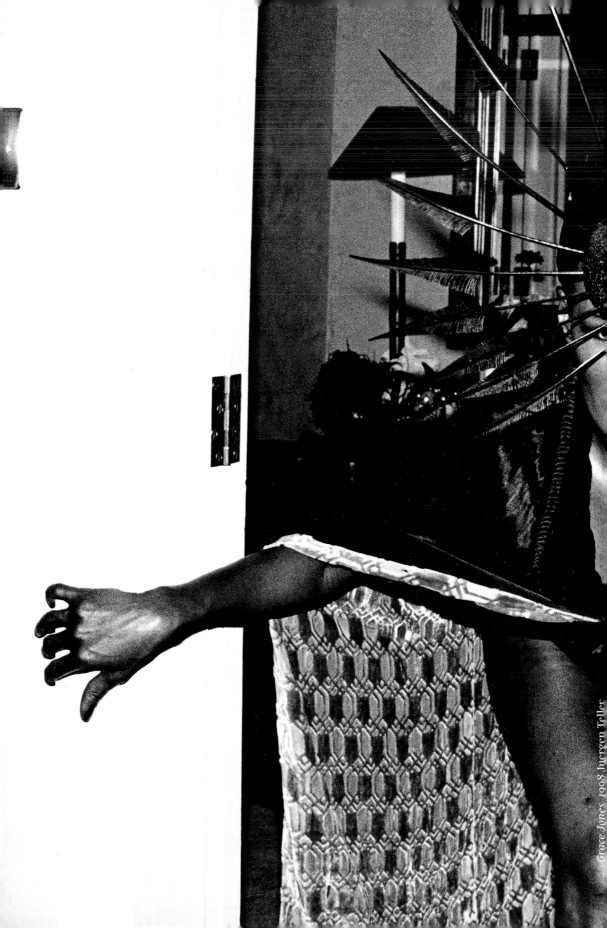

The televised flanning of Edouard Poulet, French Minister of Culture, 1991

October 1998
Introduction and interview | Mark Sanders

Over the past twenty years, Tibor Kalman's creative vision has never failed to question, challenge and provoke. From his early involvement in the student protest movement, to the formation of his own highly successful advertising and graphic design company, M&Co, to becoming the creative director of Interview *and the founding editor of the controversial and hard-hitting Benetton magazine* Colors, *his eclectic and unpredictable approach to design and the design industry has earnt him both friends and enemies.*

Characterized by the way in which he 'kidnaps' commercial techniques and then turns them back on themselves, it is his time at Colors *that best captures his unflinching desire to employ design in a way that allows people to think for themselves. Throughout the thirteen issues he produced,* Colors *became the international voice of a generation, tackling such poignant issues as AIDS, racism and ecology. In his own words, 'Editors have a responsibility to seduce their audiences with the truth. For this reason, I tried to make* Colors *as interesting and as sexy as possible, like candy or canapes so juicy you can't resist them.'*

Dazed & Confused | **So who thought up the subtitle to your book:** *Perverse Optimist*? **Was it you?**
Tibor Kalman | No, it was my wife Maira.
Is that how she sees you?
[laughs] I guess so.
And how do you see yourself? Are you an idealist? Are you 'perversely optimistic' about our collective future?
Absolutely. I really believe that people are good and not bad. I really believe that the United States may end up being the first truly socialist country in the world and that people, when given a full stomach and the basic necessities of life, will be willing to share everything together. I mean, I still consider myself to be a socialist. I even consider myself maybe to be a communist with a lower case 'c'. One thing that I say in my book is that there is plenty of food, shelter and money in this world, it's just badly distributed.
You announce right at the start of the book that you believe in lunatics; that our culture is nothing but a corporate culture and success equals boredom, so FUCK THE COMMITTEES! Does this represent the way you have always approached your work: no compromise, constant change?
Well, success can be restrictive and I think that you should always change careers once you have become recognized, or at least, change media. I've always believed that the only way to spend your life is to reinvent the things around you and try to change people's minds.
And so remain fresh and receptive to new ideas?
Yeah. I've always been more interested in the message than the medium: anything that is about communication as opposed to 'taking up space' just for the sake of it. I know this is the opposite of what Marshall McLuhan said – 'The medium is the message' – but I don't entirely agree. I see a lot of fucking media out there but I see very few messages getting across.
Is that why you decided to set up your own design company, M&Co, in the late 70s?
Not at first. To begin with, I wanted to make money. I didn't give a shit what we designed. We worked for department stores, we did bank brochures, we did trash basically – anything we could make a nickel out of. But as time went on, we managed to find some interesting clients, starting with Talking Heads, and it was then that we split the company and started working with cultural groups as well as our more orthodox clients. I would literally have a suit in the closet hanging up next to a pair of jeans and I would switch back and forth, twice a day, depending on who I was dealing with.
So what was it like working on *Interview*? **Were you given a free rein?**
For me, it was the opening up of a new medium – the same as if somebody had commissioned me to build a house. I had worked on one other magazine before, with the same editor, Ingrid

Left
Remains In Light,
Talking Heads, 1980
Right
Black Queen Elizabeth
illustration from Colors,
1993

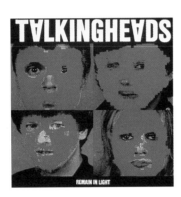

Sischy – namely, *Art Forum*, but the beautiful part about *Interview* for me was that I really didn't know what the fuck I was doing, as usual. It was scary taking over from Fabian Baron, who is an awesome designer, and it was monthly, so you had to design spreads every day. It was fascinating having to figure out how to portray Dustin Hoffman or how to portray someone like Morrissey. You know, how to have fun with them, how to make something meaningful and make something new. I tried to make my opening spreads a painting of the person that was featured, and of course, I was helped by an editor who let me experiment in very strange ways.

In what ways were you allowed to experiment with the traditional design format of the magazine?

Right from the start, Ingrid let me put upside-down type on my first issue. I was allowed to crop into pictures, work with incredible photographers such as Bruce Weber. Of course, I had some criticisms regarding the editorial content of the magazine, but I was so overwhelmed by the creative direction that I couldn't really deal with those issues at that time.

Ingrid Sischy describes you as the designer who has redesigned the concept of design with thought. Would you agree with that description?

I think what was meant by that was that I am a person who is unable to make something without thinking about it first for a long time. I try not to ever design anything that doesn't have any ideas in it, because I think that ideas are the crux of everything. And as I say in the book, once I have an idea, I've got it made in the shade. *[laughs]* **To what extent has your sense of humour played a part in your understanding of graphic design?**

Guys in the advertising world will tell you that humour is a good way to disarm people and get

Fuzzy Clock, *M&Co,*
which, according to
Kalman, 'is very good
in bars'

inside their brains; that's why there's so much humour employed in television commercials. In that respect, it's part and parcel of my work. There's always a lot of joking around the office, which is natural. But the thing that's really interesting about humour is that it's dangerous. You have to double think a particular situation so that every time you make a joke you take a chance and I love that.

In the early 1980s you were known for pushing what became known as the 'Un-design' strategy. What exactly is an 'Un-design' strategy?

That was during the period when I had been asked to become a member of the AIGA and other professional design organizations. I just wanted to stir things up a bit by promoting what interests me, what I find exciting. I've always thought that things that are ugly are more interesting than things that are beautiful. I often find my kind of beauty in say, store signs from the Bronx, or the way that people decorate their cars. You know, the type of stuff that your crazed uncle might have designed in a moment of madness, or the brother-in-law who decides to paint the store front. Something alive.

So your 'Un-design' aesthetic was a way of combating design slickness, of attacking the propagation of 'style' devoid of 'content'?

Yes, although thankfully, that sense of design for design's sake seems to have eaten itself. For me, I always thought that a T-shirt for a coffee shop designed by the owner is likely to be more interesting than a T-shirt designed by a designer. People outside the profession often do a better job because they have fewer hang-ups.

In *Tibor*, you mention that design history can teach us so much more than mere style. You argue that it can also reveal how political images are crafted, the way corporations are able to manipulate public awareness through advertising, and at one point, you even say it is the duty of every-one who works within the media to expose that level of manipulation for all to see.

I wrote about those issues with regard to the use of images within Benetton's advertising campaign.

Exactly. You raise some very important questions. In particular, the fact that images and photographs are not innately truthful or 'real' but are always dependent on the context within which they're seen. Is that why you make such a strong use of text in your design work, in order to break open the facade of the image in some way?

That's not the intention, but that might be a good result. The intention is just to create, to save space and to create some kind of argument between the image and the words. You know, to set up that argument for people to resolve.

Similar to the work of say Barbara Kruger or Jenny Holzer? I know that you worked with Jenny Holzer on the *Lustmord Series*.

Jenny's a person I've spent a long time working with and even before that, we were friends. The

Yves Klein 'jumping off a building' (*A Leap into the Void*, 1960), that's when photos began to lie. **Was your use of stock photography intended to be reflective of the media itself? The fact that you're employing images that have already been in the public domain and then turning them around in order to impart a different set of ideas or meaning?** Sometimes, yes. Sometimes, no. We never did stories per se, just as we never covered news stories. We steered clear of them so that we could deal in the big NOW as opposed to the little now. The little now is *The New York Times* today or The *Guardian* today. The big NOW is contemporary.

So you chose broad subjects to cover such as AIDS and travel? My philosophy had always been that we could do serious stuff and take the funny angle and then take the funny stuff and be serious. So we would always cover topics like sport or travel and look at them as serious cultural anthropology and then the next month we would take something like AIDS and make jokes about it. I mean, let's be positive in the face of adversity. Let's figure out how to fuck creatively so that we don't catch the disease in the first place, because we all have to live on this earth and we have to be sex positive.

What do you think of the direction *Colors* has taken since you left? Do you think it has changed from your original concept? I think the war issue was pretty good, but what happened, almost immediately the day I left, was a certain kind of cynicism regarding the photography, about the image. In all my time at *Colors,* I only ever showed one bloody picture and that was in the issue about shopping, and that was an image of a landmine. It was a tiny one-by-one-inch picture that you could easily pass over, and it showed a boy with his leg blown off at a hospital. Apart from that, I never showed any gory, negative imagery and I think if there has been anything that I have found disturbing about the magazine since I left it is that it has tended to get more and more gory.

Sensationalist? Yeah, sensationalist. I find a lot of what is covered very cynical and very negative and prurient. I tried to stay clear of that. We were always very optimistic about the world and we

Lustmord Series collaboration started right in the middle of my time with *Colors*. She had been asked to produce a special edition for a German magazine, and she suggested that we work together on the project. So I came up with the very simple idea of writing on skin, of writing on women's skin in a way that the skin became defaced by the words. And she went for it.

Who came up with the idea to print in real blood? That was something that I proposed at the last minute: that we take the cover of the magazine and print all of the type in blood. The editors wanted to do it but it was the legal people who said it couldn't be done. In the end, we had to irradiate the blood to make sure it was safe, but we stuck to our guns and got it finished.

More than any other magazine, your work on *Colors* exemplifies your innovative and subtle use of images. For instance, Reagan's computer-manipulated image as if he had full blown AIDS, or your transformation of the Queen into a black monarch. Both are positive examples of image manipulation. Anyone can manipulate an image. It used to be thought that photography told the truth, painting was a lying medium, but starting from

Opposite page
Ronald Reagan with
AIDS cover for Colors,
1994
This page
Lustmord Series, *1993*
(collaboration with
Jenny Holzer)

were criticized for it. We would show a picture of kids playing in Bosnia, instead of a person starving and crying. We would show people who believed in the future and we were a magazine that believed in the future.

By concentrating on issues such as ecology?

And covering them in funny ways by saying there is a problem to be solved here so let's work together to find a solution. I don't see that sense of optimism in *Colors* anymore. It seems to have lost its way.

Your last issue was one of the best issues of a magazine I have ever seen: *Colors 13*, or 'the picture issue': an entire magazine made up solely of images. Was that something you had always wanted to do?

Yes, it was something that I had wanted to do for three or four months before I finally got the chance to make it work. I wanted to see if we could create an issue that didn't have any language restrictions, so I decided to strip all the words out. I was overwhelmed by the question of how to sell a story. Finally, I had a conversation with a friend of mine who is the editor of *Aperture* magazine and he said, 'Why not look at Charles Eames' *The Power of Ten*?' And so there and then, the skies opened and I

suddenly understood how to organize all this information by starting outside and going in: by tracing through images a journey all the way from outer space to inside the body. The final sequence showing that outer space looks exactly like neutrons and atoms circulating around an atom. I don't know of any Amazonian Indians who saw it, so I don't have any comments from them to share with you, but I sure wish I did.

Since leaving *Colors*, you have reformed M&Co. Do you have a new vision for the company?

Yes, to de-commercialize it and use design for ideas and the conveyance of those ideas to a larger audience. That's basically it.

So you've veered more towards the art world?

I've designed a number of exhibitions for the Whitney and recently I've been doing this thing for *The New York Times*, which is called 'Op Art' and is on the Op. Ed. page, and it's kind of like visual pieces, where I do things like make all cigarette packs look alike, or make nice parts of New York full of advertising, things like that.

So Tibor, last question, where do get your energy from?

I have no idea. Maybe from my genes, from my jeans, from my genetic structure, from New York City. I think New York City is the simplest answer. I mean this is a place that is kinetic, it's a place that maybe, if you ran a wire to Chicago, it would like, blow the place up. Every day, I see people who are smarter than me, better than me, have more money than me, are more successful than me and I'm always going like, 'Shit, I could do better, I could do better.' I mean, it kills you, but it's great. It's great. I mean, it's like we're all on speed.

We are indeed. We are indeed.

November 1998
Introduction | John Robb
Interview | Jon Spencer

Maybe 1998 will go down in history as one of
the weakest years in prime time rock-'n'-roll: the
year that geeky indie acts were swamped by
goody-two-shoe boy bands and their saccharine
fuckless ballads. It is the year that misery indie
ruled and British bands fell over each other to
write the greyest, most meaningless, soulless
ballads possible, when the achingly dull
reverence for the worst aspects of the past bore
a criminally dull fruition. But, thank God no one
told Jon Spencer the news!

The Blues Explosion hit back at the nu-grey
this month with their Acme album: forty-five
minutes of raw sex played on guitars, mashing
together huge hip-hop beats with punk noise and
blues yearnings – this is Jon Spencer's best work
yet. Where the other Jon Spencer Blues Explosion
albums have been raw primal yelps, this is an
almost smoothly produced purring beast of a
record. It's the first time that Spencer has made a
record that could easily be considered mainstream and in doing it, The Blues Explosion have
lost none of their bite.

In existence for most of the 90s the Blues
Explosion were born from the ashes of New York
noiseniks Pussy Galore. Originally from
Washington DC, Spencer formed Pussy Galore in
his hometown before moving to the bad apple,
cutting a series of dirty-arsed, garage rock, filthy,
hardcore albums, the band had no choice but to
implode, its constituent members going on to
form the likes of Royal Trux and Boss Hog.

Spencer teamed up with Russell Simins and
Judah Bauer to put together the Blues Explosion
and veered off from the industrial noise root,
digging deep into the blues and soul catalogue
for the same sort of gut feeling. They crossed
this with an Elvis love of showbiz pizzazz,
their whole schtick being raw excitement, dirty

sex and a dollop of understated gold lamé
humour.

Acme is the closest they've got to making a
mainstream record – mainstream as in just great
rock-'n'-roll. Sure, there are dollops of great noise
on the album, but then there are tracks like 'Do
You Wanna Get Heavy', which is as damned close
to a ballad as they've got so far. The album is a
team effort, a whole myriad of 90s talent called
in to fuck with the tracks.

There's Alec Empire from the fab German
techno terrorists, Atari Teenage Riot; Calvin
Johnson from K records (underground US pop
noise label); Jim Dickinson the rockabilly
legend; T-Ray from Cypress Hill's mixing crew;
Dan The Automator (Dr Octagon's producer);
and Nick Sansano, who has worked on some
of the classic moments in hip-hop including
collaborating with Public Enemy back in the 80s.

And it's not like they were deliberately going
easy on the listener – most of the tracks were
recorded with Steve Albini, the Chicago-based
noise terrier, who despite recording the last Page
and Plant album and working in the big league,
still retains plenty of bite when he's sitting
behind the controls. What he brings to the Blues
Explosion record is the feeling that you're standing in the room, whilst the three-piece cut up
that howling storm of guitar-driven lust that is
the backbone of great rock-'n'-roll. Meanwhile,
overseeing the whole album is a legend.

Andre Williams has been cutting primo
sleaze rock-'n'-roll anthems right back to the
birth of the whole thing in the 50s. His life is
misted by legend, apocryphal tales surround his
dealings with women, his songs and his, let's say,
'full on' lifestyle. For purists, he is the touchstone
of the six-string guitar, fully loaded anthems and
paeons to the salacious side of sweet, sweet

'Would you like to see what I cut off?' And I said, 'Yeah' and I looked over at the table and I see this big black piece of meat with some red shit and it was still jumpin'. I almost fainted. When I got out of there I went to the temple and everybody say 'YEAH!!!!'

How important is it for you, going on stage?
Everybody has got their own opinion on Andre Williams. So I try to be what they want me to be. If you're lookin' to see a gentleman, I'm gonna come as a gentleman. But if you lookin' to see a rummy, I'm comin' as a rummy. I can drink more rum... The last time I stumbled, I was twelve years old. That was my first drink. I like to have a drink, because I've never been around a comfortable situation when I could go and do a show sober.

You have had a couple of down times, difficult times, was that due to drugs?
Cocaine. Straight up. Smoking it like a dig dog.

You worked for Ike Turner in the 70s. Was it him that got you into all that?
If you wanted to work for Ike, you had to hit it or he'd get the police.

What about Tina?
Tina was the prettiest woman in the world, a beautiful housewife. Kept the house, done the gardens and all of it. She wasn't allowed to go in the studio to try and record her voice. She didn't come in, she left the food at the door 'cause we had monitors.

Ike was pretty freaked out with all the TV monitors?
Ike had got to the point where all over the studio you could pick the nose and the tail off anything and there was a gram in it. Everywhere you walked, anywhere, there was a gram. You could have a little salt shaker and you could take the lid off and hit on it. Then if you hit on it too many times, Ike would have the monitor and say, 'I wanna talk to you.'

Ike would like point at you?
Yeah, not with his finger, but with his gun.

What kind of gun was it?
Big silver .35.

What was your job there?
I was the man that took the tapes, I paid the people, hired and fired the musicians.

How did you hook up with him in the first place?
Well, there's a guy called Oliver Saint, who plays

badaaassss rock-'n'-roll, from a man dressed as a 50s pimp hustler. For Spencer, it's this year's R L Burnside, a chance to shine some of the limelight onto a deserving cause. It's also a chance to give his own records some of the sheen from someone who really knows their shit. And perhaps it is Williams' 'production' duties (he apparently produces the whole album before it's handed over to a myriad of remixers) that gives the record its final classic sheen and edge.

Jon Spencer Blues Explosion know their shit, that much is obvious. If you're going to get on your knees and grovel to the past, then beg at the altar of soul and the blues... Sod The Beatles and sod the white-boy wishy-washy 60s. Get to the real grit. That's what Jon Spencer has done and it's paying back dividends.

Jon Spencer | **So you're converting to Judaism?**
Andre Williams | Not converting, converted. Do you want to talk about the operation? The doctor's name was Dr Wooshuwumbum somebody, the goddamn name was that long. You see, the Rabbi introduced me to him. He did a hell of a job, I didn't feel shit! He sewed it up like he was making a blanket! Then he said,

Andre Williams,
second left, with
Jon Spencer Blues
Explosion, 1998
Deirdre O'Callaghan

funky bass on 'Rescue Me, Rescue Me'. Oliver was a very good friend of mine. He had a studio in St Louis. I fell on my ass in Houston, Texas. I was fucked up, so B B King lent me ninety dollars and flew me to California. I called Oliver and he says, 'Call Ike.' So I call. Twenty minutes later, he picks me up in an MG and drives me downtown. I went in, said I needed a job. He didn't ask me what could I do, because he had already called Oliver and Oliver told him I was cool... It was the worst job I ever had.

How long did it last?
Nine months. Nine months of the worst misery that you ever thought of. I don't like Berry Gordie, but I respect him. I don't respect Ike, but I like him. Ike gave his heart, but Ike didn't know what he was doing from minute to minute. He changed every second.

And after you stopped working for Ike?
I went in there weighin' about a hundred and eighty-six pounds. I came out, I caught an aeroplane and I was weighing about eighty pounds. I was almost dead and I had to get out. I called my father 'cause I might never come home.

So where did you go?
Chicago, where I nursed myself back up. By that time I had a hell of a habit and I was tryin' to work back into the game, but by that time, everybody was saying, 'Andre Williams? Nuh uh.' There weren't no work happening for me, so I just did the next best thing to get me a new car. I went to where the white boys had money. Getting off the train, I picked (stole) me a car on the way. There's a certain stop that the white boys make, where you gotta cross a certain bridge that takes you into Chicago to go to work. Now all these people got big money. Now I'm in the shelter, I am a stone-drunk addict, like a big dog, and ain't nobody givin' me a job. So I said I'm gonna get me somethin' this mornin'. So I picked me a time, from seven o'clock in the mornin' to nine o'clock in the mornin', and I hit that corner, right on the bridge, the Randolph Street Bridge, and they even got to know me. I was there any weather, at forty below zero, with scarves all round my face, with my cup. I was given a hundred and fifty dollars in two hours, but by eleven o'clock I was broke, and I was runnin' straight to the dope house. But they would get off the train with my money already in their hand; they didn't have to stop. And I would get my hundred and fifty dollars. That's why I don't take no shit off nobody, because I know there's a way to get money, even

Andre Williams and
Jon Spencer, 1998
Deirdre O'Callaghan

if you're the lowest in the world. But it's what
you do with it... That's why I don't let money
run me, it's my heart. I stood on that bridge for
three years, every mornin'. I was livin' in the
shelter – they kick you out at five-thirty in the
mornin' – and I'd walk three miles to that
fuckin' bridge and I'd get my cash.

I don't have to steal now and I don't have to
kiss yo ass; only thing I gotta do is my job. I
don't regret none of it. I don't regret nothing I
did except the drug trip, which now, I don't
mess around with. The only drugs that I have
taken are cocaine, reefer, and one time in my
life, heroin, but plenty cocaine. I think the hallu-
cino' stuff probably wouldna worked with me. I
don't need nothin' to stretch my imagination.
What do you think of James Brown?
One of the baddest mutha-fuckers that ever
lived.
Did you ever meet him?
Well of course, I worked on the show with him
and the Flames in Philadelphia. I mean, we was
in the back of the uptown theatre together, me
and the Flames, seven days a week. You see,
when you played them theatres back in those
days, it was a house in the back of the theatre
that cooked.

And that's where the performers would hang out?

Not hang out, they'd go in there to eat and bring the food back, 'cause we had five, six and seven shows.

On your record *Silky*, there are some songs that are country influenced. Are you a fan of country music?

I was raised on country. I was out there ploughin' the mutha-fuckin' mule. I didn't hear no rock-'n'-roll till I was eleven years old.

Yeah? And then who were you hearin'?

Lloyd Price, Elmore Jennings, 'Guitar' Swain, B B King, Lou Brown. I heard them 'through the wall'. I want y'all to know what I mean by 'through the wall'. Have y'all ever walked by a place and hear a song comin' through the wall... you knew what it was because the rhythm told you what it was. You see, I was too young to go in the fish fry house, and the only place you could hear rhythm and blues was on a Saturday night at the fish fry. That was where they drank corn'n'liquor and screwed and fucked and sucked and whatever they did back there, OK. But the key is, I had to run around outside and when I went home there was no black stations, so all I heard was 'Hey good lookin', what you got cookin'; and I loved it, so my roots is country and western. But once I reached eleven, I was hearin' 'Dang, it's three o'clock in the mornin', and I can't even close my eyes' and I said 'this shit is good' you know, and then I started developing that. That's how come I got this honest feelin' and that's when I started talkin' about pussy and life, 'cause I wanna be an honest artist till the day I die. I'm sixty-one now, but I've had a party. I could use a little money and buy me somethin' nice to wear, you know, drive me another El Dorado. When I bought my El Dorado it cost me fifty-five hundred bucks, now it's fifty-five thousand – that's a house on fuckin' wheels. I'd like to have an El Dorado now and drive around with three or four credit cards, and fuckin' about seven girls a day.

But you got a girlfriend.

I'd still fuck seven girls a day.

Can you still fuck seven girls a day?

You wanna bet?

So you like to eat pussy?

I tell you what, I think everybody should taste it. You come out of one, so why won't you? You'll like it. I mean, if you're gonna be a man, if you like the girl and you want her to give you some head, then why won't you give her some too? I think everybody in the world should taste it. What it is, Andre Williams had to eat, and Andre Williams had to screw and if you're gonna screw, you gotta have money. Pussy ain't free. If you ain't got a hotel man, you gotta fuck in an alley. If you've got to fuck in an alley, there's no towels and no soap. Why would you wanna fuck the same chick with a dirty dick? If you a man, you gotta make love.

So a lot of musicians might do it so they could get girls. Is that true for Andre?

I became a musician so I did not have to plough no more god damn cotton. I didn't know nothing else to do. Just that simple. And the only thing I could do was dance.

Was it the same when you were doing business back in the 60s?

Hell no. It was all men.

So the women have all taken over?

Women ain't taking over. Women have run it all the time. Every war in whatever way, was done by pussy. That means, the king he wanted that boy for the money to go and get that whore, 'cause he didn't have enough land to go get Sheba. So he went and conquered and then he was able to go and talk to Sheba's daddy to get that pussy.

Have you ever been to Europe?

I went there one time and I made three grand in Amsterdam and left with a buck fifty. I went to the red light area. I seen the street. I went up that side, down the other. That's where I went.

You worked your way up one side and down the other?

Yes. And I do not regret it.

November 1998
Introduction and interview | Lisa Verrico

Mark E Smith must be knackered. For twenty-one years, the maverick, mouthy singer has been flying in the face of fashion, following a musical path all of his own and fighting with anyone brave enough to take him on. Throw in the fact that, as frontman with The Fall, he has written and released over thirty albums and his stamina should impress even his harshest critics.

On the day that we meet, it takes six hours to pin Smith down for an interview. By then, he has refused to be photographed anywhere other than a pub, taken offence at somebody's suit and threatened to walk out of his hotel without paying. Along the way, he has also decided that he would like his band to be sponsored by a handkerchief brand. Why? Because there are germs everywhere, obviously.

Nursing a pint in the twenty-fourth-floor bar of a hotel, looking out over London at night, Mark Edward Smith reckons that 1998 has been an excellent year. Certainly, since forming The Fall in his native Salford at the tail-end of the 1970s, his music has rarely attracted as much acclaim. Less favourable, however, was the flak that followed the very public bust-up with band members in May. An on-stage fist fight not only landed Smith in a New York jail, but forced him to re-form The Fall for the umpteenth time. Today, he calls the split the best thing that has happened to him for years. He may be right. He looks healthier, happier and more alert than he has in ages. With critics and lifelong fans alike claiming that recent shows have been the band's best since The Fall's 80s heyday, the man who is said to have single-handedly spawned indie is understandably enthusiastic about the future.

Dazed & Confused | **You are thirty-eight years old, your band is an institution of British music, you have artists as diverse as Damien Hirst, Sonic Youth, Damon Albarn and Courtney Love citing you as an inspiration. What could you possibly want from The Fall now, that you haven't already achieved?**
Mark E Smith | I want one last shot. Without wishing to sound sentimental, the last couple of times I've played live, I have actually enjoyed myself. For a long time, The Fall felt like work. Suddenly, it's as though I'm getting what I wanted from the very start. I recorded four new songs last week and they just might be the best I've ever done. I listened back to them and heard this driving beat down the centre of each song. I've waited twenty years to hear that sound. Now I feel like the possibilities for The Fall are endless.

Are you saying it has taken twenty years for The Fall to sound the way you always wanted?
Not at all. You have to understand that I never really knew what I wanted The Fall to sound like. I still don't. I can't understand groups who know precisely what they want to be from the moment they form. Those people must have the most boring jobs in the world. Some bands actually come out and say that they want to be a cross between, say, The Rolling Stones, The Beatles and electric pop music. That astonishes me. I mean, what is the point?

You must have been influenced by someone to start The Fall in the first place.
I only started the band because I wanted to write and I couldn't see myself holding down a

proper writing job. At the time, I was eighteen, working as a clerk at the docks in Manchester. Funnily enough, I'm still very clerical about most things I do. I suppose I'm still in The Fall because it forces me to make something of myself, which is a very desk-job attitude to have. That's why I record so much. The more you want to make of your life, the more you do. I look at bands who spend five years on one album, then wonder what their brains must be like. If it wasn't for The Fall, I'd be at home right now, trying to motivate myself to write, but probably doing every other bloody thing possible under the sun. It's that old writer's dilemma. Unless you're forced to work, you find yourself cleaning out the backyard as an excuse.

Surely you were influenced musically. Which musicians did you admire when you were growing up?

There were a few. The problem was, I knew I could never be like any of them. When I first got into music – which was around the age of thirteen or fourteen – I very quickly worked my way through every scene from Northern soul to glam rock to disco. Later, I got into Lou Reed and Can. I admired Iggy Pop, but he was too American rock-'n'-roll to influence me. I liked his

music, but at the same time it felt alien to me. There were no groups around that I thought represented people like me or my mates. No one was speaking to the clerks and the dockers. If I wanted to be anything, it was a voice for those people. I wanted The Fall to be the band for people who didn't have bands, for people who weren't supposed to have bands that related to their lives. I think we achieved that. I think we still do.

How did you decide what the first Fall records should sound like then?

I didn't decide. To be honest, I didn't really care what they sounded like, as long as I got to say what I wanted. Mind you, I never thought we'd take the music out of the house, never mind out of Manchester. The only real aim was to make the songs very fuckin' odd and particularly English. I wanted them to be a mish-mash of all sorts, particularly a lot of garage groups of the mid 60s. I used to go to all sorts of different clubs in Manchester, which was why The Fall had to appeal to someone who was into cheap soul as much as someone who liked avant-garde stuff like Stockhausen. I even wanted the Gary Glitter fans. I always loved Gary Glitter. I used to really get the piss taken out of me for that when I was sixteen. Everyone else was into Pink Floyd and Led Zeppelin. I hated all those guitar heroes. I still do. I detest the very idea of them, particularly since the vast majority of them are self-important little twats. It was a horrific time for me when The Fall first started to do well. I suddenly realized that the rest of the band did actually want to be rock stars. That happens all the time. It's why The Fall's membership is so random. I have to keep dismantling the band to weed out the wannabee Keith Richards. It's not only horrific, it's heartbreaking.

Have you never felt an affiliation with any other bands?

Absolutely not. That's the beauty of The Fall. Wanting to be like anyone else – regardless of who they are – is a sackable offence in my book. I watched a TV programme recently on rock family trees in Manchester. It was all Happy Mondays, Stone Roses and the like. The Fall wasn't featured at all. I thought that was a major achievement. A lot of our fans were outraged that we weren't in there. That proves

Mark E Smith, 1998
Deirdre O'Callaghan

they have completely missed the point of this band. As I watched that show, I prayed that we wouldn't be mentioned. I think that statement sums up exactly what I wanted when I formed The Fall.

Wasn't it incredibly disappointing to discover that, twenty-one years down the line, Fall fans didn't understand that?

Not at all. In fact, I thought that was great. It just means that they enjoy the music for what it is, rather than what it represents. Even a lot of the die-hard Fall fans still miss the Northern soul element or the avant-garde references in my music. It's lovely that I continue to find it very difficult to communicate with people. It gives me a challenge. Of course, it also means that I get a lot of grief. It's like when I decided on the latest line-up for The Fall. I put us on at a Catholic social club to deliberately make it obscure to get in. The fan-club turned up, of course, shouting for me to bring back so and so, who was in the band ten years ago. They were calling me pathetic, saying I was trying to take music back to the days of the working man's club. Trying to get them to accept what I'd done was so exciting. It's what most bands do when they start out, not twenty years into their career. Even friends who have worked for me for years can't understand why I would, for example, employ a country and western drummer. The reason is that I can mould them. I can make them a member of The Fall.

Do you care what other people's opinions of The Fall are?

Of course I do. Every artist wants credibility. A couple of years ago, I read a poll on the hundred best artists of all time. The Fall was in between Mozart and Puccini. I was very proud of that. Of course, the next day I can pick up a paper and be the guy with no teeth who beats everybody up, so I suppose I can't take these things too seriously. On the Internet, I've seen Fall fans write four pages on one song. That's a real compliment. It's lovely, just lovely. I read that stuff, although usually I don't have a fuckin' clue what it's about. It is stimulating though. I've also been told that German school kids have debates about the lyrics from Fall songs. They treat them like ancient Greek poems or something. That's beautiful to me. I'd never thought of myself as a Bob Dylan before.

With so many commercially successful musicians name-dropping The Fall, the band has suddenly become hip all over again.

Are we hip? I have no idea. Our standing seems to go up and down all the time. It makes very little difference to me. The hipper we are, the less money we make. Plus, if you're hip, you get lots of resentment from other bands.

Don't you monitor The Fall's place in pop?

You can't help it, can you? I mean, sometimes there's like three people in the world who like us, the next week we're massive. In Manchester, it feels very peculiar; everybody knows who The Fall are now, whereas they didn't ten years ago. I think it's because a lot of the people who

are really into us have come into positions of power. That's at least part of it. We've also started to attract a lot of the pre-student crowd, very young kids, which was our audience when we first started out. That's great because it's not because their mums and dads have introduced us to them, they've got into us by themselves.

Do you really care who buys your records?

Difficult question. Fortunately, most Fall fans are cool. They are, it's true. At least, they are not unlikeable people. The worst fans we could have are those blokes who are just into the Manchester scene. They come up to me in pubs and rave on about the band. Then you start talking to them and realize they're not really into The Fall's music, they just recognize my face. We've never had a lot of them though. I always worried that all people would know about me was my face. Naturally, I want people to know me, but I want it to be for something I've done, rather than just because they have seen my face in a magazine.

Maybe you should try moving out of Manchester.

I have never lived in Manchester. I live in Salford. It's a different town entirely. Besides, I have tried moving. I went to Edinburgh for two and a half years. I've lived in America as well. What drives me back to Salford? I don't fuckin' know. Maybe I'm mad. It must be a love-hate thing. I guess I can't get my shit together to move house.

A lot of kids form bands as a way to escape their roots.

That's right. But I left home at fifteen, so I never had that desire to get away from my family or prove my independence. I never fantasized about going to New York or Sydney, which a lot of kids around me did. Even when I did romanticize in my music, it was always about Manchester, because that's what I knew best. In the Victorian days, writers would romanticize about the Orient. They had never even been there. When they did go, they discovered it was crap. It's worse these days, though. Kids start saving up to go to Australia when they're eleven. They think they'll get there and it'll be like *Neighbours* and they'll have this great life. I say I've been, I like the place, but it's not like TV. Some people think that by getting away they'll find themselves or walk into a fantastic new life. Generally, people who keep going places just want to get away from themselves and that's impossible. Where you're living is in your fuckin' head, innit?

Do you never want to get away from being Mark E Smith for a while? It must be a bit of a burden.

It's a burden, but it's also an inspiration. I have to constantly reappraise myself and The Fall. When you're in the public eye, it's easy for people to get a fixed idea of what you're like or what the band is about. Let that happen and you become a caricature of yourself. Having said that, everyone turns into their parents in the end.

So what are your parents like?

My dad's dead. My mum is marvellous. She lives in the next street to me in Salford. She's so cool, an outrageous dresser. When she does herself up to go out she looks amazing.

Tell me what happened when you fought with your band on stage in New York. Shouldn't bust-ups happen behind closed doors?

They should, yeah. But it was the others who attacked me. I was just defending myself. They acted like kids, which I find terribly embarrassing, but I suppose is symptomatic of our generation. There's all that shit now about male responsibility being taken away. Most blokes think the only way to express themselves is by fighting.

So what happened?

They were saying I couldn't sing and couldn't remember my lyrics. They were talking behind my back. They were also coming up with all these ideas about how The Fall should sound and trying out all this strange shit on stage. I'm

the one who is unconventional, that's my racket. It was good for me though. Basically, they were middle-aged men with middle-aged minds. I'm not puking my guts out every day to make music with people I have nothing in common with.

They left you alone in a jail in New York.

Yeah, then they came home and said I was impossible to work with.

Are you?

I'm a difficult bastard, obviously. But no, I'm not impossible to work with.

Despite the critical acclaim, The Fall remains an underground band. Is that what you wanted?

Are you mad? Of course not. To be honest, I find it just incredible that we can't turn our critical standing into financial success. Most bands would die for our status. The Fall has a notoriety that you can't set out to achieve. On the other hand, I never really believed we would amount to much, so I guess we've done OK.

So what is the future for The Fall?

This sounds so crap and no one believes me when I say this after thirty-five albums or whatever, but I still approach every album as the last one. That's what you have to do. You have to imagine that you will never get the chance to record again. I think I let that attitude slip slightly a couple of years ago, but I'm back on track now.

What put you back on track?

Probably having my ears syringed. You're laughing, but it's true. I can hear everything now. It's great. I thought I was going deaf from being on stage. I was shouting at everyone. I was also very unhappy with the sound of the band. I knew something was wrong, but I couldn't hear what it was. The nurse freaked over my ears. She had to pump them out two or three times. She said she'd never seen so much wax. Apparently, I had enough for three seventy-year-old blokes. Getting it done changed my life. The other day, I was sat in my front room and I could hear these voices outside. Before, I would have thought it was people standing outside my front door, talking about me. Suddenly, I could hear what they were saying. It was only the neighbours having a chat. They didn't even mention my name.

December 1998
Introduction and interview | Chris Campion

·

John Gilmore is what you would call 'connected'.
Circulating in an orbit populated by the brightest
and darkest stars of our time, he has consorted
with movie celebrities and murderers, investigat-
ing the flip-side of fame first-hand. His journey
so far is contained in five compelling books.

Sex, crime and glamour – the staples of
Hollywood – are inextricably intertwined in
Gilmore's work. He was born in Hollywood in
1935. His mother, Marguerite LeVan, was a studio
contract-player for MGM, his father, Robert
Gilmore Jr, an LAPD cop. His parents separated
when he was a baby and he was raised for the
most part in his paternal grandmother's house.
He started acting as a child, but the dawning of
his adolescence brought home the harsh reality
of what it took to make it in Hollywood as a
young actor, where sex was hard currency. He
rejected the casting couch and his mentor, actor
John Hodiak, suggested he seek work on
Broadway. So, aged sixteen, Gilmore moved to
New York where he led a Bohemian life as an
aspiring painter, poet and actor attending Lee
Strasberg's Actors Studio.

A mutual friend introduced him to James
Dean at a Broadway drugstore in Spring 1953.
These bad-boy spirits bonded over bullfighting
and motorbikes and became close friends,
sharing knowledge, experiences and girls.
Their paths crossed again in LA, while Dean was
shooting Rebel Without a Cause (1955). Gilmore
became known as one of the 'Night Watch' –
Dean's notorious group of motor-biking buddies
and Googies' drugstore cronies – and was
subsequently blacklisted as an actor by the major
studios as a troublemaker.

In the late 1950s, Gilmore spent time in Paris,
waiting for a movie in which he was contracted
to star with Jean Seberg to start shooting. It
never did, but he met Bardot at a party and hung
out with Burroughs and other ex-pats staying at
the Beat Hotel. Holed up in a garret apartment
with a typewriter, Gilmore began writing a novel
about a young screenwriter's affair with an
actress. Maurice Girodias (who ran Olympia
Press and published work by Burroughs, Miller,
Genet and Anaïs Nin) bought the rights to
Gilmore's novel but it remained unpublished.
(It will finally surface next year through
Creation Press, now titled Fetish Blonde.)
Returning to America, writing became Gilmore's
primary occupation. He worked as a freelance
journalist, penned pulp novels – through which
he met Ed Wood Jr who wanted to film one called
Brutal Baby – wrote teleplays and screenplays.
He directed a couple of long-lost B-Movies –
Blues for Benny, a gritty docudrama inspired
by the French nouvelle vague, and Breaking
Hard, an unfinished surfing flick starring Dennis
Hopper. Later, Gilmore claims to have shown
Hopper a treatment he had written for a biker
movie called Out Takes based on his experiences
with James Dean – an idea that Hopper and
Peter Fonda apparently used as the basis for
Easy Rider (1969).

In Laid Bare (subtitled A Memoir of
Wrecked Lives and the Hollywood Death Trip),
Gilmore exactingly dissects the Hollywood
mythology, recalling his experiences with a
panoply of characters, some more famous than
others. He smashes fragile icons rooted in
fantasy and picks over the psychological shards
left embedded in memories. The clarity and
immediacy of the images Gilmore conjures up
brings these characters into sharp focus. In
some cases, their actions suggest a grotesque
distortion of pathology, in others, a bawdy
comedy: Hank Williams so sozzled he pisses
his pants in a parking lot before a show; Steve
McQueen as a virulent misanthrope stalked by
his drunk mother; Dennis Hopper trying to
ape James Dean, but going over the edge of
the abyss.

In 1959, living in a Hollywood apartment
with his second wife, a former Hungarian
freedom fighter, and their newly-born child,
Gilmore was approached by tough-guy actor
Tom Neal to script a movie based on the Black
Dahlia murder, at that time the most notorious
murder in LA. The body of Elizabeth Short, an

This page
Gilmore photographed
in Hollywood, 1955
Opposite page
Gilmore photographed
by James Dean, 1955

aspiring starlet known as the Black Dahlia
(in reference to a Raymond Chandler femme
fatale), was found naked and mutilated in a
vacant lot in January 1946. Shots of the crime
scene show the body severed in two and
positioned like two offset halves of a photograph,
legs thrown invitingly open, arms flung above
her head as if in the throes of ecstasy. It was
obviously the work of a psychopathic artist,
but the creator of this gruesome artefact was
never found. Gilmore began researching the
case using his father's LAPD connections, chasing
leads and interviewing anyone involved in the
case. Two years later, Tom Neal shot his wife in
the head and was incarcerated, effectively killing
the project.

In 1967, Gilmore was asked by novelist
Bernard Wolf to help cover a murder case in
Arizona for Playboy magazine. It was the trial
of Charles Schmid, a baby-faced thrill-killer
styled like Elvis, who had murdered three of his
girlfriends and buried their bodies in the heart
of the Arizona desert. Gilmore gained exclusive
access to the charismatic killer in prison and
developed his researched material into a book,
The Tucson Murders (1998, recently re-released
as Cold-Blooded by Feral House). During Schmid's
second murder trial, Gilmore even assisted
high-flying attorney F Lee Bailey (later to
represent O J Simpson).

Gilmore became acquainted with the
Manson Family in the early 1970s, visiting
Manson in jail for a series of prison interviews,
which resulted in The Garbage People (1995,
Amok Books), a psycho-geographical history of
Manson and his 'Family'. Charlie had read
Gilmore's book on Schmid and considered him a
suitable medium for his messianic message.
But while Gilmore remained unaffected by

Manson's hypnotic psycho-babble, he recalls
watching his partner in the enterprise, producer
Bob Levy, become progressively deadened to life.
Gilmore says he soon dropped out of producing
movies to become an insurance salesman.
Throughout this period, the Black Dahlia case
was at the periphery of his vision. In 1969, at a
party populated by Hollywood low-lifes, John
Gilmore was introduced to Arnold Smith, a man
who claimed to have known the murdered girl.
Over the years, this character would periodically
contact Gilmore to talk about the girl. In 1980,
Gilmore appeared on an evening news show in
LA in connection with the assassination attempt
on Ronald Reagan by John Hinckley, who,
amazingly, had approached the writer four
years earlier in an LA bar and talked to him
about presidential assassinations. After this,
Smith contacted Gilmore again. Over a series
of meetings, he related intimate details of the
crime, which he claimed had been committed
by a female impersonator friend of his. To
corroborate his story, Gilmore took his taped
interviews to the LAPD, who determined that
Smith was the chief suspect in the unsolved
murder. Gilmore's twenty-odd years of extensive
research on the case is contained in Severed

(1998, Amok Books), a reconstruction of the life of Elizabeth Short and her murderer, which has been optioned by producer Edward G Pressman. David Lynch has considered directing the film version.

Now in his sixties, Gilmore divides his time between homes in LA and New Mexico. He is finally being accorded recognition in his own right as a writer of what he calls 'true-crime literature' and is currently the subject of a documentary-in-progress called Fame-Eater. *In a recent photo, taken by his wife Marie, Gilmore still wears the accoutrements of his rebel stance. The bad-boy glare he shoots to the lens has, if anything, grown more intense with age.*

Dazed & Confused | **What's your first memory of the Black Dahlia case?**
John Gilmore | When the case first broke, the body was found near where we lived in LA. I lived with my grandmother in the Silverlake area. One day, these two fellows came by the house and brought this girl with them. My grandmother's sister, who lived just a few doors away, had married a man years before named Pat Short. There was a very large side of the family, which was 'the Shorts'. This girl came by

to connect with her father. As I understand it, they didn't find a connection. But this girl was Elizabeth Short, the Black Dahlia. When she came to the house I was probably only eleven years old. I can recall her very clearly. She was dressed in black and her hair was stark black, like a black shining wig. Her face was very pale. She had whitish powder on her face and red, red lipstick that clashed against everything else. And she wore tight, black leather gloves all the time. I remember having a long talk with her about magic. As a child, I was interested in magic. My father was a member of the Shriners (a Masonic organization) and all the major circuses and magic shows came to the Shrine Auditorium in Los Angeles. I had a lot of magic stuff in my room. I was sitting on the floor, squatting down, leaning against the bed. I had two beds in my room, the other was for my stepbrother. She was sitting on the other bed and I was looking at her legs. *[laughs]* When that girl was murdered, which was a matter of months after, my grandmother called me aside and told me, 'Don't mention the fact that someone had brought that particular girl here that day, because it might not be her. And if it was, it wouldn't be too good.' My father was working on the case, not in a detective capacity but on patrol. He was going round various neighbourhoods in the area where the body was found and interviewing people to find out if they had heard or seen anything. He had this police briefcase that contained a whole wad of these renderings of the girl they used to show people for identification purposes. I used to snoop in his briefcase a lot. I knew that Elizabeth Short was the same girl, because her name was Short and that was the reason she came to my house. She was so intriguing to me and was a figure that remained in my consciousness. She just radiated this tremendous amount of sex appeal. There was a dark, mysterious quality to her, as if she wasn't really real. Over the years, everyone that I encountered who had met her had the same feeling: that she just came into their lives and caused a kind of confusion. A confusion that never left; that had no answer to it.

That's reminiscent of things you've said about the effect James Dean had on people?
With James Dean, it would probably have been more direct. Jimmy had a way of tweaking people by things he would do. Because he knew they were in awe of him, he would try to shock them. Like, for example, he'd take off his jacket and drop it on the floor rather than setting it on a chair. He'd do odd things so people would remember him. Jimmy had a tremendous impact. His intensity seemed to have this penetrating intelligence behind it, which he didn't really have. He was perceptive, very bright and very intuitive about people, but he wasn't really an intellectual. He hardly read at all: he had severe reading problems. You'd be talking about something and he would say, 'Tell me. Tell me about it.' So you'd tell him something and pretty soon he had it all evolved in his own head, this whole story pieced together from people he'd talked to. He could carry the whole thing in his head as if he had real insights from it all. But he had never sat down and read the book. In particular, we talked about Patrick Mulhey's *Study of Interpersonal Relations*, which was a really great book that I loved. This one particular essay in there had to do with the proximity senses – taste, smell and feel – and how very early we try to shut these all down. We try to make the shift in our children as soon as

possible to the visual and audio, so that we can get away from shit and piss and the smells of people, which are so definitely taboo in our Judaeo-Christian culture. I love that quote by Franz Kafka that the whole structure of education is to frustrate a child's assault on truth. You begin to twist it slowly, step by step by step, until you have taken the humiliated child and convinced him of the lie. That was Kafka's guiding force and, over the years, I've had to admit that it's really true. It's just amazing how at a young age we're twisted to be conditioned in a social way. And Jimmy would try to break these patterns.

In *The Garbage People*, you talk about Manson's childhood in that way too. Do you think the reason that people like Manson and James Dean tried to break through so vehemently was due to their violent conditioning as children?
In someone like Charlie Manson's case, yes – where you throw them into a dungeon before they are even able to be conditioned and begin to condition them to that. He was beaten with a stick, kept in chains half the time and thrown in a little cell. He had intelligence, skill and talent to fall back upon – and certainly imagination. He was a highly imaginative person. So he withdraws into his own world. Then he presents himself to the world in a completely different context than we have any framework for. So he becomes a very puzzling creature.

Do you see any similarity between Dean and Manson in terms of the strengths of their characters and the way in which they were able to manipulate people?
Well, yes. But when you ask me that... if we look at ourselves, there's a part of us that wants to have a god: something that has an answer for us and that we can look up to, admire and respect; something that we are drawn and attracted to. Both Dean and Manson had a particular charisma as human beings to attract other people. It's probably something that they were not even deliberately trying to do. Although, once they learn that they can, they become very skilful at using it, which both of those people did. Also Adolf Hitler probably had the same kind of charisma. When you break off from the mainstream way, you're

Gilmore in drag in an
on-set picture from
Fame Eater, *1970s*

either going to sink or swim, and you have to fall upon your natural resources. Something that both Jimmy and Charlie had tremendously in common – and I think a great many people like this that we're talking about have – is this ability to manipulate. Jimmy could really manipulate people and Charlie was a master manipulator. I mean, you've got to find a particular type of person that's gonna want to be manipulated.

Don't you think they end up drawing the right type of people to them? Like magnetism, they attract their natural opposites.

Well, I think in the world that they are travelling in and living in, they are continually going to be coming across people who are going to be attracted to them. It's like cause and effect: it just continues to perpetuate itself; the direction being towards survival and the attainment of certain goals you might have. Jimmy was able to go from one person to another without ever having any problems. He never starved. He never had lean days. He was always able to go and get some money or something from somebody. He spent a lot of his time wandering through a labyrinth of places

and areas, which I think reflected in some way a motor activity he had. Like he was wandering around in his own psyche; wandering as a stranger in a strange land looking for something substantial that's going to give you solidarity as a human being, but really not knowing fully what it is you're after. Neither one of them – Jimmy or Charlie – ever really knew what it was they were after, but they were certainly after something.

Were you attracted to the manipulative side of Dean's personality?

I was attracted to him initially because he was a bad-boy. Not 'bad' in that you'll go out and do anything really bad or destructive, but in that you're not in the mainstream of something. Looking back at the psychological landscape of myself, I can see my attraction to the 'wrong' people. It could go back to my childhood. I used to watch the wrestling with my father and I would root for Baron Michel Leoni, who was the bad guy. My father used to get really upset because I wasn't rooting for Gorgeous George. That disturbed me greatly as a child. I had a sense of withdrawing from my father, who was a policeman. I think in some strange sense, murderers, criminals and artists (I put them all in the same category) can recognize something in me. I am not judgemental. My relationship with Jimmy was not judgemental in any sense. If when we were out riding, I had said something like, 'Jesus, slow down!', I would have found him drifting away from me and I didn't want that. I did not editorialize our relationship and haven't done that with anyone else.

In certain moments with Janis Joplin as well, there was a union. And the union was open and uncomplicated by where it was going

to go or not going, or if something was wrong or not wrong. One time, I was drinking in a bar in Sausalito with Janis and she went into the can and shot up. She came out and had blood running out of her nose. I said, 'How do you feel?' She said, 'I feel far out.' And it just went like that. I guess I was excited and compelled to go further with people. When I was out riding with Jimmy, he would go through stop signs, and there was a certain risk there, certainly if you're riding fast on Sunset at night. I was twenty years old and this was exciting and stimulating. It was kind of like we were two astronauts in a nose-cone charging through space.

My formative years as a young person were spent living through the Cold War. We had no future and the biggest thing going was to dig dug-out shelters in the backyard and stock them with Shredded Wheat, Coke and Spam. That was a major thing to do, because at any time an atomic bomb was going to be dropped. That's what we actually lived with. The beginning of the end had already started. Now we were just waiting for the end. Any time this thing was going to happen, it was going to blow us all to smithereens. So why the fuck bother

with any of this? Your entire system is wrong. You had so many people who were rigidly and sociologically conditioned to accept that only they were right. 'In God we trust. We are arrogant. We are white. And we're right.' That's what it was all about and if you weren't part of that, you were wrong and an outlaw. When the beatnik thing broke, they were the people that understood this and said, 'No! I'm not going to buy insurance policies because there's no guarantee that we're going to be here tomorrow. The only thing that's worth something is my own individual self-expression. So I'm going to express myself and try and find some meaning in a very individual sense.' I was very tightly involved with a number of those people, but I never really thought of myself as a beatnik. My original goal was to be a painter. I did a lot of paintings during that period. I had a lot of showings in beatnik coffee houses in New York and sold a lot of stuff. I was very close to a lot of people who were junkies. I was attracted to it and interested in it, but I've never really done anything to any great extent in those areas. I shot heroin, but I wasn't a junkie. I've done just about everything. In 1968, I was on extended acid trips for about three months. It was all very pleasant.

What saved you from burning out or self-destructing?

I've never had the self-destructive tendency. I always felt that I was on a journey and that I'm looking for something. I'm beginning to feel that my life is what my living has been about. That's kind of an awkward statement. It's not that I have eaten fame as a diet but it has been moving me towards something. I've sort of been in an orbit. When I was very young I used to spend a lot of time down at the Venice amusement pier. There was something called the Drone of Death, which was a giant barrel, which a guy on a motorcycle drove all the way around. I was probably about ten or eleven and I rode on the motorcycle with this guy, who was a stuntman in the movies, called Spider Madlock. He was a friend of my cousin's and used to race midget autos at the Gilmore Stadium in LA. I have always looked back at that time on the Drone of Death and felt that I was spun off into some kind of orbit. It's like I've been moving in a different type of world. I've met a lot of people and done a lot of things. It's been a learning experience and an exploration. I think that Charlie Manson, in a weird sort of way, was also an explorer. Jimmy Dean certainly was. They died, but I haven't yet. It's like at the end of that movie *The Fly*. The boy's father is dead and he asks Vincent Price, 'Why did my daddy have to die?' Vincent Price says, 'Well, your father was a scientist. He was an explorer and sometimes their exploration takes them to places where they can die.'

Some people don't die, but a lot of people do, and that's the way I think of people that I've known. Dennis Hopper felt that he was an explorer and was going to push himself to the ultimate limit. And he did. But In Dennis' case, he went absolutely bananas! I know someone who actually saw Dennis when he was locked up in a room and sat there catatonic for days. He went over the far side. Before my time, there was the 'Black Ship to Hell', and that was the romantic concept of death and poetry, of art and dying. After the war, through Existentialism, that became known as 'wigging-out'. That's what Rimbaud did. He blew all his circuits. A lot of people do that now with absolute ultra-volume. You're blowing circuits, and doing that will take you somewhere else. I feel that through seeing punk, especially G G Allin's work – he's way out there, y'know, on the crest... It's like the big wave riders I knew in the 60s. They were a breed unto themselves, nothing like what you see in the Frankie Avalon movies. These were iconoclastic outlaw people who were dedicated to one goal: to ride the waves. And it was real dangerous.

You're talking about a death trip. People that are sailing as close to death as possible. But see, the way it really is, it's a 'life' trip. You're going as close to the living truth as you can get. But there's also the possibility that if you are exploring there, that you could die as well. It's only 'death' to certain conventions that we're clinging to: the standards we're protecting ourselves by because we don't want to see. God and religion teaches you that there's only the bright side. The good is good and the bad belongs to the devil. And there isn't any between area. Now, of course, we know that there's alternatives and options to everything in the universe. Everything! Consequently, what

I'm saying is that what we've done – through people like G G Allin and Derby Crash (the late singer with LA punk band The Germs) – is to move society and experience to a fresh wave that's breaking upon the beach of reality. We're out there on the middle of this wave, and suddenly all these things that were so bloody important before are not important at all. In other words, in the whole concept of chaos, we are suddenly seeing that there might be a whole new vista of experience. In my time as a young person, there wasn't anything more to want than what you were told you needed. But I'm beginning to see that the experiences are in us. The interior journey is about being able to see that there are vast horizons of untapped territory. With some people, yes, it is a death trip. They have a very self-destructive urge. But if they have to go to that point, they have to go there for a reason. As I've walked along the ledge of life holding someone's hand – be it Janis Joplin, James Dean or Jean Seberg – something inside has let their hand go and they've gone down the other side. I've had to move on. And in that moving on I've found that the life is not meaningless. So let's just play Russian roulette.

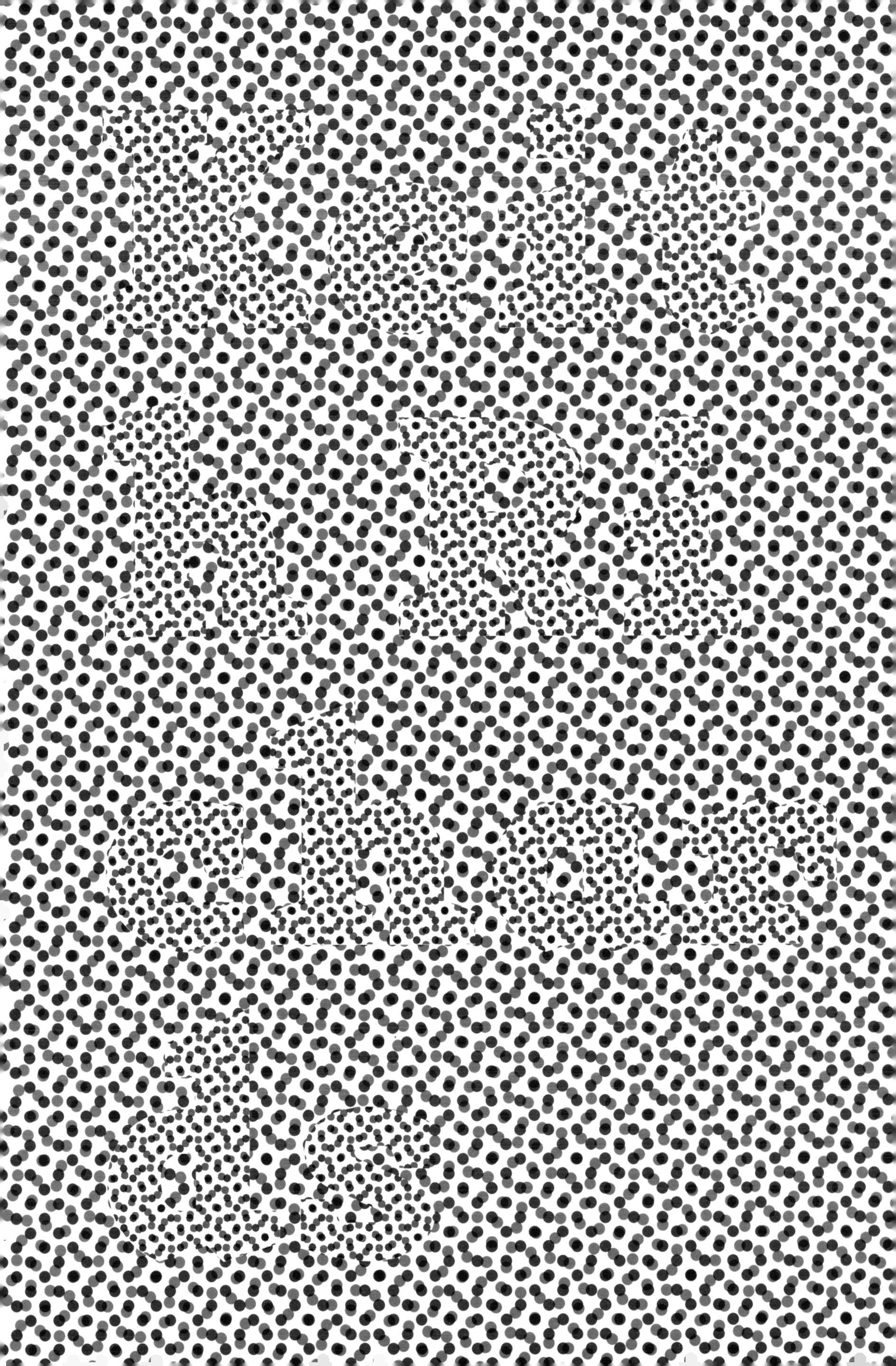

June 1999
Introduction and interview | Roger Morton

Sundown in Florida. The great burning ball drops towards the Everglades, alligators stir in the ditches and high up in a pastel palace on South Beach, Miami, the mechanical monster of the perpetually running Rolling Stones touring machine lifts one eyelid.

The inner core of the band's road regiment has annexed several floors of a brand new ice cream monstrosity on Ocean Drive. Down corridors the length of airstrips, hired hands and henchmen pad about barefoot and freaky of hair, safe in the knowledge that even though it's 1999 and the President's ex is a more fitting subject for a film called Cocksucker Blues than Mick and Keef, they're with The Stones man, and the legend still shelters.

The unearthly and venerable old blues magnates have extended their Bridges To Babylon tour for a two-month long Tommy Hilfiger-sponsored, indoor strut round the States dubbed 'No Security'. Naturally therefore, the security at the band's hotel is heavy. It's a day off in Miami but interviews are scheduled for late afternoon and a cabal of retired wrestlers are positioned outside suites around the hotel. Whether the minders are there to keep the fanatics away or the members of the band inside is hard to discern.

At the top of the faux-deco palace, Jagger swerves diplomatically through a 'commemorative' interview about Brian Jones, happy to talk about anything as long as its not Brazilian nymphets and his 'old lady' problems. Deeper down, 'new boy' of twenty-four years service Ron Wood twitches like a hyper schoolboy in detention, gabbles incoherently and considers drinking a lava lamp as a way out of facing another hack.

It is not however the singer or the other guitarist that has drawn us into the maw of the waxwork beastie currently defying the laws of biology as the Ripest Rock-'n'-Roll Band in the World. It is the promise of a conversation with The Man Who Invented Twentieth-Century Rock Cool, the Twelve-Bar Lord Byron, the Human Riff, the last British swashbuckler, mad, bad and magical to know Mr Keith Richards. And for that you have to wait.

It isn't a matter of Keith making an entrance. It's more of a space launch. Half an hour before he emerges, The Stones' propaganda apparatus starts crackling as news of Keith's stirring is passed down a chain of walkie talkies. Fifteen minutes before launchtime, an escort marches your interviewer into a disturbingly pastel suite. At last the countdown signal comes: 'Keith has left his room...'

Some weeks later, the door opens and a very mortal, grey-haired man twinkles into the room accompanied by the merry clinking of ice cubes and a flurry of press representatives, minders and assistants' assistants.

'Oh shit, the entourage!' exclaims Keith, spinning in the middle of the room, apparently surprised to discover the small army on his heels. With eyeballs rolling he lurches puppet-like towards the sofa, deposits cigarettes and fizzy orange drink and settles back.

'Ah, another day at the office! Welcome to Miami, the sun's nearly down.'

It's a full moon tonight.

'Yeah it was looking pretty much there yesterday. We lock half the band up when it's a full moon. Hahhaaarrrch! Probably why we're not working today. A full moon's impossible.'

As the entourage shuffles out, it's possible to get a closer look at the werewolf opposite. The in-the-flesh, in-cashmere-black-v-neck-and-jeans Keith Richards confounds a number of clichés. His average physical size is far from intimidating and his gouged features are less wasted, and more weathered like a healthy boatyard worker. The silver handcuff bracelet and skull ring clamped onto a bulbously veined hand confirm his identity, as does his bearing which is part Peter O'Toole part cockney Clint Eastwood. But there's an immediate openness and warmth which you don't expect from the Prince of Darkness. It's like meeting Keith Richards' lovely brother, the one with a laugh like the distant sawing of teak.

How's your day been?
'Fairly short.'
Late start today?
'Yeah, well my old lady's here too so that kind of hahahhhhrcchhh kept me occupied for a bit. It's almost like getting serviced, this kind of gig. It's very rare I see my old lady for more than two days in a row!'

In 1969, during the six-month gap between Brian Jones' drowning and the hippie horror of Altamont, author of the True Adventures of the Rolling Stones, *Stanley Booth, looked at Richards and saw 'an insane advertisement for a dangerous carefree Death'. That was before the heroin fog of the 70s and several more decades of beyond the call of duty reckless living, encompassing driving like a suicidal baboon, carrying a .38, setting fire to stately homes (his own), fighting murderous thugs and befriending psychos.*

Richards, however, never believed his own advertisement, outliving three generations of stellar outlaws from Morrison and Hendrix to Vicious and Cobain, and ricocheting through to the millennium's end to merrily booze on, play the best meat cleaver blues riffs on the planet, wind up Elton John (he recently described his talent as limited to writing songs for dead blondes) and confound expectations.

Last year when the neighbourhood around his moated Tudor pile in Sussex launched an appeal to save West Wittering Village Hall, he donated £30,000.

At fifty-five, and a grandfather, Richards has to be one of the most beautiful people alive. His only rival as a still working British exotic with an equivalent depth of experience of the twentieth century is probably Elizabeth II (whose type he despises). Her Majesty has a clearer memory, but she didn't hang out with Burroughs and Warhol, spar with Dylan, get stoned with Marley and get punched by Chuck Berry.

It wouldn't be hard to make a case for Richards as some kind of über-archetype. The globalism, hedonism, racial blurring and bad motherfucker style that permeate the present culture were all innate to Richards as he clawed his way out of monochrome post-war Britain heading for Mississippi via Morocco.

There are however twenty more reborn again performances left before The Stones finish their 1999 American tour. Richards – at least in his

own head – is still in full flight, tracking down transcendence through the infinite grid of six strings and twelve battered frets.

Dazed & Confused | **Is this a happy and creative phase for The Stones?**
Keith Richards | We're very happy together when we're playing together. I mean knowing these guys like I know them they don't do anything they don't want to. You couldn't talk Charlie into doing something he didn't want to do. It'd be like walking into the Great Wall of China. Boom! Forget about it. So my presumption therefore is that they actually enjoy it and they want to do it. I mean, eh, we were freezing our balls off last week up in Fargo or somewhere so this is already semi paradise to us after that. It's then that you go, 'Why? Is it just because you've got used to it?' But in actual fact it is what you do, and what you like to do.
Does it bother you why people come to see The Stones now, like if they're just coming for the nostalgia?
Not really, when I'm up there looking at them, they're coming from everywhere, there's a lot of kids, there's a lot of the old crowd there..

Whatever their motivation is, any musician will tell you, you've got a show to do and if they're there, sod the motivation! Hrrrrch! As long as there's somebody there!

What interests me more is the band's motivation for doing it. The last thing you want to ever do is go up there and feel like you're doing it by rote. If it ain't fun for you you're not going to project much for everybody else. After all, basically it is entertainment and hopefully it's good. Really, we go up there to have a damn good time ourselves and screw it if you blow a few notes. You know, Segovia I ain't! Haahurrk!

What's the deal with you and Mick at the moment, are you getting on OK?
Well, hey, we're getting on with the gig. I mean Mick's a bit preoccupied these days as you can well imagine.

Does it affect the band, that kind of 'personal difficulty' thing?
Only as much as its affects Mick. We go 'Hrrrhrrr, good one Mick! Whooops-a-daisy, eh!' Hurhurrrh! So he's a little preoccupied. But apart from that yeah, we have a lot of fun on stage. Basically that's where we get peace and quiet and we can actually hang out a bit together. Its the only place where the phone doesn't ring and nobody else gets in the way. And then when shit hits the fan you give somebody a little space.

Is it true that you didn't like Jerry?
No. I admire her very much. I mean any woman who can live with that man, I tip my hat to. Let me put it like that. Hrrrrurhur.

Does the money mean anything these days?
Well you don't go out not to make a profit. But it's not so much the money, it's what you do with it. I mean nobody's going to turn their nose up at money, they're not stupid, but at the same time you couldn't buy it. None of us are that greedy. I mean really you look around for things to do with it. Where can you help here? Who can you help here? Without going into that huge charity foundation bullshit that they're so fond of in England, and all that licking arse in order to get tapped on the shoulder with a sword...

Which isn't imminent in your case, I think.
Oh I doubt it. Hrrrchhhchchach! I wouldn't let them near me with a pointed stick let alone a sword! They know how I feel about them.

I read that one tour you walked away with fifteen million pounds personal profit. That's insane.
Yeah.

What does that feel like?
Great. Hahahaaach! But as I say it's what you do with it. I don't know why they pay me so much, quite honestly. It's quite a task dealing with it, having that much money is a bit embarrassing in a way. So what do you do?... See I was a bloke who used to save the money for the hair cut, so that's why the long hair. It was to save half a crown so you could spend it on cigarettes. So I've been there. But at the same time I've been incredibly well paid since the age of nineteen.

Sometimes I kind of resent it because automatically with that amount of money to deal with you have to start thinking like and becoming like the empty suit with the tie and you have to get into their minds, because you're dealing with big business and you have to actually listen to tax legislation and you have to get into things which really have nothing to do with what you want to do. Ever since I've been in the game, you make a record, there you are a pure, idealistic young musician, and the next minute you're in a pool full of sharks. And you can get eaten or not. You just sort of learn. You get burned here and there and you get a few scars on the way. But that's that whole other area that you have to deal with and really you're trying to write another song.

So it's a kind of ambivalent thing. I try and keep the business down to a minimum in my life. Mick really enjoys to get in there, sometimes to his own detriment. I suppose in a way it affects us all but we never talk about it amongst ourselves, business. Our idea of hell is going to business meetings. You sit around with the tax lawyers and you feel like you've been called into the headmaster's office. Hahaharch! They're like droning on and on and on.

So you nod off in the corner?
Yeah. I nod off, and then they say, 'So what do you say?' and it's like, 'Yes. Like I said two hours ago.' Also the other thing is with this game you're on a permanent night shift, even when you're not doing it the internal body clock takes an incredibly long time, you still get up at two in the morning, get up and stay up all night, and if you've done it this long, that's a bit

disruptive. Especially when you've got kids at school and you're just going to bed. It's like, 'Put dad to bed and go to school. And then I'll get up and pick you up later...'

Are you not any better at fitting into the, erm, 'straight' world?

No, you see, my wife says I'm semi-domesticated at best.

Patti Hansen, the American model Keith married in 83, has been given much of the credit for his comparative stability in latter years. His previous central relationship with Anita Pallenberg was a Narcotics Anonymous parable of getting it wrong, but Hansen who came from a devoutly Lutheran family helped tone down the most insidious problems while still happily mixing Keith his wake-up vodka and orange.

Keith, his 'old lady' and their two young daughters live off-the-road life mostly on a country estate in Connecticut. Richard's father who he reunited with in the 80s lives nearby. No doubt the Prince of Darkness, the man mostly responsible for The Stones' former image as that of 'sado-homosexual-junkie-diabolic-sarcastic-nigger-evil unprecedented in the annals of pop culture' (Albert Goldman) permits himself a cackle when he takes his kids to the local Sunday School.

His current stability is not, however, without a few wobbles. Last year he fell off a ladder in his library cracking a rib, puncturing a lung and causing £35 million worth of Stones gigs to be cancelled. In 97 he intimated to a journalist that he might have dabbled with heroin more recently than, well, his big late 70s bust in Toronto. After years of friendly interaction with HM Customs, he was then promptly stopped leaving Heathrow and strip searched.

After too many years of being tackled by the media as The World's Most Famous Junkie rather than the man who wrote the chords to 'Satisfaction' it might be expected that Richards would be bored of the drugs topic. That doesn't seem to be the case today. As dusk settles on Miami beach the sound of drilling buzzes through the window over Keith's shoulder. There's con-struction work going on next door and despite the fact that earlier in the day The Stones offered to pay the site developer $10,000 to shut up for the day, the drilling is going on..

They're building in Miami Beach. This isn't the first hotel in thirty years to be built from the ground up, and look what a piece of crap they built here. So over there they're building another piece of crap. The area's changed, they've cleared out the drug dealers and moved them somewhere else. Cleaned up this area, badabingbuda-bangbudaboom.

Did you take any interest in the emergence of house music and ecstasy culture when it took off in England?

I wasn't there much but it was very interesting that it was going on. When I was there people would tell me about it and I thought, that sounds like the old house, rent party thing. But London is changing all the time on me, I don't get there a lot but at the same time it's my home town. That's the weirdest thing about London. It's the only place I feel like a visitor. Every time I go back to London it's changed somewhere.

You went through the whole 60s drug culture experience but in a way it happened again in the 80s/90s with a million people a week taking ecstasy.

Well drugs are... I think probably the first thing the human race ever looked for was how to get high. After screwing, the next thing was, 'Right, how can we enhance this?' People have been taking this, drinking that for ever. And it's a fairly recent thing people trying to stop them, governments trying to stop people.

I mean the idea of someone taking a pipe out of your mouth because you're smoking this or that! It's all very recent. Which means that money's involved in there somewhere because the human race has taken just about everything it can get its hands on, for ever. I mean poppies! Who would imagine! You know what I mean, hahhahahrrch! Who would imagine that guys would sit around in a field until they found out how to make opium? Can you imagine the work that went into finding out about opium? You know, and then growing the weed? That's a lot of work and intense scientific and horticultural effort over the years. And whether they're now made synthetically or not. I mean ecstasy... and then there's your Egyptian jelly, which is apparently pretty good, although I've not actually got my hands on any, hahahuchuch!

What's Egyptian jelly?

Oh it's a powerful herb, so they say. They

probably make it synthetically in some Mexican laboratory by now. The funny thing about drugs is that there are some that are legal and there are some that ain't and it's very difficult figuring out why... And why bother to put all the money in to take the high out of something?

Did you get on with William Burroughs?
Yes, yes, I knew Bill, off and on. An evening here and there, usually at dinner or somewhere, with Robert Fraser (the art dealer). Yeah, we used to swap cures, hahahrch... Gram Parsons and I used his old nurse, a little old biddy from Devon called Smitty. Oh she was a cruel woman! I don't know if it was Bill Burroughs' joke on us. His tried and tested method of kicking smack! And we're sweating. It was like Bill said, 'Well have you tried cold turkey? No, you must try Smitty from Cornwall, it's even worse!' This little old lady, you know, she's really sweet, grey hair and this lovely smile. And then she's whacking this shit into you that makes you puke up and if you didn't obey, she'd put you in an arm lock. Hurhurch. She could deal with anything. She was unbelievable. And there was Gram Parsons and me in a bed together going, 'Oh man I can't take much more of this bitch!'

Does it annoy you when people want to typecast you from your drug history?
Well, you know. I kind of take it for granted, I'm pretty much typecast in somebody's eyes before we sit around and talk. With some people you can chat and then with others you know that you're not going to be able to change their mind whatever you say. You know what they want and what they're after, because they're like ferrets, and you feel like sticking a ferret down their trousers. But it's quite amusing too because you can joust with them, and sometimes you can just be outrageous and lie your head off. I mean I'm not under oath here, know what I mean? Hahaharrch!

I read that you were doing heroin when you were in Switzerland and you learned to ski on heroin. What the fuck is that like?
Well it's actually very good because it slows everything down. Huhuhurrrch! You start very slowly and then, on smack you're used to being about three feet off the ground anyway so it's no problem. But anyway I was in Switzerland and it's very boring not skiing in Switzerland in the winter and I had to live there.

First I was cleaning up and then it was taxes or something like that. I spent one winter there in total gloom from October to March and then it was, well that's enough of that. And then I found myself living there again the next year and I thought, 'Sod it! We're going up above the clouds and we're going to start skiing!'

And it's very nice up there. It's sunny and it's not so difficult once you get the hang of it. It's a bit embarrassing at the beginning when you've got little four-year-old kids zooming past you and you're on your side trying to get up. Harrrchcuh! But eventually we used to have a good time. After that I quite enjoyed Switzerland. But they're funny people. Strange attitude.

All that sliding stuff, skateboarding, rollerblading just wasn't meant to be.
Not really. I diced with death on ballbearing steel rollerskates when I was a kid and that was enough. Skiing was about my last attempt at athletic, daredevil activity. I mean you could hear legs breaking like rifle shots up there. And then you see these little tubes going with somebody and it's like, 'Nahh, I'll give this up.'

One of the magical aspects of Richards' slalom through the decades is that despite his many stumbles he's held onto a basic core dignity. No matter how out there he got, his saving grace was his evident commitment to a pure tradition of primal guitar music. It was Jagger who had the Chuck Berry and Muddy Waters albums when the pair bonded over blues on the train from Dartford in 61, but while swivel hips has slipped into the VIP enclosure for celebrity Lotharios, Richards has survived as the player and 'soul of The Stones'.

Jagger's solo projects (the backdrop to the pair's acrimonious feud during the first half of the 80s) have looked like career moves. Richards' have been happy-go-lucky accidents. His 'X Pensive Winos' pick-up caper has been dormant, but a couple of years back he released Wingless Angels, an Afro-Rasta Celtic marvel put together with his smoking mates from Steer Town, Jamaica. 'Jah Keith', who's had a villa on the island since late 72, maintains that the album was recorded by chance, mostly because his house is the only safe place round there to keep a drum kit.

The other recent Richards showing outside The Stones was equally unplanned. Jagger and Richards are on the recent Blues Blues Blues *album celebrating Jimmy Rogers, the 'first electric blues man from Chicago' who died while the album was being completed. The Stones happened to be in the studio next door recording and Bridges strolled in for two songs. If Keith's never quite got his head around hip-hop and house music that's only to be expected – he wrote the game plan for British kids getting into black American music.*

I don't know what the affinity is with the Chicago blues cats, I mean I'm steeped in it myself but at the same time they kind of all know us. I know Mrs Muddy Waters! Hrrch! I know Mrs Howling Wolf. Those kind of things, when you're a kid you kind of think, 'Yeah one day if I could play with that guy...' You dream about it and then you get to do it. And in that respect, I mean, hey, do dreams come true? From my point of view in many respects they have.

What was the deal with you and Chuck Berry?
That was a sort of nightmarish dream. Nobody gets on with Chuck. The fact is that there's a great guy inside but there's a big chip on his shoulder and it's too much energy and bother to actually go in there and find it. I mean he's such a cheap sonofabitch. Hhhrhhhhchaha! And that's about the nicest thing I can say about Chuck. But bless him, I still love him dearly, with all his warts and faults he made some of the best fuckin' rock-'n'-roll records ever. I mean there's a one-man machine there. What he forgot was that he did need a good band.

Did you get any reverse prejudice when you were going to America in the 60s, dealing with blues musicians? Did nobody say, 'You're from Dartford what the fuck are you doing in the Delta?'
S'funny, never. Always expected to run into it. I might have run into it from a couple of guys who weren't players, just guys on the street. But you almost automatically expect that, and I never found it, never found more peace and quiet and generosity than hanging with the brothers quite honestly. They just like to hang! Hahahrch! You don't have to go, 'Oh good evening, and how are you?' and worry about whether you've upset the table arrangements. There's a wonderful warmth and generosity even from people who've got nothing.

It's something that's missing amongst a lot of other people. And it's even if they don't know who you are, especially if you're white. You become like a little mascot. 'Oh here he comes, our white one. Let's buff him up a little bit!' It's great. Hahharch.

You got a musical education from black musicians but did you get a sexual education from 'the chicks'?
Oh The Ronettes? Yes. Hrrch. Well that's where we started. Well of course, black gurrr... You know playing the music that we were playing you started very early on gravitating towards that side of town. When I first came to America it was full-blown segregation down here, down South. Guys you were working with, or chicks, people like Patti Labelle, you'd have to separate just to get something to eat. It was all that stuff about, 'Oh well then we'll come into your bit' and they're like, 'No man, it'll make trouble.' So then you end up: nobody eats. But yeah my sexual education is multi-racial... Chinese ain't bad either. Hahharch!

Don't know much about Chinese sexuality.
No, well, hahhahrrch! There's a lot of them. Know what I mean...

The cultural pirate in Richards cannot sail so freely these days. His family (four kids including the grown-up Marlon and Angela) and The Stones' sprawling empire make it less easy to slip off to the other side of town. But amidst the luxury archive-prison of the band's end-of-the-century phase he's found a way to stay impressively human.

One theory has it that all the drugs were just a way for a shy, stubborn, working-class kid to kick against his stardom. Certainly, now he doesn't have to be so much the bad motherfucker, it's easier to catch sight of the insular council estate boy who picked up his grandfather's guitar aged fourteen and found his way into the universe.

An evening breeze is making treble clef shapes with Keith's cigarette smoke, but the ice cubes are still clinking and now we're talking banjo lore, it's like he could talk all night.

Do you find yourself still at this stage wondering what you're doing surrounded by glitterati?

I try and avoid it but at the same time you know that from the minute you walk out of your door in a way, you're on. You go down to the lobby, and you're kind of performing even the minute before you get out of the door.

So does it get tiring having to do the 'Keef Richards' performance?

No, in a funny way it kind of wakes you up. Because you've really got to laugh at it. I mean you can't take it seriously. The only things I find that I don't do any more is I can't go to the movies. I'm waiting for the asshole who's going to go, 'It's him, Keef Keef!' And everybody's going 'Shhhhh!' So I had to cut that out, because I feel like I bugger it up for everyone else.

But apart from that you take it with a grain of salt. And people just coming up and saying, 'Thanks for the music.' In a way it's very humbling. It's like, 'I changed your life? I don't even know you!' And you're like, 'Take it easy. I hope I changed it in the right direction!'

Well nobody's going to believe the crazy satanic motherfucker bit after you donated all that money to save West Wittering Village Hall.

Aaah. But I'm turning it into a satanic temple! Hahaharch! You won't believe it. Wait until it's finished.

Everybody should have a guitar. It doesn't matter whether you pick it up once a year, but it's a great little thing to have around, and it's just the right shape. I sleep with mine sometimes. Haaarurch! I've always wondered if it was something to do with the shape... But no, it's an incredible instrument.

The minute you start to do something for a living maybe you're taking half the real joy out of it. You lose your innocence by getting paid to do it. And that's something you've got to deal with. Because the real joy of it is just sitting around with the thing for no particular profit: except that it soothes the heart. For a while you don't have to worry about a thing. Nothing.

For years and years my guitar never sounded right to me. Other people liked it. I hated it! But lately, I don't know if it's experience or the joys of senility – hahahach – I can pick the thing up and it sounds like I want it to sound.

So you're coming into your own now?

Yeah I'm like a late bloomer. I actually enjoy playing the thing probably more at the moment than at other periods. It's such a frustrating instrument. Six this way, twelve this way – it's all in there, figure it out.

With a final dusty twirl of his pronged fork, Richards acknowledges the pleading of his press minders waving from the back of the room and prepares to face the photographer. The old devil's work isn't done yet. The next century's rock-'n'-rollers will need pointers for how it's done, and having made it through the crazed years he's cruising quite steadily through to the other side of millennial chaos.

'I've got two fifty-millimetre machine guns and enough gasoline to run my generator,' he cackles. 'And a lot of tinned fruit!'

The quintessentially beautiful Keith Richards lies back on the sofa and for a few seconds closes his eyes.

The drilling has stopped and as twilight glimmers over Miami, the mask of his features dissolves into an expression of deep serenity.

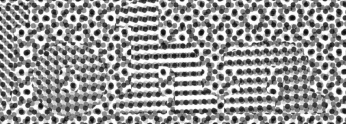

February 1999
Introduction and interview | Wendy Ide

It is 1972. The unfocused anger of the disaffected post-hippie generation erupts into sporadic bursts of direct action worldwide. After a bombing campaign, the key members of the Baader-Meinhof gang are arrested in Germany. Two members of The Weathermen accidentally blow themselves up in a Greenwich Village town-house. The Manson family are being tried for the Tate murders. Watching the progress of the trial from the public gallery is an unknown filmmaker called John Waters. Two weeks later, he makes the film for which, even now, he is notorious.

The film in question was Pink Flamingos *(1972) and featured a pivotal scene in which a 300 lb transvestite called Divine ate a dog turd. Waters sees his style of filmmaking at the time as a direct response to the counter-cultural movement of the era. 'It was like joining a crime scene. It was influenced by the Yippies and Baader-Meinhof, all the insanity of the left-wing. The influence on that movie was comic cultural terrorism; that's what we were trying to do.'*

Crime has always fascinated John Waters. When we arrive at his house in Baltimore, he sends the photographer off to choose a location for his portrait shoot. 'Have a look around, just don't steal anything. I have had journalists steal things, books mainly. I don't blame them actually – if I was a journalist I'd probably steal things.' He gives the impression that he'd be secretly impressed if we tried. He is famously quoted as saying, 'Everybody looks better under arrest.' It's not surprising then that crime, and in particular, terrorism, is a recurring theme throughout Waters' films. But it's not just terrorism that makes him tick. As he explains here, his cinematic themes are many and varied, covering his home town, Baltimore, the art world and countless variations of sexual deviancy and perversion.

John Waters | Testing, testing... I think I'm getting a cold, as you can hear.
Dazed & Confused | **Nobody likes the sound of their own voice.**
Well I think that's a good sign – people hate their own voice. The only person that probably doesn't is Barbra Streisand. That's because she never had a bad take.
What happened to the film you were planning to make, *Cecil B Demented*?
It was a development deal with French money and it fell through due to casting, which many movies do. They wanted one person to do it and she wouldn't, and the people I wanted, they didn't accept.
Are you still going to try and get the project off the ground?
Yeah, absolutely, but it's hard because it's a comedy about teen terrorism against the movie business. In Hollywood, that's not the easiest sell because in the movie they punish producers of bad films and those are the very people I'm approaching for money.
It sounds a fantastic idea though.
Yeah, everyone says that when they haven't got any money. *[laughs]* People who have the funds to invest usually prove to be the same people who are a little nervous about a terrorist comedy.
All of your films seem to be twisted love letters to Baltimore. Would you agree with that assessment?
Well yes, they all are, but in *Pecker* (1998), Baltimore plays by far the biggest character. Christina Ricci actually kisses the ground in that film. When I asked her if she would really go through with it, she said 'sure'. All these people at the time were commenting, 'God, Christina Ricci kissed the *ground*!' Of course, I

really appreciated that she did that for the film, but then I've had people eat shit in my movies before, so it's not that big a deal.

Would you ever consider making a film outside of Baltimore?

Well, I shot parts of *Crybaby* (1990) in LA and I shot the amusement park scene in *Hairspray* (1988) in Pennsylvania, although you are right, not by choice I wouldn't. I just know it better here and the extras are more interesting. See, in Hollywood, all the extras look like the people that didn't get the speaking roles. In Baltimore, the extras look like real people you see on the streets. All the people who work behind the scenes with me here are very important to me, although I suppose I could have shot my movies anywhere. *Serial Mom* (1994) could have taken place anywhere.

I liked the parody of Spielberg's idealized suburb in *Serial Mom*.

Well, it was certainly the neighbourhood I fled. It was very strange when we filmed there because I grew up in that neighbourhood and so did Divine, and we left there very quickly and very hated. When we went back to make that movie, we were greeted with open arms by the community, and that's because it was their parents who had hated us. The children all live in the houses now and their parents are dead, or without influence, let's put it that way.

Would you ever make a film that you hadn't written?

No, I hope not. I just wouldn't be very good at it. I don't know how to direct somebody else's work, I don't get what the job is. What do you do? Just say 'cut' and stand there? For me, the most fun is making up your own script. From then on it's downhill because you have to turn your spontaneity into reality and trying to

Divine in Pink Flamingos, *1972*

make anything real is never as good as when it was first in your head. The most fun is always thinking about it.

A personal question: are you the most famous person in Baltimore?

No, I'm not the most famous. Barry Levinson is probably the most famous person in Baltimore. People yell Barry Levinson at me all the time. He's the other director, who made *Rainman*. He also made his own series of Baltimore movies: *Diner, Avalon, Tin Men*.

But he hasn't had a city holiday named after him like you do: he doesn't have a 'Barry Levinson Day'.

He might have; he might have turned it down. *[laughs]*

So what happens on John Waters Day?

Nothing in particular. John Waters Day only happened the once. It's not like every year there's a parade down my street or something! The year in question, the powers that be proclaimed a John Waters Day and even a John Waters Week. In fact, when I come to think of it, when *Pecker* first opened in Los Angeles, the mayor of West Hollywood proclaimed it *Pecker* Day and gave me the key to the city. So I have a lot of these keys to these cities. I don't know

exactly what they open. The bars after they close? The prisons to let my friends out? All the places that I want to get into, these keys don't seem to work.

I just had this image of you being the Lord of Misrule for a day – proclaiming all your own laws.

Giving out free hairdos. Movie tickets and hair-do-stamps for the poor. Um, no. I don't have any power on that day and unfortunately it doesn't happen every year, although I do get fan mail sometimes wishing me a happy John Waters Day. That always shocks me because I don't remember when it is, although I do recall that when I was awarded this proclamation, it was exactly like in *The Wizard of Oz* when the scarecrow gets given a brain.

You have a longstanding interest in odd sexual tendencies: there was chicken sex in *Pink Flamingos*, foot-stomping in *Polyester* and tea-bagging and Dutch oven in *Pecker*. Do you ever worry that you're going to run out of strange deviant behaviours to put into your films?

No, I heard a new one: helicoptering! That's like when you have a hard-on and you hit someone in the face – WHAP! Whap, whap, whap, whap! That's the best one I've heard since, but people tell me this stuff all the time. I once had a glossary that went out to all the foreign countries who needed to produce subtitles for *Pecker* and you know what, it was over six pages long! England is the only other country in the world that has as good a slang as the USA. Nobody has such great slang as English. In some languages there are only two words for shit. There are over seven hundred terms for that here. I think we're so lucky that we have such a creatively filthy language. *[laughs]*

I think that Christina Ricci swears brilliantly in *Pecker*.

She does; when she said 'fuck wad' she said it very well. And you know what, that was me on the phone. I was the obscene phone caller saying 'Put your vagina up to the phone.' Someone actually said that to a friend of mine. It's really the most ludicrous pornographic phone-sex thing you can say. And then she heard 'Slap! Guess which part of the body that is? Slap!'

So that wouldn't be helicoptering, that would be telecoptering.

I hadn't thought of that but you're exactly right!

We've coined a phrase!

Oh, and a 'beef curtain', that was another one, but you probably have heard that one before. No one had heard that one in America. That's Australian – that's punk Australian – but when I used it in the film, everyone was laughing so hard that they don't hear the line. That's something I hadn't counted on. It's one of my favourites. I once heard a punk girl say, 'She kicked me in my beef curtains!' and I thought: 'Gosh, what's that?' I just think that phrase is especially obscene. Tough girls can say it. It's a good new dirty word for me.

You once wrote an essay entitled '101 things I hate' back in 1985. Is there anything you'd like to add to that list now?

There's lots of things from that list that I don't hate anymore – like I love Brussels sprouts now; but that was ten or fifteen years ago that I compiled the original list. Of course, there's millions of things I hate. I hate New Age everything. I hate astrology – I think that was in the original. Faeces is my star sign and I hate it more now than I did before. Old hippies are bad enough, new ones really get on my nerves. What else do I really hate? It's hard – hating takes up so much energy.

You've made use of celebrity criminals in some of your films – Patty Hearst for example.

Yeah, but I don't do that anymore, because after *Crybaby* I thought everybody expected that.

Do you think that today's criminals just aren't as glamorous or interesting as they used to be?

In your country they are. For instance, I was obsessed by the childhood killer Mary Bell even before her book came out.

Did you hear about the outcry when the book came out in the UK?

Oh yes, that's because you have such great tabloid press. I'm jealous of a country that has five tabloid newspapers. Usually each city only has one newspaper here, so there's no competition. I've been in London when the tabloids have printed complete lies, like Patty Hearst was going to give all her money away and Patty said 'Huh, yeah *right*.' They print stuff that I know was completely made up, but I think that makes your newspapers so exciting – when they have these wars. I'm all for that. You know, I think Princess Diana *should* have slowed down and waved. She

Opposite page
Christina Ricci on
the phone in Pecker,
1998
This page
Kathleen Turner
and family in
Serial Mom, *1994*

was a princess for Christ's sake: it was her job to wave. So I'm not against the tabloid press. They have the best kind of gossip and star stuff. I do think they should have page three boys though.

But what about the way Mary Bell was treated in the tabloid press?

I agree, she was treated very unfairly. You know, for years I had the other book, *The Case of Mary Bell*. I didn't even realize that it was the same woman who wrote both, so basically, she's been obsessed with this case for all this time. I understand that and I think that nobody could be more qualified to write about it. Sure there is no fair answer – if the victims were

your relatives it would be hard to stomach, but that's why the whole situation was so interesting, because there is no real answer. But I have to say, you have so many great criminals in England.

What about the guy who shot Gianni Versace? Didn't you rate him?

No, I didn't; he was like a dreary circuit queen. It was more the chase that was scary. When he was on the run, they had on the news a headline, 'Have all gay local celebrities been warned?' And they called here and I thought, 'Oh Christ, yeah, I'm in a fallout shelter with armed guards out front.' I couldn't believe they called here. That must have been a slow news day. And the whole thing was, the reason he might be coming this way was because there is only one road to go north, Route 95. That's like a pretty tenuous connection.

A lot of your earlier collaborators are no longer with us; has that changed the way you work in any way?

I used to write parts with certain people in mind and I don't do that anymore and haven't since *Polyester*. I look back at those early films and I'm very proud of them, but I don't miss running from the cops. I don't miss having to steal the props. I've done that and it's fun to do when you're young. To do it now – I'd get caught, that's the problem. I look back on that almost like my 'mental institution' days. It's like looking through a high school yearbook in an insane asylum. No one sent me their résumé, no one had head shots when I made *Pink Flamingos*. People said, 'I have a singing asshole, can I be in it?' Has it changed? I guess so. I've been doing this for thirty-five years – I hope something's changed otherwise I'd be making the same movie over and over again.

In the 1920s, Aleister Crowley took some time out
from his furious schedule of demonism and
debauchery to declare to the world: 'Every man
and woman is a star.' Crowley knew something
about infamy and celebrity, being, as John Bull
magazine had assessed him, 'the wickedest man
in the world'. At the dawn of the twenty-first
century, it is becoming clear that the gift of post-
Cold War late capitalism is an acceleration in the
fame industry. Now you don't have to be famous
for a mere fifteen minutes, you can construct
your own icon for eternity. And the money and
media people will help you. Children understand
this transformation intrinsically. No longer do
the young want to be astronauts or train drivers,
they want to be stars.

Of course, the abundance of new constella-
tions will eventually implode into a thousand
carefully distinguished and academically
endorsed categories. But for the moment, star
culture provides an avenue into identification,
empathy, irony and simulated idolatry. Thirty
years ago the world was a very different place:
the young imagined, perhaps foolishly, that
fundamental change was a possibility. War was
not a series of computer-game images on the
screen, but a reality of burning, wretched flesh.
The brutality of the Second World War was a relatively recent collective memory. Faced with the
threat of a rampant Soviet Union, capitalism was
cautious, less cunning and substantially more
tolerant. In this world, a number of young mili-
tants launched their own revolutions against the
state. Of these urban revolutionaries, the Baader-
Meinhof were amongst the most notorious.

Although the original Baader-Meinhof group
was only active between 1970 and 1972 and its
leadership has been dead for twenty-two years,
Andreas Baader, in particular, retains much of

his infamous legendary status. In West Germany,
Baader, Meinhof, Ensslin and their comrades
symbolized a fundamental series of transgres-
sions. They were young, they were hyped and of
course, it all rapidly spun out of control. Indeed,
described in that form, they sound like pop
musicians or footballers. Nevertheless, however
misguided their actions, they at least understood
the importance of negation. Revolution, resistance and transformation are predicated on a
refusal to accept what passes as social consensus.
Of course, Baader-Meinhof's demise also meant
that it avoided the passive, sagging, self-satisfied
consumption that eventually overtook the rest
of their generation. If Baader and Meinhof had
survived prison, they would be fifty-seven and
sixty-six respectively.

Violence remains one of the few areas of
modern life that has not been colonized by
capital. Sex is now used as a marketing tool
throughout the world. The personal is political
and yet somehow the political has lost its personality. Meanwhile, a botched vision of perpetual
youth is heralded as the purest ideology of our
age. But where aggression on the football park
or the pop arena is rewarded and recognized as
commitment and passion, political militancy
continues to be condemned as hysterical, infantile or self-defeating. The teenage Communism
of the Baader-Meinhof group might appear
outdated, but the agency, the defiance and the
determination echo the needs of the present. Our
childhoods have perhaps fallen under the cosh of
free-market economics, but our buried potential
for violent transgression remains as uncommo-
dified now as it has ever been.

Astrid Proll was an early member of the
Baader-Meinhof group; she stole fast cars, she
photographed her compatriots and she was

amongst the first to be arrested and subjected to isolation treatment. She offers one of the few remaining avenues into a moment in time when youth culture, politics and bombs came together in a confusing mass of conflicting signifiers. Her memories of the 1970s might appear dislocated and, to a certain extent, distant, but if genuine stardom depends on individualistic difference and originality of authentic experience, then her voice demands to be heard. In an age where history has been relegated to one channel amongst hundreds, it is essential to remember that if we forget the past we are doomed to repeat it.

Dazed & Confused | **How were the 'survivors' of the Baader-Meinhof group treated in Germany over time?**

Astrid Proll | It took years to establish the fact that there would be survivors. For a long time there were only terrorists, which concerned German society. The choices were: death, incarceration and betrayal. The concept of survivors was established as terrorist-histories became more complex over the years. It was mediated through the press, of course. Individual stories became more interesting, people made themselves available. When I became a picture editor I learned about the pressure and the needs of journalists. There hasn't been an analytical book published in Germany on the Baader-Meinhof. People were arrested quite young and when they came out of prison they were still able to integrate and get jobs. The question was what do you do after being a terrorist? Would we live only through our stories from the past, or would we be able to adjust to a new life? That also depended on how the outside viewed you – would you be allowed to be something else rather than a projection of their fantasies?

Gudrun Ensslin and Andreas Baader in Paris, November 1969

The bottom line is that the Baader-Meinhof group was a constructed fantasy not just for the German media, but for the global media. As much of the iconography of the Baader-Meinhof group came from external production as from the group itself.

Certain symbols were created by Baader-Meinhof, but were then appropriated and used by others. Socialism within the student movement was what people opted for as an 'anti-strategy' to address capitalism. Our generation picked on sources from the 1930s. We had a very purist take on Communist ideology. The Baader-Meinhof group was only one faction of the German student movement. To many,

perceived in retrospect, it was the faction that led to the most terrible consequences, but at the time, it was the most radical option.

And the most exciting one?

I don't think we entered into it for excitement. People tended to be very serious about the cause. We were the most determined. We were into the creation of a new kind of being, of living, of existing. For us, it was more philosophical, asking questions like: 'What is a revolution?', 'Are we in a revolutionary situation now?', 'Are we revolutionaries?' This had nothing to do with image. The Baader-Meinhof was creative in its thinking because we had to confront new ways of living: 'How do you live undercover?', 'How do you pretend to be a normal member of society when actually you are an urban guerrilla?' In that sense, it was very creative, but at the same time it was also very repressive. It forced us into confined structures and behavioural patterns. People had to give up their identities, which had developed over the last twenty-five years. They threw their passports in the toilet or burnt them. We simply disappeared and gave up all connections with our families. We stopped seeing our friends. At a time when there was a fashion for leather jackets and blue jeans, we wore office clothes: ties – maybe not that far – or a dress. The Baader-Meinhof group started as an experiment. Some of us had a premonition that it could have a deadly outcome.

Nowadays, capital has invaded right down into our very souls. The point about the Baader-Meinhof group, flawed though it might have been, was that at least it had the energy to say 'No', to try and do something, anything, against what it saw as being wrong. In some respects, Western societies view that as the greatest crime that you can commit – to challenge the very basis of the society in which you are living.

The state portrayed us as being more dangerous than we were. Over time, it worked like a spiral, a coil: the consequences became more and more serious. But I think that it is true to say that the Baader-Meinhof's greatest asset was that it was against and that it was not afraid to act.

Was it sucked into that coil? I appreciate that it might have started climbing up the coil, but as the state and the media picked it up, was it spun further and further?

Very quickly the confrontation became deadly, but it was totally unequal. To quote Heinrich Böll, the German writer, here was a war of sixty million against sixty. In the early 1970s the media was sympathetic to the Baader-Meinhof's cause. At that time, we lived in a period of transition that dominated people's ideas. Everybody wanted to be a part of this sense of change. What fascinated the media was that the Baader-Meinhof were either talented students, or individuals who already had a career. That's what was so outstanding about Ulrike Meinhof and Horst Mahler: Ulrike was a prominent TV journalist and Mahler had been a successful lawyer.

The arrest of Baader, still wearing his sunglasses as he is dragged out of the building, talks directly to modern culture. He is aware all the time that it is an act: 'I'm playing a game – I've got to look right, I've got to play it right.' He is invoking lots of themes, for example Latin American machismo.

I think that had an impact on all of us, although not to the extent that you would accentuate nowadays. There was the great influence of Latin America: Cuba, Ché Guevara and the Tupamaros. We were particularly fascinated by the Black Panthers and their visuals. I remember we looked at pictures of them in the Californian magazine *Ramparts*. They stood in military formation with their arms and berets. This sort of militancy we found inspirational. By that time the Eldridge Cleaver book *Soul on Ice* had been published, which described how Huey Newton drove his car, and that influenced Baader.

The Baader-Meinhof group were never like orthodox terrorists...

When the Baader-Meinhof took off as a group there were never more than twenty people at one time. We wanted to be an armed faction of the existing German revolutionary movement, but once settled underground, it became harder to participate in necessary discussions with the others. We did not trust the security arrangements of those living legally, as we had undergone a unique, unshared experience in having to operate underground. Mentally, this moved us into the avant-garde mind-set. In 1972, before the arrests of Baader and others, there had been a bombing campaign across Germany focused on certain Vietnam-related targets. Baader-Meinhof took up their own programme.

Tell me about the PLO connection.

In the early 1970s, some factions within the PLO became extremely militant. The Baader-Meinhof group were invited to go to Jordan for training. We took up this offer when most of us were in hiding and stuck in flats so that we could debrief and think about our next move. This opportunity was also offered to other political activists who operated legally. At the time it was quite popular to visit the Palestinian revolutionaries and to shoot a few Kalashnikovs – a form of revolutionary tourism.

To what degree do you think the Baader-Meinhof group were terrorized in prison by the German state, and were they murdered or did they kill themselves?

I have been asked this question many times in the last twenty years. I can only say, I don't know because I wasn't there.

But you can speculate.

I don't like to speculate. I knew the people concerned too well. I do believe now that Ulrike Meinhof killed herself, she simply had no strength left. In prison, the Baader-Meinhof were very hard on each other. They became obsessed with their strategies and would not listen to anyone from the outside. Under strict confinement in prison, they mutated into an isolated corps. Inside the core group there was a series of clashes. I knew Ulrike in prison; I was kept with her in the same prison and subjected to the same circumstances as she was.

When she describes the cell she was locked in and the whole torture of having no stimulus at all, you experienced the same thing?

Yes, I had been kept in the same cell before she was arrested. All Baader-Meinhof prisoners were put in isolation after their capture – we were not allowed to go to work and we were not allowed to mix with others. After my arrest, they put me in a cellhouse where there was nobody – it was empty and had never been used – and that was hell. There was nothing to see and you couldn't hear any sound.

What did you do to handle that?

Nothing, I had no strategies. It fucked up my nervous system to the extent that it took years for me to recover.

Have you recovered now?

Yes. At certain moments things come back. I was only twenty-two when I was put in isolation, and I couldn't understand what had happened to me. In fact I was very eager to accept my

Andreas Baader
February 1972
Klaus Mehner

situation and to deal with it. One thing that
members of the Baader-Meinhof group had was
a very strong sense of self confidence, which
stemmed from a theoretical preparation for a
prison situation. Most of us didn't break down
under interrogation even when in isolation. In
the 'dead wing', where I was kept, I was totally
alone. It was as if I had been buried alive. Before
being captured, I had lived a very active life on
the run, so isolation was a shock to my system.
When Meinhof was arrested a year later, she
was immediately locked in the dead wing and I
was moved to a male wing, where at least I
could hear people talking outside my door,
which was a relief.

**Did the prison authorities punish Ulrike
Meinhof for being a professional person
who had engaged in terrorist activity?**
Yes, she became Germany's most prominent
and therefore most restricted prisoner. Even
the longest-serving prison warders had never
seen a prisoner treated in such a repressive
way. They didn't beat her, but observed her
twenty-four hours a day. They tried to drive
her mad.

**Do you think that young people are less
political than they were in the 1970s?**
I think the 1970s was a time of change, young
people wanted to be part of it. A lot of people
got involved, even to the extent of Baader-
Meinhof, because of friendship networks. Things
are very different now. In Germany the Greens
have entered into mainstream politics. It could
create space for a new opposition. In England
many interesting things happen on a grass-
roots level, but with no perspective towards real
power. England is more American-orientated
than the continent. Capitalism seems to embrace
every aspect of life here.

Good
+
Evil

December 1999
Introduction and interview | Rachel Newsome

On the top floor of a private apartment block off the main trunk road to Florence in a room with three different views of Rome's famous hills, Ilona Staller ('Cicciolina for you') reclines on a leather sofa, lips forming another scarlet pout for the cable TV crew. This afternoon, the ex-porn star/Radical Party MP/wife of artist Jeff Koons and the current mother of Koon's son/director of the recently established We'll Be Famous artist management agency, is wearing a crushed velvet baby blue mini-dress. It has a barely discernible but there all the same stain of an indiscriminate nature to the left of her chest and is teamed with her hosiery of choice, white hold-up stockings.

Ensconced in an avalanche of teddy bears, Ilona heaves out her chest and sucks in her cheeks. Each new take for the TV an opportunity to fan out her hair, curl up foetal, drape her legs just a little too far apart. Reducing her forty-seven years under camera lens and panstick to more like thirty, each move is stage-managed for maximum come-to-bed effect. But with a bath-room full of eyebrow dye and hair bleach and a jaw line which is taut in the way only knife on skin can effect, it is never quite clear whether all this is motivated by desire or desperation.

The TV crew currently focusing on Ilona's best and most charitable angles are here to report on We'll Be Famous, which Ilona operates out of her apartment with her tarot card reader – a self-styled reincarnation of an Egyptian soothsayer, Princess Saba, and Roberta – a hermaphrodite, for whom it seems keeping his/her blue sequinned dress attached to his/her body is a perpetual struggle.

With Ilona retiring from porn in 1990 following her marriage to Koons, leaving politics following a disagreement on drugs policy (Ilona is, she emphatically repeats, anti) and divorcing Koons in 92 following an acrimonious marriage, it is TV appearances and interviews such as this which these days, Ilona says, keep her from impecunious obscurity. It is during these appearances that she tells of how as a country girl from Hungary she would make a living from modelling. Of how she moved to Italy, where her manager introduced her to the world of porn. Of how she reinvented herself as La Cicciolina (meaning little dumpling) and developed her dreams of reconstructing 'the nude symbol from one of sin to one of peace' while promoting free love for all. Of how she canvassed votes for Italy's Radical Party parading topless through the streets of Rome. And of how she offered to sleep with Saddam Hussein during the Gulf War in the name of world peace. Then of course there was all the terrible trouble between her and Jeff and all the battles over who should have custody of the now seven-year-old Ludwig. This is what, that afternoon, she had to say:

Dazed & Confused | You've retired from porn, but you still perform erotic shows.
Cicciolina | I do erotic nude shows accompanied with songs where I speak about Paradise, others about life, peace, drugs and liberty.

It's a pity I don't do my shows in England since I'm transgressive in character and work similar to *The Rocky Horror Picture Show*. I do talk shows everywhere, two days ago I was on French television speaking about my life. It's incredible because everyone can relate to my work and recognize me in the street.

How does it feel to be so well known?
I feel that I'm an icon. Some people hate me, some love me, that's natural. But I am the first person to change the concept of sexual purity into the freedom of sexuality. This has made a

deep impact for men and women, it's very important because I feel that I started a road for young women to do similar shows to me. After fifteen years these girls have a reference point to me. Next March I'm going to Hungary, where I was born, for television interviews and photographic shoots and disco shows. They are looking forward to my arrival as I symbolize sexual freedom to young girls as Madonna does in her music. I think that it's very important that they practise sex, as it strengthens our instincts and recharges our energy. It's like a battery that you charge with sexuality.

Do you still enjoy sex after all these years?
I love sex. There is a song that I sing against drug abuse which says that I love sex, not drugs! I also have a song that's against war but again pro sex and love. Just do a lot of sex not war!

Does it get better as you get older?
Life naturally evolves, this is normal. It's natural to get older, I accept this and I have had so many experiences. Before, I was a very naive woman, even now I'm naive. After my wedding I am much stronger. Even though my husband who works in New York has just sold a piece worth one billion lire, he still can't cough up the money to pay for Ludwig his son. His art secretary asked me why I don't accept Jeff the way he is, despite his difficult nature. I have maintained my sweet character as always but have just strengthened from my experiences.

Did you have any idea that things might end so badly when you and Koons first met?
No, because we loved each other. From 1988 onwards I was staying in Germany as I couldn't get into the States, I was considered like an Arab. I was black-listed and I didn't know why. Jeff would come and see me there where I lived in an apartment with thirteen bedrooms, we had a wonderful time together frequenting the theatre, movies, eating Thai food, never arguing and having loads of sex. Then after a few days he would return to New York and I would return to Rome. But on the first day of our marriage we argued!

Why do you think the change was so sudden?
My friend and tarot reader Princess Saba foretold everything including the breakdown of the marriage. Jeff wanted to dominate and be in control, he didn't understand that I was not an object to be pushed around. I wasn't going to cut my hair or throw myself from the balcony just to suit his whims. I am very sensitive and I loved him very much but he wanted to undermine my confidence because he was so insecure.

How did that make you feel?
This didn't really upset me because I didn't want to jeopardize the safety of my unborn son. I fell pregnant with Ludwig four months after having a miscarriage. After the miscarriage I went to pray to St Anthony to fall pregnant again.

Do you believe in God?
I'm a believing Catholic even if I don't go to church all that often. I also love the beliefs of the Dalai Lama and I probably believe in the Buddhist religion more. I hear that Richard Gere is Buddhist and others from America.

Did you ever question whether Koons ever really loved you?
I don't know if he truly loved me, or if he used me. He wanted to separate Ilona Staller from Cicciolina. We had sex in various forms. I remember in the first month we had sex about eight times a day. I suggested going to the movies as I was in quite a lot of pain by that stage as we were going at it for three-quarters of an hour at a time.

This page and overleaf
Cicciolina, Princess Saba
and Roberta, 1999
Katinka Herbert

What do you think the difference is between your porn performances and Koons featuring your porn movies in his artwork? Didn't he get you to sign a pre-nuptial agreement stating that you would receive no money from his paintings and no maintenance entitlement if you had a child together?
One day I asked Jeff what he thought of the difference between a porno star and his making me a porno star with his artwork. I told him to tell me the difference between the way he licked me and sucked me and how we used all the different forms, and to tell me what the difference is between my art work and his art work. The only difference is that he sells his art work with me in it, Cicciolina porno star in it, for millions of dollars. I have mixed feelings about this as he was very hard, and yet at times I feel he did love me. After our divorce I didn't do as the American women do and sue him for three million dollars. He didn't even give me money. He would tell me how much he loves Ludwig but would never even send him gifts of clothes like a pair of blue jeans or a T-shirt. He would complain about all the clothes I would buy Ludwig when living in New York, but I bought what was necessary for him. Because of

the way I have been brought up I believe that Ludwig must grow up loving his father and it's not necessary to know all the bad points about his father. Sometimes we would argue about money matters on the phone and Ludwig would hear this. The other day Ludwig asked me why Papa won't give Mama money for schooling. So Ludwig said in his own words that Papa is mad and that he doesn't love Ludwig and that Ludwig doesn't love him back. I was left upset at this. The other day I was finishing off an article to fax off to a newspaper, and Ludwig asked me why we don't ask Papa to send us money. I have to do talk shows and interviews and write articles on society and sexuality for a magazine in Palma. One night I was writing at eleven-thirty p.m. and Ludwig was watching a cartoon on television and asked me why I was still working at that hour.

It must have been very distressing for Ludwig to see such animosity between his parents.
For the boy and the mother. In 1993, when Jeff came to Rome to see Ludwig and ended up abducting him, I saw that my husband was very nervous. Ludwig was in pyjamas and I had to dress him whilst I was crying. Mothers are telepathic about their children and I could sense that something was wrong so I called the police and asked them to telex all the border controls to stop Jeff and Ludwig from leaving the country but it was too late. I was told that an American judge forbade me to see Ludwig. I couldn't believe that such an order could be made so I went to New York to appeal.

How did you feel when you were told that Koons used footage of you having sex in court to show that you were a bad mother?
They played dirty because those films belonged

to the past and they wanted to reveal what I did as opposed to what I do. Sometimes when Ludwig is sleeping I stop and think about all that has happened and feel like I'm going to have a nervous breakdown. I feel things very deeply like cuts of pain. At that time I wanted to be calm and have a normal family life, but he didn't want to give me that. One day I remember I was in New York, and I walked into a room with Koons blaspheming and telling Ludwig that I was a prostitute, a shit, a bitch, everything! I stopped him and told him never to shout like that in front of my son again. Jeff became rich by exploiting my reputation, he became popular because I was popular. He sold work of us having sex and I certainly didn't receive a penny from any of it.

I spent five months in New York trying to get custody of my son. During that time I was made to stay in Koons' servants' quarters measuring two metres by one and made to eat left-overs. So after this I decided to take Ludwig back to Italy and if Koons interpreted it as kidnap, the reality was that I was just taking him home.

What would you say to Ludwig if he found out about your past?
He has found out. Two weeks ago he asked why his friend showed him a picture of me putting his father's dick in my mouth. I said, 'My love, it's because we were making love.' What can I tell a seven-year-old about these things? He asked me if I liked sucking his dick. I explained that when two people love each other they do sex in various forms, and finished with that.

What would you say if Ludwig told you he wanted a career in porn, too?
He said he wants to become Ricky Martin, a rock star and a lion hunter. It's a hard world and I would dissuade him from being a porno star. If he insisted I would let him see for himself, at a certain age he is allowed to do as he wishes. I would prefer him to become president of the republic for America, Italy or Hungary!

A lot of the dialogue between yourself and Koons has happened in public; your personal problems are in the public domain. And on top of that, you're now writing your biography. Do you not feel sometimes that some of your dignity has been lost during this?
It's hard to keep privacy. I used the media to help me fight the battle of my son's custody, asking the public what they thought on the matter, basically to put pressure on the Italian judges otherwise I would have lost Ludwig. I decided to write the book because so many things happened to me that a woman with a normal life would not experience these things and I want to show these women that they can happen. It's a true life story.

Can you remember a point in your life when you became aware that your body could be perceived as an object of male desire?
It's something that developed step by step. In 1975 I started Radio Luna talking about liberal

sexual issues. After that I started doing discotheque shows in the nude. I wanted to change the nude symbol from one of sin to one of peace. I have always remained a child inside, and Jeff used this in court saying that I was like a child and was therefore inappropriate to be a good mother. I may be infantile, but I am very pure in my person.

How did all that attention from men make you feel?

Beautiful, it's not a sin to be desired. From desire life is borne. My agency name is We'll Be Famous – I like to employ people who do eroticism, acting, strippers, anything.

So how do you make people famous?

People who come to me want to be famous. Plus I have a lot of contacts in Argentina, the Americas, Spain, everywhere. It's easy to become famous if you have the right contacts. We have this agency to try and alleviate the negative social stigma attached to our ways of life. Hypocrites are just as grave as Yeltsin's politics which result in people not having any food to eat. In Italy and everywhere in the world we all need the Dalai Lama, because he only gives and never takes. We need to learn by this.

Can anyone be famous if they want to be?

No, they have to have talent. This is Princess Saba's opinion.

Princess Saba | If a person has talent and you have the right agent then maybe you'll have success.

How many people belong to the agency?

Twenty-five and growing, we have many phone calls from other agencies all the time.

So why did you decide to have this agency?

Roberta | To cultivate progress so someone like myself who is a hermaphrodite can move forward. Also being associated with Cicciolina's name helps me move up the ladder.

Is social justice one of the reasons why you joined the Radical Party?

Yes, because it represents my beliefs of anti-woman abuse, anti-abortion, anti-famine.

When you were campaigning, did you ever worry that people might not take you seriously?

No, some probably voted to compete against other party members and some because they believed in me.

I hear you are thinking of opening a chain of discos and restaurants?

I'd like to do something like Planet Hollywood incorporating discos and restaurants where women waitress topless with their bums out.

What would you say to people who think it's distasteful?

Everyone has a choice to do as they please. I'm not a bigot, I don't tell people what to do. We live in a difficult society with all the stigmas attached. There are poor people who live in South Africa and Kosovo and Lebanon, and we need to understand that politicians are only there for fame and power and I don't accept these terrible people. We only want happiness..

'I always wanted to meet you. I have always
wanted to thank you.'

An outstretched hand is thrust towards the
off-guard Malcolm McLaren. We have just
finished dining at the Soho House when a twenty-
something, besuited city boy, with chattering
teeth and a hyperactive demeanour, approaches
the table. He insists on shaking McLaren's hand
and thanking him. But who is he? A second-
generation punk turned corporate lackey? A
rampant admirer of Paris, Paris? What part of
McLaren's past, what moment of truth from
McLaren's archives has so touched this thankful
fan? After a few minutes it transpires that his
father had been the proud owner of a safety pin
factory in Wales and as a result of the punk
explosion in the 1970s, the business was sold for
a small fortune, enough for him to put his son
into private school, through college and into a
slick city job. He hands McLaren his business card
as he leaves and there is a moment of silence.
'I thought I'd heard it all,' McLaren says and
then laughs to himself at the surreal nature of a
world in which someone could profit so directly
from anarchy and turn revolution into con-
formism. It is an ironic twist of fate, not lost
on McLaren, that someone, somewhere may be
having the last laugh on him.

For McLaren is usually the one who is
typecast as profiteering from somebody else's
creativity, and not the other way round. It's
usually McLaren that is seen to be having the
last laugh at the expense of the industry, the
machine and the spectacle. Indeed, in a world of
entertainment über alles, to label McLaren a
conman, a charlatan or Svengali is far too
simple. 'Only artists or criminals defy the rules,'
McLaren claims, quoting from Diderot, and by
this he means that the artist like the criminal is

an outsider, he has to invent his own anti-world.
That's the only role McLaren has ever played.

Now just past the half-century mark in his
life, McLaren is launching his ultimate self-
portrait in time. The Casino of Authenticity and
Karaoke is an interactive multimedia video
installation at the Bonnefanted Museum in
Maastricht, Holland, which features four cus-
tomized, one-armed bandits that incorporate the
images and sounds connected to the key events
and figures that have featured in his life.
Collectively, they signify the various gambles and
payoffs that have marked McLaren's colourful
and chaotic career, a testament to success
through diversity which seduces the player into
a direct engagement with McLaren's unique
creative process. You hit a flashing button, the
one-armed bandit spins and the icons align; a
row of anarchy signs triggers a Sex Pistols clip
on a giant video screen which is replaced by a
sound-bite, a piece of text or music, as one of the
other three gaming machines cuts in with a win.
The axes of time and space disintegrate as the
fragments, memories and romance of the past
are reconfigured in random order. For this is
none other than the Malcolm McLaren road
show, a larger than life, digitally enhanced,
karaoke re-enaction of a man and his past.

When questioned on his past exploits,
McLaren is nothing if he is not precise. He's
relived, recounted and refined his anecdotes at
multifarious dinner tables, nightclub booths and
lecture halls. He's played the Situationist who
had a twelve-year relationship with Vivienne
Westwood; the savvy shopkeeper of Nostalgia of
Mud who dug a six-foot trench by the entrance
door so customers had to leap to get in; the rock-
'n'-roll swindler who put the New York Dolls in
Communist red leather and the manager who
famously mismanaged The Sex Pistols, who wrote
the film, the play, the record and even the rule-
book to accompany it.

Probe further and you will be introduced to
McLaren the wannabe film producer who once
hired soft porn director Russ Meyer to make the
film that never was, called Who Killed Bambi?;
the schmooze operator who escaped to France in
the middle of a court case just before his bank
assets were frozen; the pop impresario whose
metaphorical take on rock-'n'-roll propelled his
protégés Adam And The Ants and Bow Wow

Wow into the British charts; the producer turned artist who mixed world beats with dance music in Duck Rock and transposed the lifestyle stance of Buffalo Girls into our popular consciousness; the scene stealer who brought hip-hop to Britain; the darling who waltzed among the Hollywood set or player who dated supermodel and actress Lauren Hutton, 'flirting on contract' as a scriptwriter with Spielberg's Amblin Productions.

Malcolm McLaren has been all this and more, but for the purposes of this interview, conducted at McLaren's relaxed HQ in Fitzrovia, he is no longer to be considered simply as 'an operator' but rather as an acute cultural attitude. In the last decade his activity has become less explosive and more self-reflective, producing Paris, Paris, *an Eric-Satie-inspired album featuring Catherine Deneuve and Françoise Hardie, launching a group of all-singing, all-Kung-Fu-fighting Asian babes called Jungk on an unconvinced and uninterested British music industry while still working on his autobiography and art installation* The Casino of Authenticity and Karaoke. *He may play the rent-a-gob armchair renegade for TV arts programmes but his unique take on contemporary culture, that of the 'flamboyant failure, as opposed to a benign success', has never been more worth re-evaluating and exploring. Enter Malcolm McLaren, archbishop of pop whose vision of contemporary culture has defined a generation.*

Dazed & Confused | **Let's talk about your theory of karaoke versus authenticity?**
Malcolm McLaren | Karaoke is a product that can be sold and the authentic is something that isn't as easily assimilated by capital, so therefore what is authentic isn't necessarily what the culture wants on location, because it's complicated, it's messy, it's difficult.

You mean the authentic is rendered useless in a consumer-driven society?
You could say that the authentic in some ways is almost art for art's sake, you are not necessarily doing it as a pursuit to create a product, to create success.

So the authentic is about failure?
Exactly. In the 1960s, careers were never authentic, rather it was the noble pursuit of failure that was authentic. Authenticity is to be found in the ruins, in reclaiming the past. That was how you preserved the authentic, but society just isn't programmed to develop flamboyant failures like Malcolm McLaren, it's programmed to produce benign successes like Alan McGee. It fits much better. When you're a member of the golf club you get Tony Blair to co-opt you, you've finally become friends with everybody and you have a seat at every single dinner table throughout the planet. By contrast, authenticity is dirty, it's horrible, it's disgusting, it has built into it this uncomfortable idea of chaos where anything can happen, but we don't want *anything* to be possible, we want *these things* to be possible. This division has never been more clear than today.

What lessons can we learn from this?
That the machines that have made us suddenly believe in all this karaoke are going to become more and more human and we humans are about to become more like machines. It's a new kind of biology which we are all going to have to deal with. If you think we've had anarchic explosions in the past, just get ready for the huge big bang that will happen in a few years from now as people get more and more dissatisfied with the fact that they can't get any satisfaction. Karaoke culture is a blind and dead alley. There's no romance in that lifestyle. That's why so many contemporary artists try and struggle to make themselves as real as possible within a karaoke world by creating something that you can't pin down and sell on the stock market but it always ends up being sellable. People were pissed off with all this concept crap – we're bored with Tracy Emin's bed. We don't want to be her psychiatrist.

Do you think that contemporary pop culture has lost its political edge?
It's gonna flair up – there's no two ways about it. There's all of that social unrest and that's

interesting. You've got Brit Art on one level which is being deemed now by new generations as a kind of art that is packaged and ultimately run by TV and advertising executives. It is an art that is ultimately establishment, it's controlled and modified. Then you go to the alternative called 'political art' which seems to be lost in time. Today it now looks fresher and far more exciting, far more interesting. Art that has a presence to lead someone into action.

How would you place David Bowie within your theory?

He has made himself into a brand where everything is for sale and therefore can be reproduced.

And Damien Hirst?

You too can go and put a shark in formaldehyde if you wanted. You too can copy the dot paintings. Paperchase have done it so why not you? All it means is that Hirst has been accepted into the mainstream and therefore become a part of it. If you can be imitated in this world today you are worth a lot more than if you can't be. That was never the case twenty-five years ago. That's the real difference.

Why does no one opt for romance anymore?

Because romanticism is not for sale. It deals with the messy process of creativity. It doesn't fit in. It doesn't have within it the ability to be sold. It has only the ability to create something called romance. We used to adore it as a noble pursuit because we used to put the notion of romanticism as a very high cultural adventure, as something we should look to, as something we should try to follow. Today it bears no sense of purpose for what governs the way we want to – or think we want to – live.

Is that maybe because we are living in an age that is less pretentious? There's nothing wrong with having money. There's nothing wrong with being successful, with playing the game.

That's quite right. There's nothing wrong with it. However, for those who have lived in a different world with a different set of references it's very difficult for them to understand.

You mean yourself?

Yes, me or a taxi driver over the age of forty who wanders around London and thinks to himself [*McLaren takes on a mock cockney accent*] 'Why are all these people going to all restaurants run by Terence Conran. I walk in there, it costs you an arm and a leg, there's no atmosphere. It's all a load of bollocks.'

The reason for that is that the food and the atmosphere is always already programmed, Conran's put it all together and sold it to you as a package. We don't believe in it. It doesn't feel real. It's corporate. It's part of the cappuccino culture and boom economy that Prime Minister Tony Blair is talking about. What does it mean if you walk around Soho today? Cab drivers don't understand it. And yet people are travelling to it in hordes. They're all buying into it.

So who's being duped? Are these changes being dictated to us by a market based on consumer choice or by a market led by propaganda?

I think it is because people do not want the struggle. To be romantic, to find a place that has a particular, unique ambience is a struggle. To actually create it is a struggle. To actually deal with it is a struggle. People don't want to struggle. They have been told they can have everything they want by just sitting in bed. If you are living in a culture like that then the last thing you are going to want is something you are going to have to walk ten miles through muddy fields to find. We live in what is easy. In answer to your reference to propaganda: we have all already been told we are all a nation of middle class. No struggle. If we are all a nation of middle class then we are all celebrities. The person who first tried to invent that concept was Adolf Hitler.

The Nazi Party were ultimately responsible for the invention of media. They were the first to actually brand their country and tell everybody that they were fabulous. In some respects, America took that up after the war and so did the Russians. I reckon in ten years' time we will look back at the twentieth century and realize we are all godchildren of the Nazis. We live basically within a system that they helped set up. Just look at America. Nowhere in the world has a country been so believing in its total superiority after the war as the US.

The symbol of choice and freedom of expression. The ultimate democracy but all dancing to the same tune?

Exactly. It was never a coincidence that Andy Warhol's artistic vision was co-opted within seconds. He was deemed acceptable because he created the art of the reproducible. He believed that people were, without a shadow of a doubt, able to be channelled and reproduced. He was right. We will all be stars for fifteen minutes.

Although in Warhol's universe you had to be beautiful and buy into the image in order to be famous. Punk took that notion and subverted it. Punk was never about having to be beautiful to be famous. It was about the democracy of being ugly...

It was making ugliness beautiful. The Sex Pistols' whole premise was: I'm going to be an artful dodger. I'm not going to accept that. I'm going to search for the authentic. I'm going to fucking write songs that I believe in. I'm going to write lyrics that haven't been used before. I'm not following the old-fashioned template. I'm going to declare the ultimate culture: DIY.

An inclusive subculture rather than an exclusive corporate one.

Absolutely, and for a while the industry was shocked because punk undermined everything that they had built up. In the end that moment of madness was just a blimp on the map. What they didn't realize were the repercussions within a new generation.

You could say that The Sex Pistols, by struggling with their authenticity within the industry were accepting the fact that they were caught in world of karaoke. They couldn't fight it, it was impossible.

The past is always rewritten through the eyes of the present. The history of punk has been rewritten. Your past has been rewritten. Our own histories have been rewritten, almost as something that is a *fait accompli*, without any mention of the real struggle and chaos that make these things happen.

Exactly. Exactly that. It is impossible to realize that it is the accident that we all cherish. Manifestos are often written after the event, never before. You articulate it after it happens.

Whilst it is happening it is a purely instinctive, chaotic, romantic thing. You just allow it to happen.

When you saw New York hip-hop and saw all those kids in the Bronx wearing *Never Mind the Bollocks* T-shirts, did you have any idea how successful hip-hop would become?

I thought it was going to be, without a shadow of a doubt, the biggest thing that was going to happen in the 80s. I saw it and I genuinely thought that what was fantastic about hip-hop music was that they didn't need music. They decided they could make music out of other people's music. They decided they could just grab anything. They could put their rubber stamp on anything in pop culture by reclaiming the past and turning it into something they could claim as their own. It was a way of grabbing culture by the balls and spitting it out. They could control an industry and bring it back to the people. It was a continuation of the DIY phenomenon and that again is why it was hated by an industry who decides who its stars are and how it works.

People who rewrite history like to write the parallels alongside drugs and say the accident happened with explosions of drugs cultures. Are the drugs another element of the accident or are they another symptom, another product?

That's a difficult question. I think if you go back to the guy who invented the T-shirt as something cool to wear, the guy who decided to go on the road, the guy who wrote about the ultimate first outlaw culture of the post-war – Jack Kerouac. The guy who made Levi's jeans cool, the guy who took the black leather jacket and white T-shirt and walked around the fucking world... You think, 'Jesus Christ, that image is still with us.' How come that image has never ever left us as a signal, as an icon of what is supposed to be the outlaw? What is that about? It's also about drugs. It's about the fact that we are going to be living in a world which we would prefer to drop out of. Drugs were always a way of trying to accept the fact that the world was shit. They were a form of escape.

You ever went there?

Well, I dabbled. I'm afraid I never became an addict. I certainly took heroin, I certainly took

cocaine, I certainly took LSD in the 6os, I certainly took hashish – I did it all but I never became an addict. Why? Maybe because I couldn't afford it. Maybe because I felt I didn't really need it. I felt quite happy in my own personal anger at the world and that was sufficient to prompt me to act. I didn't need drugs to force me to act. I didn't need to escape.

Do you love England?

I don't know if I love England. It's not that I've never felt at home here – because I do – but I've never really loved it because it's always been a constant battle. The problem with England is that the English have great difficulty in appreciating someone whose constant way of life or thinking is contrary. They don't see that as a pursuit. England is about good old blokes. England's about people who confess. England loves old queens confessing. England doesn't like it if you remain an outlaw. They think that at a certain time you have to accept the fact that you must no longer rebel. The difference between England and France is that they like their outlaws to *remain* outlaws.

Would you say that France is more your spiritual home whilst England is your psychological battlefield?

That's a nice way of putting it. It's a very romantic way to put it. Basically the French are a lot of tossers in many respects but they have that one thing: they don't like their outlaws becoming members of the establishment. You're never too sure ultimately whether England really believes in the counterculture. It's like, 'Get your gold chain after twenty-five years' work as a signalman.' Whichever way you look at it you have to join the club: you have to lecture at the RCA, join the board of the BBC.

But that's where I find your position

interesting. You've been invited to advise corporations and give lectures to heads of government and industry. You're the ultimate marketing guru who argues that the only way to get people to want more is to sell less. I'm not detracting from you as a countercultural figure, as someone who likes to throw a grenade into the middle of the party, but at the same time I do find it funny that you are invited to advise these people.**

But I don't advise them. Not really. I walk away and people think, 'That's very nice. That's very interesting. But answer me one question, "How do you make money out of all this anarchy?"' That's always the question from director after director. And when you say that that's not really the point, you've lost them completely. They feel like you've genuinely wasted their time. Unless you can appear as a millionaire having made money out of all this anarchy, they think you're a dead loss. When I came back to England in 1990, everybody thought I was about to join the club. I'd been away and done my time. I was now coming back home to join the boys. 'Come on, Malc, come and join us...' I was invited to polo trials. I couldn't believe it.

You once told me about *The New Yorker* tour when Tina Brown hosted a forum on behalf of Disney.

Yeah, it was called something like 'What's Next?' It was extraordinary. It was held in Epcot, you know at one of their big think-tanks. We were all flown over to the US and housed in these little rooms in Disneyland where you wrapped yourself up in Mickey Mouse towels and you went to sleep in Mickey Mouse sheets.

What was the idea? To bring together all the captains of industry and impresarios of pop

culture so that they could discuss the future of entertainment and how it was going to develop commercially?

That's right. Quincy Jones was there, Chris Blackwell, even Vice-President Al Gore was there! Bill Gates refused to show but he did send all his heavy boys in.

Were there moments from the discussion that particularly struck you?

The main battleground was between Disney and Microsoft. Disney argued for a new language based on signs. They wanted to do away with the idea of reading altogether. They wanted to do away with writing.

They wanted to Disnify everything?

Exactly. Microsoft tore them apart. They believed in people who want to write. In fact Disney came out of the whole event looking like this fascist organization that wanted to remove all alternative viewpoints.

And what was the conclusion?

It was left open-ended. Everybody who had a private jet – and many did – sort of flew off. And those of us that didn't have a private jet were sent on a tour of this local Disney town that they had built called Celebration. We were all supposed to have dinner in whatever part of Celebration that we wanted.

Sounds like the ultimate karaoke town, a sort of futuristic utopia, essentially a Disney-controlled community?

Yeah, somewhere you are not allowed to buy anything without going through an audition with the Disney Board. Not anybody can go there. You know, you have to be of a certain type. You have to believe in Disney. You have to swear allegiance to the Disney Corporation.

And how did that make you feel?

It was extraordinary! We were driven around with a guy who was like some kind of Disney park attendant. He told us that the local police force were run by Disney and that even the town's laws would be formed according to Disney's wishes, although apparently they plan to hand back the town to the state of Florida at some point in the future. I remember watching all these kids rolling down the pavement on their skateboards, children of people who had been recommended so that they could live in this town. They'd all hang out in this 'mom and pop' soda store in which there was a glistening old jukebox which only played 1950s music. It was really funny to see these kids hanging out in this environment because you would have to take a double take and think, 'Oh wow, They're just part of the scenery. They're like – part of the movie.' That's the whole point. Even the bank was called 'The Bank of Celebration'.

That's outrageous. It's obvious that that is not your world. It's everything that you have ever fought against.

It's impossible to be programmed into their way of thinking. I'm a complete product of the world I arrived in at art school in 1963. I was a total and utter believer. I believed in art for art's sake. I bought the entire ideology hook, line and sinker. I just went with that and swam with it.

Who are the people you identify with now?

I think the huge problem is that you continue forever to have to remain young. It's a very difficult thing because you don't want to get into Dorian Gray syndrome. The problem is that it is the way you worked when you were twenty-one. I've set up a certain sort of *raison d'être* and it hasn't changed. At times you don't like it because as you get older the friends you had in your generation have left you, have gone overboard. They're running Granada, they see Michael Green at Carlton, they see Charlie Saatchi. You think, 'What are you doing?' You end up with your friends getting younger and younger. It's a very weird trek. As you get older, your friends get younger. You suddenly are not able to relate to people of your own generation at all. They look on you as some total and utter madman. A lunatic. Weirdo. Fucked up. Crazy one. And I guess that's happened to other people in their time. The difference today is that that notion and way of thinking is extremely unfashionable. But you can only work that way and you are forever optimistic because that's the way that makes you care about life the most. If you live the way others want you to you just end up caring less and less about life. You become more and more selfish and forget to fight back. You merely accept.

Additional photo credits

Research Assistance

Sam Knapp and Melissa Louca

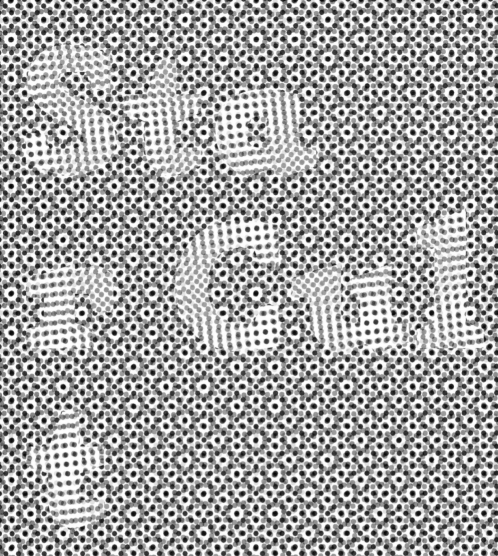